Deconstruction
Reframed

Deconstruction Reframed

Floyd Merrell

Purdue University Press
West Lafayette, Indiana

Published in 1985

Library of Congress Cataloging in Publication Data

Merrell, Floyd, 1937-
    Deconstruction reframed.

    Bibliography: p.
    Includes index.
    1. Deconstruction.   I. Title.
PN98.D43M47   1984   801'.95   84-13348
ISBN 0-911198-72-5
Printed in the United States of America

∫ʷᵉ 6-17-85

To Araceli,
for her patience and omnipresent inspiration,
and to
Susy, Alex, and Danny.
They all knew how to hang in there.

Table Of Contents

Preface

This inquiry is about deconstruction. But it is multifaceted, presenting an array of views, all interrelated in one respect or another. The objective is twofold: to bring perspectives from a number of disciplines to bear on the deconstructionist controversy in order to demonstrate that it is but part of a larger Western World intellectual movement, and to focus on certain problems inherent in deconstruction, not as an all-out-critique, but as an ongoing process of questioning the minds of those I have investigated as well as my own. Consequently, this book is directed chiefly toward scholars in deconstruction, literary criticism and theory, Peircean semiotics, and, more generally, philosophy.

Two disclaimers must be initially forthcoming. First, scholars specializing in the areas of inquiry to which I address myself are exceedingly more competent than I. Although usually critical of blind overspecialization, still, I do not follow the naive dictum that an expert should never be trusted. Both the specialist and the generalist can offer valuable contributions. The latter may lack the particular disciplinary commitments of the former, but his breadth of scope can aid his counterpart to an increased understanding of his own work. I do not always agree with those I have cited, yet I respect their opinion, and, aware of my limitations, I beg their forgiveness if I have not been able to represent them faithfully. Second, my concerns are generally theoretical, but the following pages do not contain theory in the orthodox sense. This book, from the viewpoint of some, might be called critical theory, yet it only tangentially focuses on literature. Neither is it philosophy, in the phenomenological sense at least, since it incorporates some mathematics and logic, and a few ideas from contemporary physics. Perhaps the most appropriate label might be, to use Johnathan Culler's (1982, 8) terms, "textual theory," or simply "theory," for the writings found herein are at once a curious heterogeneous mixture of diverse theories, an expanded (re)interpretation of a contemporary intellectual movement, and a challenge to numerous disciplinary boundaries.

Specifically, chapter one introduces basic Derridean concepts and their relation to Charles Peirce. In chapter two, the relevance of current radical hypotheses in physics and the philosophy of science are discussed. Chapter three encompasses developments in mathematics, especially Kurt Gödel's theorems of inconsistency and incompleteness insofar as they relate to what I will call the *deconstructive principle*. In the next chapter, I offer a series of "thought experiments" in an attempt to illustrate that some concepts propounded by Jacques Derrida are generally compatible with certain aspects of the "new physics." Chapter five relates the deconstructionist's notion of "writing" to Karl Popper's philosophy, and especially to his notion of "objective knowledge." Critique of key terms from a Derridean passage in the following chapter reveals some problems inherent in the deconstructive "method," as well as in all human thought. And in chapter seven, I attempt an account, derived in part from the "new physics," of a fundamental Derridean principle—*différance*.

Samuel Beckett's dilemma concerning language is relevant to my goals, especially in his trilogy, *Molloy, Malone Dies*, and *The Unnamable*. Beckett, significantly, also reveals an anti-Cartesian strain in certain ways commensurate with much deconstructionist thought. To introduce Beckett, I have interspersed quotes throughout the inquiry, juxtaposing them with key points in my arguments. Then in the final chapter, I discuss Beckett more fully, with the intention of demonstrating his importance to the general thesis being presented. It must be kept in mind that I never pretend to "deconstruct" Beckett or Derrida, nor do I claim to offer ultimate solutions to the problems I raise. This inquiry is, it might be said, more descriptive than critical, more synthetic than prescriptive. Beginning with a brief discussion of deconstruction, it then widens the parameters of its vision with each chapter, while building, helicoid-like, a set of variations on the same and similar themes.

I must add that references are weighed heavily on the side of the sciences, mathematics, and logic. This is for an important, and I believe necessary, reason. I assume the general reader to be familiar with the basic tenets of literary study, semiotics, and philosophy. Consequently my discussion of deconstruction will bear references primarily to Derrida, though this is no indication that I have simply ignored works by his followers. And, since discussion of the more abstract disciplines will in some cases take the reader onto untrodden ground, I have referenced them more thoroughly.

Acknowledgments

In the course of composing this volume, I have received assistance from various sources. First and foremost, I owe a special debt to the many theorists and scholars who have written directly or indirectly on the issues I discuss. Without their work, my own would have been impossible. Virgil Lokke's ongoing seminar here at Purdue University offered me a sounding board for some of my initially vague and tenuous ideas, as did the many private conversations with Dan Jaeckel. Calvin Schrag read some of the chapters, providing me with further insight into my shortcomings and omissions. My gratitude must also be extended to Purdue University for a sabbatical during which time the first draft of this book was written.

Substantial portions of chapter three are from my article "Deconstruction Meets a Mathematician," *Journal of American Semiotics*, 2, No. 4 (1984), which appear by the permission of the editor; and portions of "On Understanding the 'Logic' of Understanding," *Ars Semeiotica*, 4, No. 2 (1981) are incorporated into chapter seven by permission of John Benjamins. I also wish to thank the University of Chicago Press for permission to quote from Jacques Derrida's *Writing and Difference;* Dover Publications for quotes from Erwin Schrödinger's *Science, Theory, and Man;* Grove Press for numerous passages from Samuel Beckett's *Molloy, Malone Dies, The Unnamable;* Harvard University Press for quotes from Charles S. Peirce's *Selected Papers;* Johns Hopkins Press for passages from Derrida's *Of Grammatology;* and Indiana University Press for a section from my *Semiotic foundations.*

Finally, I cannot overlook the valuable assistance from Verna Emery, Darle Griffith, Janice Becker, and Lynn Gastinger in editing and designing this volume.

Introduction

1

The following preliminary words on Derrida and deconstruction are, I believe, necessary since chapter one presupposes familiarity with them.

For Derrida, traditional metaphysics bears on an erroneous assumption about language. According to this tradition, meaning is embodied in an immutable connection between signifier and signified to form a unified whole, which is like, to use the Saussurean analogy, two sides of a sheet of paper. Derrida, in contrast, argues that signs cannot incorporate any absolute, univocal meaning, nor do signifiers directly refer to their respective signifieds. Signifiers can do no more than relate to and become other signifiers which are divorced from the world "out there." In other words, there are no definite meanings prior to the system of signifiers. Hence there can be no immediate presence *in* consciousness *of* a single, isolated, and absolute signified in all its fullness. The mistaken notion that there *is* Derrida terms the "metaphysics of presence."

In addition, with respect to language as a whole, there can be no determinate *center* nor any retrievable *origin*. Belief in such is no more than nostalgia, says Derrida. What actually exists is a complex network of *differences* between signifiers, each in some sense carrying the *traces* of all others. Ironically, it is due to this very important fact that the traditional "metaphysics of presence" has been able to pervade all aspects of our thought, for our body of knowledge, Derrida asserts, actually consists of a differentially interrelated fabric of signifiers set down in texts as if they all composed One Text: a vast monolithic totality sometimes called "intertextuality."[1] Caught within this totality, inaccessible for us due to our human limitations, escape becomes impossible. From inside the totality, however, we can at least attempt with some degree of success to point out what is absent in our partial perception of it, what part of it has been repressed, and what part of it appropriately should be accounted for. And yet, from within, the realm of signification becomes potentially infinite in extension—i.e., a finite but unbounded whole. And hence the ultimate parameters of the totality will always be unknowable. That is, if language is not inherently determined by a limited set of univocal meanings, then rhetoric, given the possibility of an unlimited number of contexts over an indefinite period of time, becomes an unrestricted interaction of signifiers (Derrida, 1978a, 278-93).

Unfortunately, according to Derrida, the object of repression by Western World metaphysics has concentrated chiefly on writing (Derrida, 1974a, 3-93). The Saussurean tradition in particular, and metaphysics in general, have placed emphasis on speech to the detriment of the written sign.[2] Also, due to the "metaphysics of presence," of the supposed simultaneity of Being and consciousness *of* Being, and of the concomitant notions of identity, contradiction (or opposition), and the excluded middle, rhetoric has been systematically pushed under the rug. As a result, all languages, mathematical, logical, and natural—particularly in the Chomskyan sense—are usually conceived to be context free, potentially embodying univocal meaning and truth in the transcendental sense. In contrast, Derrida stresses the dangers of overlooking contexts, particularly when considering readings of texts in diverse time and space frameworks. We must, then, reconsider writing, for it can give us a handle with which adequately to consider contexts. *Grammatology*, Derrida's "science of writing," is assertedly more fundamental than the traditional notions of mathematics, logic, and natural languages (that is, speech). It will ultimately demonstrate that there is no absolute univocity. Then the plurivocity of the sign will finally become evident.

3

the suggests an origin,
" *the*" suggests a Pre-sense. Derrida
does not suggest this.

What we must do for the present is find the *flaw* in all texts.
We must discover that certain point in a text where its duplicity of
meaning, its dialogical character, its *aporia*, become apparent, and
it becomes "undecidable," indeterminately plurivocal, multiply paradoxical. Derrida and the deconstructionists, consequently are readers and interpreters of texts, and the texts they place under study
must be particular texts, interpreted within the context of particular
readings in order to disclose their subversive act which places them
and the entire metaphysical tradition in jeopardy.

Yet at the same time, it is admitted, deconstruction cannot itself
completely escape Western World metaphysics. In fact, it inevitably
suffers from the same problematics and pitfalls as the language of the
texts it deconstructs. However, the presumed advantage of the deconstructor over the traditional metaphysician is that while the latter
continues to build the walls of his prison-house of language ever
higher, hermetically sealing himself from the outside but with the
illusion that he enjoys transcendental accessibility to it, the former
finds a weak spot in the wall, and by removing a chink here and a
stone there, he breaks out, only to discover himself immediately sur-
rounded by another concentric wall. There can be no escape, only
oscillation, at the edges of language, with the knowledge that the
"outer" realm is never accessible. And, since there purportedly can
never be a fixed method for deconstruction, it must constantly put
into question even the product of its own activity. It must at least
partly dismantle itself. But this dismantling is/becomes at once an
affirmation: evidence that what is constructed at the moment of deconstruction is/becomes itself deconstructing.

In this light, deconstruction appears to entail the following:

The univocal text is undecidable; the decidable text is not
univocal.[3]

In other words, the sole criterion of decidability with respect to
Western World texts, inevitably embedded within the "metaphysics
of presence," is that they are always, already, and decidably plurivocal. Let the above statement, which will be qualified extensively
throughout this inquiry, be called the *deconstructive principle.* NO!

Principle suggests
method — in fact
it wreaks of it.

2

In this study discussion will rest chiefly on Derrida's early works, especially his three books published in French in 1967 and cited in English translation: *Speech and Phenomena* (1973), *Of Grammatology* (1974a), and *Writing and Difference* (1978a).[4] This selection is for two reasons. First, Derrida's later production appears most basically to consist of a set of variations on his earlier themes, and second, I believe that these themes are most adequately developed in his previous writings. I have chosen for special consideration four of Derrida's key concepts: *différance*, the *trace*, what I call *mediacy*, and *play* (all of which will be defined below). Throughout this inquiry, constant reference to another term, "consciousness," may aggravate the deconstructionist. It must be kept in mind, however, that I do not use the word in the phenomenological sense of "present consciousness." It is a "deferred consciousness" whereby all perception and conception is mediate rather than immediate, where "consciousness *of*" some-*thing*-as-such-and-such is always and invariably separated by a temporal interval from immediacy.[5]

Since I attempt to place deconstruction within a broad Western World context, it is difficult to avoid the problem of occasional misrepresentation. Nevertheless, I have conscientiously strived to select as faithfully as possible, and then branch out into other areas, likewise selecting from them, in order to exercise valid comparisons and contrasts. Never do I propose that Derrida and deconstruction are simply "the same as" intellectual endeavors in contiguous disciplines. The underlying thesis is that though we are often and unfortunately overspecialized in our miniscule fields, and though we may be relatively ignorant of other areas of specialization, still, we are never alone. The Western World mind, indeed the Human Mind—and I cannot use *Zeitgeist, Weltanschauung*, or other vague allusions here—is itself an interrelated and continuous fabric, whose parts lose their essential meaning when isolated from the whole. In this I follow the American philosopher Charles S. Peirce.

CHAPTER ONE

Introducing Some Unnamables

1

Let us first speak of Jacques Derrida's *différance*.

There is a "difference" between that which *is* and consciousness *that* it *is*, for consciousness *of* such-and-such is inexorably "deferred." In other words, consciousness can *be* only slightly after that which *was* was immediately before it. Hence Derrida's term *différance*, which embodies, as is now well known in deconstructionist circles, two meanings: to "differ" and to "defer."[1] And, it must be mentioned, this word, according to the Derridean formulation, must be placed "under erasure" (i.e., written and then crossed out) since it reportedly not only refers to no-*thing*, but also being unnamable, it cannot properly exist *as* a sign.[2] The linguistic sign, then, can be such only by virtue of its being a *différance* (hereafter DC).[3] The entire production of signs is made possible through the/a DC between one sign and its contiguous signs, as well as between it and all other signs in the system. But DC itself is neither a *word* nor a *concept*. To "differ" signifies both non-identity and the order of sameness. It is a sameness which can never be identical, for it implies simultaneously a "deferral," a temporal increment separating word from thing, word from thought, sign from meaning, and sign from other signs.[4] The signifier and signified can never be copresent.

5

The problem of definitions here is that DC elusively slips through our fingers when we attempt to grasp it conceptually. It is "unthinkable within the authority of the logic of identity or even within the concept of time" (Derrida, 1978a, 329). It makes the opposition between presence and absence possible, but it is neither the presence nor the absence of anything (Derrida, 1974a, 143).[5] Providing for the movement of language, nevertheless, it cannot be represented phonologically, only graphically, and even then in an indirect manner, for it is properly speaking neither temporal nor spatial (Derrida, 1973, 132). But neither is it existence nor essence, though it does constitute "the essence of life" (Derrida, 1978a, 203). In fact, life without DC would be unthinkable: it would be death, because DC provides for movement, the very life-giving principle (Derrida, 1974a, 71). In other words, since the moment of DC produces a subject which could not *be* before that moment, the absence of DC—which admittedly is an anomalous phrase, since nothing cannot be absent and remain *as* nothing—is at the same moment the absence of that subject (Derrida, 1973, 82). In this sense, then, "the living present is . . . *in* fact, really, effectively, etc., deferred *ad infinitum*" (Derrida, 1973, 99).

How, as precisely as possible, does this so-called dynamics of language through DC occur? By means of a *differential* between none other than what must be qualified as physiological processes and psychological processes; that is, in the DC between sensory impressions and mental impressions, and between one mental impression and another.[6] Without there being a deferred, temporal increment between these impressions, "the temporalizing synthesis, which permits differences to appear in a chain of signification, could not operate " (Derrida, 1974a, 66). Consequently, there can be no real *presence*—i.e., consciousness *of* in simultaneity with presence *of*—before the semiotic DC or outside it (Derrida, 1973, 141). "Originary being," or one's being simultaneously conscious *and* self-conscious, reduces therefore to no-*thing*—in other words, to DC. It is the "nonfull, nonsimple 'origin'; it is the structured and differing origin of differences" (Derrida, 1973, 141). To claim that DC is "originary" is also "simultaneously to erase the myth of a present origin," that is, to erase the "metaphysics of presence," or the notion that what is is immediately in consciousness. Since, according to the *deconstructive principle*, the notion of pure and simultaneous presence is a fallacious doctrine, the very term "originary," like DC, must appropriately be "crossed out," placed under "erasure." It is none other than a "non-origin," which is "originary" (Derrida, 1978a, 203).[7] More appropriate than "origin," then, DC should be termed the "production" of differences, and differences between differences: the *play* [*jeu*] of differences (Derrida, 1973, 130).

Obviously Derrida, like the early Ludwig Wittgenstein[8] and Lao-Tzu,[9] can speak/write rather extensively *about* that which is presumed to be ineffable. To speak/write *about* DC implies that on so doing it has some sort of existence, even though diaphanous, therefore it must somehow *be* something *about* which one can speak/write. We must return to this problem.

2

Derrida's notion of the *trace* (hereafter TC) is involved in and essential to thought or consciousness *of* something never absolutely present. A sign can never be fully present because it always relates, by means of the TC and through deferral, to something other than itself, something which it is not—and hence the Saussurean notion that language consists of differences among signs without positive terms is at least partly upheld. That is, the TC potentially accounts for what can never be present—potentially we must admit, for it is, like DC, unavailable to immediate consciousness *of*. This is because the above mentioned interval separating signs from other signs— that which provides for DC—must always reconstitute itself. The TC, like DC, is, properly speaking, "not more ideal than real, not more intelligible than sensible, not more a transparent signification than an opaque energy and *no concept of metaphysics can describe it*" (Derrida, 1974a, 65). And consequently, since both the TC and DC entail contradiction, they are "not acceptable within the logic of identity" (Derrida, 1974a, 61). This is an important point. Derrida contends that since Western World metaphysics contains no language with which adequately to describe the TC, attempting to speak or think about it "*can no more break with a transcendental phenomenology than be reduced to it*" (Derrida, 1974a, 62). It appears that in this sense transcendental phenomenology and the notion of the TC entail incommensurable levels of discourse, each enjoying a distinct frame of reference. And, since there is no necessary overlap between their respective domains, there can be no point-for-point translation or reduction from one to the other. From within one, the other is ineffable, and, for all we know, vice versa.

For example, to define the TC as a simultaneous and ambiguous presence-absence is inadequate, "for the word 'ambiguity' requires the logic of presence, even when it begins to disobey that logic" (Derrida, 1974a, 71). Moreover, the TC is not a presence, but a "simulacrum" of a presence, for it always dislocates, displaces, and refers beyond (Derrida, 1973, 156). Neither is it exactly an absence, for, as described above, it is a presence effaced at the very moment of its being-becoming present: it is atemporal, but at the same time it provides for DC, and hence for temporalization (Derrida, 1973, 154). Nor is it spatial, yet by means of DC spatiality is generated conjointly with temporalization (Derrida, 1973, 152). In fact, there is presumably no outside vantage point from which to conceptualize the TC by means of any Kantian-like categories of time and space: paradoxically, its frame of reference contains itself, it is *immanent* rather than *transcendent*.[10]

Perhaps the most effective illustration of the TC is a line which traces out a circle dividing and differentiating what is "inside" from what remains "outside." The line, in the sense of it being a mathematical construct, is ideal, imaginary: it occupies no space and exists irrespective of time. The physical aspect of the line as so much graphite on paper is real, but layers of laminated and interconnected carbon atoms are not what the ideal line *is*, or what it represents. In order properly to perceive the circle *as* a circle, the line must in a sense be effaced. That is, consciousness becomes the transparent medium giving rise to the imaginary line of which the graphite layers are no more than a signifying entity. This imaginary line is a line of differentiation without it actually being anything at all. It is a no-*thing*, which yet distinguishes "inside" from "outside." And as soon as that which it distinguishes comes into existence *for* consciousness, the line's presence as so many graphite layers on paper, at the moment when it becomes "present," is effaced; it "vanishes."

In addition, the TC is at the interface between all physiological and metaphysical (or psychological) questions. That is, it must precede all conscious sensory perception, audible or visible, phonic or graphic, and it can be neither consciously seen nor heard, for it is properly "inside" (Derrida, 1974a, 65). At the expense of oversimplification, it might be said that at the brain-level the TC must be somehow real—a vast complex set of neuronal firings. Therefore the TC is never, and can never be, actually present to immediate consciousness (Derrida, 1974a, 62). In contrast, with respect to consciousness, consisting of multiple hierarchical levels, the TC must admittedly be "mental," but that does not imply that it is derived from "another realm" in some ideal transcendental sense. Depending upon and in interaction with the brain-level, sense is made possible by the TC somewhere along the hierarchical chain of command between brain-level and conscious mind-level.[11] The TC consequently becomes *"the absolute origin of sense in general,"* which amounts to saying that *"there is no absolute origin in general."* It is a generator, a producer of sense in the chain (or better, network) of signs, but it is neither *in* time nor *in* space, for they are also generated *by* it (Derrida, 1974a, 65). The TC, therefore, makes possible the opening of the "outside" as opposed to—an imaginary rather than real opposition—the "inside," and ultimately sense *becomes* sense with respect to some-*thing* which is now presumed to be actually, potentially, or imaginarily in the world.

3

Derrida's *mediacy* (hereafter MC) of experience and consciousness in part follows directly from his critique of the "metaphysics of presence." If the TC entails an interval, and DC a difference between one sign and other signs in/through that interval, then conjointly they both imply non-presence. A critique of presence is a critique of the presupposed immediacy of the signified with respect to the signifier, and the Cartesian "I" with respect to the world (the other). This "myth of presence," Derrida claims, is due to the emphasis on speech and to the avoidance of writing. Speech, it has been traditionally assumed, entails hearing (understanding) oneself speak immediately: the presence of the voice, which is the focus of Derrida's attack against Edmund Husserl. This erroneous assumption has contributed to the false "inside/outside" dichotomy (Derrida, 1974a, 7-8).[12]

In reality, the "I" as an assumed immediacy can be no more than an abstract ideal, an impossibility which has continued to nurture the illusion of self-presence, of full consciousness, and a nostalgia for origins (Derrida, 1973, 95; 1978a, 292). Given Derrida's notion of DC and the TC, instead of embarking on an impossible quest for pure presence, the only reasonable alternative is to posit an equally elusive pure difference which "introduces into self presence from the beginning all the impurity putatively excluded from it. The living present springs forth out of its nonidentity with itself and from the possibility of a retentional trace. It is always already a trace" (Derrida, 1973, 85). Consequently, signification is a corresponding progression away from self-presence, away from the ideal identity of meaning. It is a successive progression of deferred differences which, ironically, has made possible the mistaken concepts of self-presence and identity. The proper notion of meaning, in contrast to Western World thought, is not that of pure presence, which allows for identity and contradiction; the proper notion entails signification, which is generated over time, by means of convention, and within particular contexts. Meaning, then, is ultimately language-bound, perception-bound, and bound to a given world-view or ideology.[13]

Therefore, there can be no transcendental or privileged signified (univocal meaning or content). The signified is never copresent with the signifier, it is always a deferred, delayed presence. In this sense, the subject can become a speaking/writing subject only by entering into the system of language; that is, of DC. Moreover, there can be no self-presence or consciousness before speech, for this supposes that "prior to signs and outside them, and excluding every trace and difference, something such as consciousness is possible" (Derrida, 1973, 146). In reality, consciousness is an "effect" rather than a "cause"; it is produced only after DC and the TC, and then it is not, nor can it be, any more than an MC (Derrida, 1973, 147).

4

But it seems impossible to speak and yet say nothing.
(Beckett, 1955, 303)

It will become increasingly evident throughout this inquiry that the concept of MC is not exactly original with Derrida, nor properly speaking, are the TC and DC. Derrida of course comments extensively on various precursors to his thought, most notably Martin Heidegger, Friedrich Nietzsche, and Sigmund Freud. Interestingly enough, he also admits that Charles S. Peirce "goes very far in the direction that I have called the deconstruction of the transcendental signified, which, at one time or another, would place a reassuring end to the reference from sign to sign" (Derrida, 1974a, 49).[14]

The Peircean sign is, simply stated, something that stands for something to someone in some respect or capacity.[15] Nothing can be a sign of and by itself. To be a sign it must be understood as such; that is, it needs its interpretant. But all signs are interpreted only in terms of other signs (through, so to speak, their DC), and these in terms of others, and so on *ad infinitum* (Peirce, 1960, 2.303 and 2.92).[16] Likewise, the object of representation of the sign becomes (by a displacement or deferral) yet another representation and "an endless series of representations, each representing the one behind it . . . [becomes] nothing but the representation itself conceived as stripped of irrelevant clothing [much like the movement of DC]. But this clothing never can be completely stripped off; it is only changed for something more diaphanous. So there is an infinite regression here" (Peirce, 1960, 1.339) (brackets mine).[17]

In addition, all thinking is necessarily with signs, and since thoughts are signs that refer to other signs, cognition also becomes an infinite series (Peirce, 1960, 5.260, 5,753 and 6.338). Hence no thought can be considered either self-sufficient or self-confirmatory, for all thoughts necessarily require the existence of each other. However, this existence is not a simultaneous presence. Reference of one sign-thought to another sign-thought is not instantaneous, but occurs over a certain increment of time (much in the Derridean sense of the DC) (Peirce 1960, 5.253). In this light, Peirce's dictum that the mind, as generator of thoughts, ultimately *is* a sign leads to the notion that mind and signs interact reciprocally, and therefore "each increase of man's information involves and is involved by, a corresponding increase of a word's information" (Peirce, 1960, 5.313). Peirce concludes with the statement no less enigmatic than many of Derrida's, that: "my language is the sum total of myself; for the man is the thought" (Peirce, 1960, 5.314). In other words, like Derrida would tell us, the speaking subject enters, and becomes part of/with the system of signs, or better, of DC.

Against the Cartesian belief that knowledge is based upon a set of primitive intuitions, of axiomatic simples, Peirce tells us that there is no knowledge that is not mediated by prior knowledge. The cognitive process is a chain of thoughts, a process of flowing inferences, "but the beginning and the end of this chain are not distinctly perceived" (Peirce, 1960, 7.337). That is to say, the end cannot be known, for, as Derrida also maintains, there is no teleological, transcendental, and absolute end. Moreover, the beginning (or origin) cannot be fully grasped until the indeterminate end is reached, until the system can be seen in its totality — admittedly an impossible dream, but a possible hypothetical construct. In this sense, the beginning can be clear only from some mythical, absolute perspective.

Peirce's notion of MC is significant, then. Whatever might be called the "Immediate . . . runs in a continuous stream through our lives; it is the sum total of consciousness, whose mediation, which is the continuity of it, is brought about by a real effective force behind consciousness" (Peirce, 1960, 5.289).[18] It must be remembered, of course, that this "force behind consciousness" is not immediately available *to* consciousness by intuition or direct introspection (Peirce, 1960, 5.213 and 5.238-49). For instance, we can never think *"This* is present in my consciousness," since as soon as we reflect *on* the event our consciousness *of* it is past. Once past, we cannot "bring back the quality of the feeling as it was *in and for itself,* or know what it was like *in itself"* (Peirce, 1960, 5.289). This notion gives rise to Peirce's hypothesis that all *thoughts-signs form a continuum.* But here we confront a paradox. If one sensation is simply displaced by another, then that other can be displaced by still another, and so on indefinitely. Yet even though thoughts-signs embrace temporal intervals, there is no way actually to isolate any given interval, no matter how large or small, from the continuum of thoughts-signs. *There is no way to work our way to an original, a first, a central thought-sign.*[19]

Peirce illustrates this point with an example similar to Zeno's Achilles and the Tortoise paradox (Peirce, 1960, 5.263). A triangular-shaped object representing the sum of one's thought-signs is inverted and dipped in a liquid which leaves a horizontal line (a TC?) on it. Suppose it is first dipped in one-half the distance from the apex, then one-fourth, then one-eighth and so on. There is no point in this process where we can state that we have reached the line representing the first thought-sign. Peirce justifies his example thus:

> Explicate the logical difficulties of this paradox . . . in whatever way you may. I am content with the result, as long as your principles are fully applied to the particular case of cognitions [or thoughts-signs] determining one another. Deny motion, if it seems proper to do so; only then deny the process of determination of one cognition [thought-sign] by another. Say that instants and lines are fictions; only say, also, that states of cognition [or thoughts-signs] and judgments are fictions. The point here insisted on is not this or that logical solution of the difficulty, but merely that cognition [or thoughts-signs] arises by a *process* of beginning, as any other change comes to pass. (Peirce, 1960, 5.263) (brackets mine)

Hence, Peirce's inaccessible last "line" in the triangle, an infinitesimal segment, cannot be some-*thing*; it is necessarily no-*thing* to finite consciousness, like the line tracing a circle in the above illustration of the TC. The contradiction here, as Zeno aptly demonstrated, stems from the fact that infinitude cannot be interjected into finitude, nor continuum into discontinuity.

Peirce's notion of the continuum is further corroborated by his complementary idea that some or many of the thoughts-signs which lead us to a conclusion from a set of premises are non-conscious. That is, the premises, or initial assumptions leading to an inference, are by and large consciously generated; then other supporting premises or arguments are successively introduced to lead one, vaguely as it might be, toward the final result. But there is invariably a non-conscious mental leap over some aspects of the general development of the argument. It is well-nigh impossible to make sure that these non-conscious aspects of the argument actually passed through some part of the mind. If they did, then there must have been a "resting place" for them, because subsequent to arriving at the desired conclusion many or most of them could be consciously generated. But they could have had no actual "resting place," for if so, there must already have been consciousness *of* them. They must have been "there," as "part" of the continuum potentially and mediately available to consciousness (Peirce, 1960, 2.184).

In short, Peirce's thesis is that ideas come to consciousness in succession. They are necessarily discontinuous—albeit by somehow overcoming the inevitable paradox—but since "there is no such thing as an instantaneous consciousness," then all consciousness must relate to a process (Peirce, 1958, 7.351). But this process can only be made continuous by the mergence, through consciousness, of intervals of time into one another (Peirce, 1960, 6.111). Consequently, with respect to consciousness, and in light of Peirce's triangle example, there can be for consciousness no real "instant at a point," at an infinitesimal "point"—and this notion that experience is never exactly present to itself nor identical with itself is precisely Derrida's argument against Husserl (Derrida, 1973, 65).[20]

Consider a "thought experiment" to illustrate this non-instantaneity more concretely.[21] Suppose someone tells us: "I am dreaming." If indeed dreaming, can he be awake, or must he be asleep while making the statement? And if either awake or asleep, can he make this utterance consciously? If while emitting the utterance he is asleep, the dream is not immediately available to his conscious awareness, for it can be so only mediately, after awakening. And, if he is awake and consciously uttering the statement, then he cannot at the same instant be asleep and actually dreaming, for if so, images would be passing through his head, consciousness *of* which would not be available to him immediately, and hence he could not immediately be dreaming and making a statement *about* his dreamt experience during the same "point" in time. So he, if conscious, is lying, or spouting out an absurdity. And if nonconscious, he cannot at the same time make a statement implying that he is conscious: hence the statement from this perspective is equally absurd (see Malcolm, 1959).

Consciousness *of*, according to Peirce, and Derrida would certainly concur, can only exist after the fact of immediacy. And consciousness *of* always retains a trace of the past tinged with a projection into, or as Alfred Whitehead tells us, an anticipation of, the future. The dream-state/waking-state dichotomy is a macro-level illustration of a discontinuity which, at the micro-level of consciousness *of*, becomes continuous, paradoxically. More on this later, after an adequate foundation has been set.

5

*The best would be not to begin. But I have to begin. That is to
say I have to go on. (Beckett, 1955, 292)*

Reconsider a key, perhaps the principle key, to Derridean
thought: the absence of presence of origins, or of a first. This concept can be discussed in relation to Peirce's categories of Firstness,
Secondness, and Thirdness, which are, admittedly, complex, confus-
ing, and at times outright contradictory. Yet they bear on the importance of Derrida's critique, and should be discussed. First
however, I must be clear on one point. Peirce calls his doctrine of
signs "phenomenology," a theory of consciousness (Zeman, 1977).
But it is a "phenomenology" very much unlike the twentieth-
century conception of the word. Consciousness, according to
Peirce, is not a manifestation of presence; it produces a sign, by
means of a DC, in much the Derridean sense.[22] At the core of
Peirce's non-intuitive and non-presence "phenomenology" is his
system of categories. Of these, Firstness, appropriately, is the most
difficult to describe, for it implies origins, or beginnings, before
there is any consciousness *of* anything.

Firstness is, in a vague sense called "feeling." It is:

> an instant of that kind of consciousness which involves no analysis,
> comparison or any process whatsoever, nor consists in whole or in
> part of any act by which one stretch of consciousness is distin-
> guished from another, which has its own positive quality which con-
> sists in nothing else, and which is of itself all that it is, however it
> may have been brought about; so that if this feeling is present during
> a lapse of time, it is wholly and equally present at every moment of
> that time. (Peirce, 1960, 1.306)

The immediate presence, could we fully and consciously grasp
it *as something present*, would be Firstness. This is not to say that
the erroneously conceived "immediate consciousness"—which
Peirce calls a "pure fiction"—is Firstness. The idea of the First
must be entirely separated from consciousness *of*, conception *of* or
reference *to* anything else. In a way, in a fictitious way of speaking,
it is the "now," the "present" between past and future, the "original,
spontaneous, and free" (Peirce, 1960, 1.357). It is like the Oneness

which precedes differentiation or distinction into parts, it is a unary rather than a binary "existence." As such it cannot be subjected to articulated thought: it is, practically speaking, unnamable. If we assert it, "it has lost its characteristic innocence; for assertion always implies a denial of someting else. Stop to think of it, and it has flown!" (Peirce, 1960, 1.357)[23]

Secondness, on the other hand, is binary. It entails relation and hence the idea of something *other*. Just as we become aware of our self only on becoming aware of the non-self, so also we, on distinguishing something *from* Firstness, must become aware of that something *with respect to* something else which it *is not* (Peirce, 1960, 1.324).[24] Firstness is feeling, pure spontaneity, potentiality. Secondness is *what* is experienced, the actual. When one has developed at least a rudimentary idea of "reality" as apart from one's self, Secondness is predominant, "for the real is that which insists upon forcing its way to recognition as something *other* than the mind's creation" (Peirce, 1960, 1.325).

Thirdness is cognition, which is necessarily constructed on the foundations of Firstness and Secondness. Thirdness entails representation, the third leg of the triad including *relations* between things (Secondness) and pure *quality* (Firstness). Essentially it can be said that Firstness is potentiality, a "might be" without yet there being any awareness *of what* it is *that* might be. Secondness, the actual, is a "happens-to-be," through consciousness that what *is*, is, *with respect to* something which it *is not*. Thirdness, then, is a "would be." It is a hypothetical, a conditional, and it includes consciousness *of* an absent "happens-to-be" (Greenlee, 1973, 36-38; Peirce, 1960, 2.667, 1.304 and 6.327). In other words, if Firstness can be termed "seeing" and Secondness "seeing *as*" in the sense of Wittgenstein, then Thirdness is "seeing-*as*-it-could-have-been." Secondness and Thirdness, then, include temporal continuity—and hence their relevance to Derrida's DC, MC, and the TC.[25]

Significantly, Peirce (1960, 1.342) tells us that dreams have no Thirdness. This must certainly be so, for in light of the above comments on dreams, consciousness *of* a dream-state can exist only after the fact. Dream is free and spontaneous; it does, so to speak, whatever it pleases without any necessary or direct relationship to the "real world." When one is in the waking-state, on the other hand, this relationship can be recalled, and then spoken *about*. Now, Thirdness comes into play; the dream is related to a Second, the "real world," and the relationship is established by a Third, the hypothetical or imaginary, which can be reconstructed by the dreaming subject only after the dream is already past. In this respect also mediacy (like Derrida's MC) must be admitted.

In sum, Peirce's Firstness, or *"immediate* consciousness" (for him a fiction, since we can never know it—think about it—directly) is comparable to Derrida's conception of the absent presence. In both cases the "presence of the perceived present can appear as such only inasmuch as it is *continuously compounded* with a nonpresence and nonperception" (Derrida, 1973, 64). For both Peirce and Derrida, any ill-conceived "now" is actually "not-now," a perception which is "now past," and part of the flow of sensations. Yet the "now" can mediately become a consciousness *of*, a deferred thought or sign. And, as we shall observe below, through repetition, deferred thoughts and signs can potentially become embedded in our conception of the "real world" such that they are accepted uncritically to be simply *the ways things are*, as if they were presence, pure immediacy. Thus what Peirce calls "habit" risks becoming, by repetition, blind dogma, or the "myth of presence" (Peirce, 1960, 5.338-410). Peirce and Derrida in their own way launch a comparable attack on Western World metaphysics.

6

This time I know where I am going, it is no longer the ancient, the receding night. Now it is a game, I am going to play. I never knew how to play, till now. (Beckett, 1955, 180)

Derrida's brand of *play* is purportedly a jubilant sublimation, but unlike any rule-governed play, the *play* of deconstruction virtually enjoys total license. *Play*, centerless and ruleless, is, like DC and the TC, indispensably ineffable. Yet, if we desire more adequately to come to grips with these Derridean concepts, G. Spencer-Brown perhaps can offer at least a partial insight. In *Laws of Form* (1979) he begins with a *mark* which he calls the *mark of distinction* (comparable to DC), and proceeds to construct a beautifully powerful system from two initial and elegantly simple axioms. In other words, Spencer-Brown reproduces the basic universal forms, the mentally constructed building blocks with which to account for the principles underlying traditional logic and computers—both based on Boolean algebra—and for erecting the foundations of particle and quantum mechanics. From pure form, from no more than an unbroken continuum, or from what in quantum mechanics is called a "state function," which gives information concerning the probabilities of a potentially infinite range of events, this initial *mark of distinction* is made. Since it is the originary—though irretrievable—*mark*, it contains within itself the coded possibility for distinguishing all potential distinctions from all other distinctions, which, in very much of a Derridean and Peircean sense, eventually entail also the demand for seriality (that is, temporal increments separating successive *marks*: DCs).[26] Hence this *mark* can be considered "informed in the sense of having its own form within it, and at the same time informed in the sense of remembering what has happened to it in the past" (Spencer-Brown, 1979, 100).[27] However, Spencer-Brown qualifies his words by suggesting that he does not presume this to be the same as a human or even an animal form of memory. His formulation accounts for, at the most fundamental level, the so-called "memories" in computers. Yet the principle can be looked upon "as a precursor of the more complicated and varied forms of memory and information in man and the higher animals" (Spencer-Brown, 1979, 100).[28]

Comparable to Spencer-Brown's "forms" is what Peirce calls the "evolution of forms" from an "initial condition." This evolution has its beginning, or at any rate, its early development in a primordial potentiality, "an utter vagueness of completely undetermined and dimensionless potentiality" (Peirce, 1960, 6.193).[29] It must be, Peirce says, by some contraction of that vagueness containing everything in general but no-*thing* in particular, that these "forms" come about. After such contraction into particulars, we can now experience and be conscious *of* sense-qualities and feelings which are, we can hardly but suppose, "relics of an ancient ruined continuum of qualities, like a few columns standing here and there in testimony that here some old-world forum with its basilica and temples had once made a magnificient *ensemble*" (Peirce, 1960, 6.197).

With this in mind, contemplate the following integration of Spencer-Brown and Peirce with Derrida:

The ("evolution of forms") ("operation of differing") producing successive ("marks of distinction") ("DCs") from the ("initial condition") and by an ("informing of the form") ("simultaneous division and delay, through DC"), accounts for the lack of immediacy ("consciousness *of*"), the ("continuum of qualities"), or the ("initial mark") ("DC").

At this juncture the deconstructionist is undoubtedly gnashing his teeth. Derrida, he might counter, would deconstruct this use of "form," for: "As soon as we use the concept of form—even to criticize *another* concept of form—we must appeal to the evidence of a certain source of sense. And the medium of this evidence can only be the language of metaphysics" (Derrida, 1973, 108). But does not Derrida allow himself liberal use of much nineteenth-century physicalist or corpuscular-kinetic jargon such as "dislocate," "displace," "condense," etc.—primarily from Freud, who is to a certain degree a holdover from the mechanistic world-view, a "romantic mechanist" (Matson, 1966). So why not "form"?[30] Spencer-Brown, certainly outside the traditional language of metaphysics, uses what he calls the "imaginary state" (derived from the imaginary number, $\sqrt{-1}$). And, he asserts, this "imaginary state," not in space but through something akin to Derrida's "repetition" in time, gives incessant movement to "form." In this sense "form" has hardly any relevance to the same term as it is used in metaphysical parlance.[31]

Actually, Peirce qualifies his use of the word "form" such that it is not entirely incompatible with Derrida. The "magnificient *ensemble*" Peirce speaks of above does not consist of "forms," Platonically speaking that is. "Forms" are actualized from what is no more than a cloud, a vague potential. Moreover, what becomes actual at a given moment participates in the evolution of related "forms" by pure accident. And if the continuum of possibles is infinite, then it must be admitted that whatever might be teased out of that continuum must be the product, at the deepest level, of freedom, chance, spontaneity (*Play!*) (Peirce, 1960, 6.217).[32]

Peirce invites us to use the number system in creating a "thought experiment" with which to illustrate his "evolution of forms." He begins with nothing, pure zero. But this nothing is not that of negation. *Not* means *other than* and *with respect to* what *is*. Peirce is aware that negation, in spite of the trend in modern logic, is a binary rather than unary relation (see Cowan, 1975). Pure zero is unary, prior to every other, every First. It is what has not yet seen the light of day. The pure nothing of negation, on the other hand is death; it comes second to everything, after everything has been. Zero, then, represents an "event" "in" which there is "no individual thing, no compulsion, outward nor inward, no law. . . . As such, it is absolutely undefined and unlimited possibility—boundless possibility. There is no compulsion and no law. It is boundless freedom" (Peirce, 1960, 6.217).

It bears mentioning that Peirce, one of the most important precursors of modern logic, was in many respects beyond classical logic. He himself was working in a sea of possibilities, where little was fixed or structured, and many of his speculations could not bear fruit until the appearance of other preparatory work. Consequently, the implications of his logic are only today being realized.[33] One "logic" which since Peirce's time has been by and large forgotten is his "logic of relatives" (loosely speaking, of DC).[34] This Peirce calls a "logic of higher type," a logic of the continuum. It is, itself, a "logic" governing the "primordial beginning," and all lesser "logics" follow from it. For example, on reviewing the course of logic as a whole, Peirce remarks that it proceeds "from the question to the answer—from the vague to the definite. The indeterminate future becomes irrevocable past" (Peirce, 1960, 6.191). In other words, the undifferentiated homogeneity takes on heterogeneity; the cloud condenses into a clock. Our classical logic is an inferior logic of minute parts, inadequate for describing the real universe, which requires a vastly superior logic, the logic by which originary distinctions are separated from the continuum (Peirce, 1960, 6.192). Peirce continues:

> It is true that the whole universe and every feature of it must be regarded as rational, that is as brought about by the logic of events [i.e., Hegelian logic, which Peirce in a way "deconstructs"]. But it does not follow that it is *constrained* to be as it is by the logic of events; for the logic of evolution and of life need not be supposed to be of that wooden kind that absolutely constrains a given conclusion. (Peirce, 1960, 6.218) (brackets mine)

We can get a tentative grasp on the slippery handle of this "higher logic" through Peirce's notion of *quality*—Firstness. *Quality* is, to reiterate, not yet an actuality. For example, if a person can see only blue, then all things will appear of one color. Nothing will attract his attention, or surprise him—with respect to colors at least—because it has not been *differentiated.* In other words, nothing, to become something, must have been actualized as *different from* something else, but the person seeing only blue is incapable of making such distinctions. Colors, at this more primitive stage of perception, Peirce calls *quale*-consciousness, a sort of First Consciousness. It is lifeless, static, passive. Now, if this person is suddenly able to perceive red things in his world, a shock of surprise occurs. He becomes conscious *of* blue things *as* blue things in counterdistinction *to* red things. This consciousness is lively, dynamic, active, a Second Consciousness (Peirce, 1960, 6.222). Each item of *quale*-consciousness, then, "is in itself what it is for itself, without reference to any other. It is absurd to say that one *quale* in itself considered is like or unlike another" (Peirce, 1960, 6.224).

Generally speaking, in *quale*-consciousness there can be no more than one *quality*: it is *unity*.[35] It is truly the "now." It is one, and but one. Peirce demonstrates how the principle of contradiction can be conceived as a formal juxtaposition of *quale*-consciousness (Peirce, 1960, 6.231). Any object, X, cannot be both blue and not blue. It can be blue and hard, for blueness and hardness are two *qualities* that can be conjoined in consciousness. And, if it is, say, blue and yellow, then the two *qualities* merge into one another to produce green, another *quality.* Consequently, "the positive truth in the principle of contradiction is that *quale*-consciousness has but one element" (Peirce, 1960, 6.231). *Quale*-consciousness, therefore, cannot be a consciousness of binaries, of duality. If the *quality* could be double, the principle of contradictions would vanish.

Moreover, from the above blending of two *qualities,* blue and yellow, it becomes evident that *quale*-consciousness "cannot blend with *quale*-consciousness without loss of identity" (Peirce, 1960, 6.235). This is indeed significant. It implies that the blending of *quale*-consciousness is analogous to the movement of DC through the TC and by means of MC. An item of non-conscious experience must be all that it is in and for itself, for it is not available to conscious awareness except mediately. Then what is the difference between Peirce's and Derrida's conceptions? It might be contended that Peirce retains confidence in logical systems, whereas Derrida overtly attempts to subvert all logic. However, there is no need to engage here in the trivial criticism that Derrida questions the value of logic while using logic to develop his arguments.[36] The important question is: What is the meeting point between Derrida's logical deconstruction of logic and Peirce's reserved qualification concerning logical principles?

Notice that according to Peirce's use of contradiction, a given entity, A, cannot be both blue and not blue at the same time. This implies that if a *quale*-consciousness contains A as blue and only blue, it exists in total separation, as a oneness, and independent of any color other than blue. If, subsequently, another *quale*-consciousness exists containing, say, B, which is green, then this not-A (not-blue) content is distinguishable from the blue A. Then, and only then, relations can be established by a subject to complete Thirdness. The point here is that during the "instant" of the first *quale*-consciousness, what it is *not* cannot be in consciousness, and hence the principle of contradiction is not, and cannot be in effect immediately. Contradiction is only available, so to speak, through something akin to MC by means of DC and the TC.[37] So the law of contradiction does not really apply here. Though Peirce does not exactly bring up this argument, in his terms contradiction and duality (or difference and binarism) can only apply *after* the transition from oneness to dyadic and triadic relations. DC entails precisely this "instant" of transition, or in Peirce's terms, the "instant" of passage from the unbounded potential, from the oneness to contradiction, and ultimately to *differentiation*. And *successive differentiation* eventually evolves into a complexity from which contradictory opposites must now be artificially abstracted.[38]

7

Yes, even then, when already all was fading, waves and particles, there could be no things but nameless things no names but thingless names. (Beckett, 1955, 31)

The task now at hand is to develop an image with help from Peirce, with which provisionally to account for the passage from the potential to the actual—that is, the *play* of DC. Such an image must also entail the mediacy of thinking and speaking *of*.

Peirce (1960, 6.193) tells us that the process of deriving an actual from the potential is "a process which extends from before time and before logic." Consider the "thought experiment" he offers. A clean blackboard can represent "the original vague potentiality." For practical purposes it is a continuity, a generality, an indeterminate multitude of possible dimensions and points, just as the ideal continuum is an indeterminate multitude of possible *qualities*. If we draw a line on the blackboard a discontinuity (*mark of distinction*) is produced, but this discontinuity is itself a continuity complementary with the continuity of the blackboard—that is, it consists also in an infinite continuum of points. But the chalk mark is not really the line, for a line ideally is of infinitesimal thickness, and it is not visible. It is actually a narrow plane, a white strip which severs and displaces a segment of the black surface:

> Thus the discontinuity can only be produced upon that blackboard by the reaction between two continuous surfaces into which it is separated, the white surface and the black surface. The whiteness is a Firstness—a springing up of something new. But the boundary between the black and white is neither black, nor white, nor neither, nor both. It is the pairedness of the two. It is for the white the active Secondness of the black; for the black the active Secondness of the white. (Peirce, 1960, 6.203)[39]

Generality, then, is viewed as analogous to geometrical continuity. The original generality of the blackboard is, "like the ovum of the universe," broken by the first mark. This mark, however, is the product of an arbitrary act, for it could have been drawn in an infinity of different ways. And after having been made, it can be "erased" (i.e., through the function of the TC). After "erasure," it will now not interfere with a subsequent mark drawn in another way, for there is no necessary consistency between the two. However, by repetition of similar (but not identical) marks, "habit" can be established such that the arbitrary, accidental mark "acquires some incipient staying quality, some tendency toward consistency" (Peirce, 1960, 6.204). In other words, through "habit" the mark can come to be perceived as sameness, or even identity, without the subject being aware *that* the marks are different and separated by an interval. To revive the geometry metaphor, the distinct line marring the blackboard's suface, in conjunction with a set of similar lines, has brought about a reversed transition from discontinuity to continuity. Or, to use Peirce's graphic illustration, a series of slightly divergent marks produces a new line, a curve, which is itself a continuity derived, like each of those marks, from the continuity of the blackboard:

The curve (an actualized universe) is formed from the original potential. The marks, "as they multiply themselves under the habit of being tangent to the envelope gradually tend to lose their individuality. They become in a measure more and more obliterated and sink into mere adjuncts to the new cosmos in which they are individuals" (Peirce, 1960, 6.260). It is metaphorically at this point, we might concur, that resemblance or sameness can be construed as identity, that the Derridean "myth of presence" potentially begins to emerge.[40]

Now, reconsidering Peirce's notion of the transition from Firstness to Secondness, I will attempt to go one step further in order to demonstrate Peirce's relevance to DC, MC, and the TC. In Peirce's blackboard example, the boundary between black and white separates Firstness (the white segment) from Secondness (the white segment *in relation to* the black or vice versa). The key phrase is *in relation to*, for the *relation* entails, like the boundary, neither whiteness nor blackness, but both of them *simultaneously*— though, like the figure and the ground in Gestalt diagrams, they cannot both be an item *for* consciousness *in simultaneity.*

Admitting the relational properties whiteness and blackness into our scheme, let W stand for white and B for black, W-ness for the property possessed exclusively by the mark, and B-ness for the property possessed exclusively by the blackboard. Corresponding to these positive properties are the negative properties, unW-ness and unB-ness. Since there is nothing except the actual mark and the potential (the blackboard), unB-ness pertains solely to the mark and unW-ness exclusively to the blackboard. Hence, the mark and the blackboard appear to be united by nothing. It seems that the only property they can have in common is the compound property, WB-lessness. But nothing else besides the original unW-ness and unB-ness is either unW or unB, so they cannot share properties with anything else even through the compound property. Yet since WB-lessness is jointly possessed both by the mark and the blackboard, they have something in common, but the commonality is a disjoint—incompatible or mutually exclusive—property. Hence W and B cannot *be* in *simultaneity*, nor can the mark *and* the blackboard exist *simultaneously* and totally divorced from one another. The mark, a discontinuity, depends upon the blackboard for its coming into being, and once into existence, it possesses a continuous nature which is shared with the blackboard. On the other hand, the blackboard contains, within itself, the mark as a potential discontinuity, but, since this discontinuity is incompatible with the blackboard's continuous nature, it might be said that the blackboard does *and* does not contain the mark. Once the mark is drawn, however, there *is* a boundary which separates one continuity from another and establishes the discontinuity by means of which divergent properties come into being.

Let this boundary be represented by a "slash" (formally written: W-ness/B-ness).[41] The "slash" implies that what is a continuity cannot possess both negative properties, unW-ness *and* unB-ness, since there is nothing in the universe at this time possessing both of these properties (this can be formally written: $\sim$ W-ness $\wedge \sim$ B-ness—i.e., not both not W-ness *and* not B-ness). Replacing the logical connective *and* with *or*, the equation becomes doubly negative: not not W-ness *or* not not B-ness (formally: $\sim (\sim$ W-ness$) \vee \sim (\sim$B-ness$)$). And finally, dropping the negatives, we have, W-ness *or* B-ness (formally: W-ness $\vee$ B-ness).[42] This "slash" or "cut," then, embodies within itself identity *and* opposition. Like DC, or like the chalk line marring the blackboard, it is no-*thing*, it can never be totally present; and after it is asserted, it remains contradictory, as an "invisible absence."[43]

Peirce provides a useful hypothetical model to illustrate what is being discussed here. We can imagine the total realm of possible assertions (i.e., possible worlds) as a "book of separate sheets, tacked together at points, if not otherwise connected" (Peirce, 1960, 4.512). The first sheet in this book is the standard "sheet of assertions," a "universe of existent individuals," different sections of it representing propositions asserted concerning that particular sub-universe. A "cut" in this sheet enables one to pass into a successive sheet, into "areas of conceived propositions which are not realized" (Peirce, 1960, 4.512). Further "cuts" in this and successive sheets then allow one to "pass into worlds which, in the imaginary worlds of the other cuts, are themselves represented to be imaginary and false, but which may, for all that, be true, and therefore continuous with the sheet of assertion itself, although this is uncertain" (Peirce, 1960, 4.512). Peirce invites us to regard the "ordinary blank sheet of assertion" as a film upon which there exists the as yet undeveloped photograph of the facts (propositions) of the universe. But this is not a literal picture, for when we consider historically the range of "facts" which have been asserted to be "true," we must conclude that this "book" can be none other than a continuum which:

> Must clearly have more dimensions than a surface or even than a solid; and we will suppose it to be plastic, so that it can be deformed in all sorts of ways without the continuity and connection of parts being ever ruptured. Of this continuum the blank [initial] sheet of assertion may be imagined to be a photograph. When we find out that a proposition is true, we can place it wherever we please on the sheet, because we can imagine the original continuum, which is plastic, to be so deformed as to bring any number of propositions to any places on the sheet we may choose. (Peirce, 1960, 4.512) (brackets mine)

Hence, Peirce goes on, this original photograph is, more appropriately, a map in which all points of a surface correspond to points on the next surface, and so on successively, and the continuity is preserved unbroken. In this manner, each point, each "cut," corresponds to the initial sheet of assertion where the "real" state of things (that is, perceived and conceived to be "real" at a given time and place) is represented. All successive sheets, then, represent an infinite set of potential facts or propositions many or most of which can, at another time and place, become "real." Expounding on Peirce's "cuts" and other ramifications of his "existential graphs" does not fall within the scope of this inquiry, though they will be sketchily cited in following chapters. The important point is that Peirce's "cuts" provide an approximate abstract formulation of what Derrida calls the "originary" DC and TC, though without any reference to what is conceived at a given time and place as the "real world." In addition, given the boundary separating what is "inside" the "cut" from what remains "outside" it, we have further illustration of the above-mentioned "slash," which, like DC, is itself no-*thing* but provides movement for the generation of some-*thing*.[44]

But there is still a problem here, a "logical" problem which also concedes validity to Derrida's general hypothesis. Let us return for a moment to the chalk mark on the blackboard. It must have been made by someone. The mark, of course, cannot simply appear out of the clear blue. So, considering the blackboard to be the initial unbounded continuum of possibilities, how is it possible to account for the existence of something (a subject) which has been separated, has separated "itself," from the continuum?—the term must be in quotes, for the beingness of this self cannot exist at the same instant that it is part of the continuum (or the world). And if separated from the continuum (or world), this act must have occurred before it could see the world as *apart from* "itself." Its very beingness can, paradoxically, be no more than an MC.[45]

We must return to this paradox at the propitious moment.

CHAPTER TWO

Whose Science Are We Speaking of When We Speak of Science?

1

I like to think I occupy the centre, but nothing is less certain.
(Beckett, 1955, 295)

The library is a sphere whose exact center is any one of its hexagons and whose circumference is inaccessible.
(Borges, 1964a, 52)

What is a center anyway? For instance, where is the center of the ocean? Everywhere *and* nowhere, if we follow Buddhist doctrine. Let us arbitrarily posit the center in a particular wave. The totality of the ocean is embodied in that wave, and that wave simultaneously embraces the entire ocean. Like the ocean, it is indivisible. It is the manifestation of the ocean while being, itself, no-*thing*. Without the ocean this physical manifestation cannot be realized, and the ocean, without the wave, without all its waves, cannot be the ocean. So the center is simultaneously everywhere *and* nowhere in an amorphous mass in perpetual motion, and the summation of this motion is *stasis;* all particular motions in the mass are, in their composite, *mutually cancellatory.* (For every change there is an equal and opposite change.)

28

This might appear to be useless ethereal talk. Yet it illustrates an essential point to be developed throughout this inquiry. Samuel Beckett's uncertain portrayal of a universe of "relativity," and Borges's universe in "The Library of Babel," an infinite, unfathomable library, are comparable. And, they are also comparable to the Buddhist conception of the universe, or, concomitantly, of the mind. What remains to be seen is how this analogy, at the most general level, is in a strange way compatible with Derrida's "anti-metaphysics."

2

... or a circle and a center not its center in search of a center and its circle, respectively, in boundless space, in endless time. ... (Beckett, 1959, 129)

Derrida's critique of origins, of a center, has been dutifully celebrated. Derrida argues, to repeat, that faith in the existence of a center, for instance, the center of a text, implies a metaphysics of teleological and transcendental character. According to this metaphysics, there is an absolute end which must be perceived *a priori*, and if this is the case, then there must be a definite beginning, a center from which that end emanates. To reveal the structure of a text, therefore, it must be given a center, which amounts to embodying it with a presence, a fictive presence so to speak, resulting from an artificial act. This center, presumably a rock of stability, founds and generates the text's structure, allowing for certain combinations and permutations while prohibiting others. The center thus becomes "the point at which the substitution of contents, elements, or forms is no longer possible" (Derrida, 1978a, 279). The centered text is now believed to possess some absolute meaning, and this meaning is necessarily transcendental. It must embody, ultimately and ideally, Truth.

This privileged status of an absolute perspective founded in Truth contradicts Derrida's principle of immanence. Derrida tells us that the constraint set up when a text is centered closes it to any real *free play* of elements which could have generated other meanings but did not. The text, says Derrida, is never to be closed. A potential infinity of meanings is possible for each text, given an indefinite number of *repetitions*—readings. This must be essentially the case, since meaning is ultimately culture-bound, language-bound, world-view-bound, and above all, dependent upon particular contexts. Whatever meaning is derived at a particular time and place could always have been otherwise. Whatever is interpreted could be other than what it is. There can be no *a priori* order, crystallized for all eternity. Selection of a text's center, then, is in a sense arbitrary.

Moreover, classical thought, argues Derrida, is founded on the tacit supposition that the center of a structure is paradoxically "within" and "without." That is, according to classical thought the center is "within" the structure, but does not belong *to* it, for it is "transcendental." Yet it is specifiable, though not really part *of* the totality being specified. It is a center which is in reality *not* a center at all. The very concept of a centered structure is, therefore, "contradictorily coherent." It follows, in light of Derrida's thesis, that logic, and hence Western World science and metaphysics, can only be coherent on the grounds of a deep-seated contradiction, or better, inconsistency, due to the historical suppression of DC, or writing.[1] Such contradiction, as always:

> expresses the force of a desire. The concept of centered structure is in fact the concept of a play based on a fundamental ground, a play constituted on the basis of a fundamental immobility and a reassuring certitude, which itself is beyond the reach of play. (Derrida, 1978a, 279)

The desire always for a "reassuring certitude" compels and motivates the arbitrary positioning of a center about which the play of signifiers can be anchored. This provides at least the illusion of permanent meanings embodied in the signifieds, and hence in thought, experience, and the world. But at the very heart of this game contradiction must invariably lie, or better, paradox; it is essential paradox however, which points tangentially in multiple directions. Without it words, and language, could never convene and the game commence. Thought would be eternally unthinkable, experience could never be more than an innocent "seeing," and at most only occasionally "seeing *as*," without the possibility of "seeing-*as*-might-be-or-could-have-been." There would be no anxiety and hence no need for a "reassuring certitude," and no need, either, for an origin or an end. History as such would remain a mere potential. The *play* of language or of signifiers, would be reduced to grunts, gestures, and perhaps a limited set of primitive icons and indexes. It appears, at the outset, that Derrida has discovered the core of what makes human semiotic distinctly human.

Let us extrapolate from Derrida's formulation. If the center of a text can always be arbitrarily chosen, and if in fact, as Derrida seems to imply, there is an indefinite number of possible centers for a given structure, then any "reality" we can speak of must be pluralistic. It consists in the potentiality for the actualization of an infinity of structures. Any presupposed "meaning" and "truth" can enjoy no correspondence with this pluralistic "reality," for each "meaning," each "truth," is context-dependent—language-bound, culture-bound, and world-view-bound. "Meaning" and "truth" can only exist solely and exclusively within a paticularized framework entailed by a given actualized structure, which has been constructed from that infinite realm of possibilities. And each of these structures, following Derrida, must be inventions and not discoveries, constructions rather than gifts from on high, for they must be derived from within the unfathomable potential. Hence, with respect to the potential, each and every "meaning" and "truth" is relative to and dependent upon all others. The text, then, incapable of housing The Center, cannot possess univocal Meaning and Truth.

This assertion, as will be discovered, is actually nothing new. The important question for the moment is: Considering this pluralism of potential structures, each with an arbitrarily given center, must they not belong to some kind of nebulous, non-essential, universal set? Must not all potentially actualizable structures pertain to some all-encompassing Structureless Structure? Perhaps we should call it the Non-Structure. This Non-Structure must embrace, somehow and simultaneously, the multiplicity of all potential structures. Such would also be properly a Centerless Structure, like the ocean which embraces, in simultaneity, each and every wave. That is, if the collection of all potential structures can be construed as One, then this One may in turn be construed as many, or the many as One. And if the many contain "meaning" and "truth" from within their respective frames of reference, then the collection of all "meanings" and "truths" into the One gives, ultimately, a *static* balanced equation, an array of *mutually cancellatory* "meanings" and "truths."[2]

Now, the One I speak of, like the unnamable, unthinkable *Tao*, must be construed as simultaneously Order *and* Chaos. For example, in a uni-dimensional system each element has only one degree of freedom: back and forth along a line. In a two-dimensional system, or a plane, two degrees of freedom are possible, and in a many-dimensional system, many. As these systems become more complex, greater freedom is allowed and concomitantly there are fewer constraints. It follows, therefore that in a system of infinite dimensions, there must be total freedom, and complete unpredictability, or randomness, must prevail. But if this is the case, we have, once again, reverted to chaos: the original One. That is to say, the infinitely structured (ordered) system is synonymous with an infinitely unstructured (disordered) system. Infinite order is tantamount to infinitely random disorder. *Play*, then, can be viewed as at once absolutely free (indeterminable) *and* absolutely structured (ordered). Therefore, *play is* and *is not* free. From the broadest perspective, the notion of structureless free *play* is somewhat of a misnomer.[3]

A good deconstructionist might applaud this "undecidability" at the heart of a—any, even his own—framework. Hence, to purport, as mentioned above, that it constitutes a legitimate criticism of deconstruction would be trivial. On the other hand, it might rightfully be contended that the deconstructionist's acknowledgment of multiple possibilities with no firm foundation can solve no problems; if one is aware of all possible meanings simultaneously, how can one put this awareness in a book. Continual and successive dwelling within multiple frames of reference actually generates no perspective at all. Neither can awareness of many meanings with no definite perspective be a valid starting point. Criticism must at least commence from some definite frame of reference which, ideally, is broader than and includes the frame incorporating that which is being criticized. But the deconstructionist aggravatingly continues to choose what appears to be the equivalent of something approaching the One as his frame—*play*. Nothing can contain this frame; paradoxically, it can only be contained by itself. Consequently, if *play* is beyond good and evil, then it must be beyond criticism. There is not, nor can there be, any Archimedean point of fulcrum from which to move it. But actually the entire universe is the coliseum where this game is played anyway. Hence it must be possible to find a fulcrum point anywhere. Perhaps this is the problem. An infinity of criticisms of deconstructionist texts may be possible, but, in composite, they would be, themselves, also *mutually cancellatory*. They would become, themselves, synonymous with the One. And valid criticism of that One is impossible, for it is already contained within the deconstructionist's infinitely interpretable text— which, according to his own admission, self-deconstructs anyway.

The intriguing question now becomes: Is it possible that the *deconstructive principle* is constructed on its own central bedrock, its Center?[4] Let us journey briefly through Jorge Luis Borges's "Library of Babel" in search of a provisional answer.

3

The library is unlimited and cyclical. If an eternal traveler were to cross it in any direction, after centuries he would see that the same volumes were repeated in the same disorder (which, thus repeated, would be an order: the Order). (Borges, 1964a, 58)

But the best is to think of myself as fixed and at the centre of this place, whatever its shape and extent may be. (Beckett, 1955, 295)

Borges admits that there is a more satisfactory alternative to his cumbersome library. It is a single book consisting of an infinite number of infinitely thin leaves with an "inconceivable middle page" that has no reverse. This middle page can have no reverse since, if the book contains all possible sentences and their countersentences, it must be the mathematical equivalent of zero. And, like zero, that mysterious "non-number," it is at once the center *and* no-*thing*—unthinkable. Just as there is no negative zero, so there can be no opposite to the central page.

This should remind us of the Buddhist concept of *Sūnyatā*, the void or emptiness, a word also derived from "cipher" or "zero" in Sanskrit. Zero is at once no-*thing* and it "contains" the possibility of every-*thing*. That is, it is not merely some-*thing* empty, but rather it is dynamically, the potential for the generation of all integers. In the same way *Sūnyatā* does not mean complete nothingness, it has both negative *and* positive facets simultaneously. Hence the void, or zero like *Sūnyatā* is unthinkable.

Significantly, the ancient Greeks' *horror vacui* and their *horror infiniti* compelled them to surpass the concepts of zero and infinity. If, according to Derrida, the suppression of writing and DC has deterred human creativity and bred ideology and violence, so also hiding zero and infinity under the rug thwarted the growth of Greek mathematics for centuries. But is the zero actually a worthy counterpart to the potentially infinite *play* of DC?

Gottfried Leibniz imagined the Unity, the Monad, to represent God, and zero the Void. God, he deduced, drew all things from the Void, just as Unity (One) and zero potentially express all numbers. Is the deconstructionist somehow playing God, drawing a potential infinity of interpretations from the *play* of DC?

"No," says he, "for I am finite and an 'immanentist.' That is to say, I must inexorably remain within the apparently all-encompassing cosmos of metaphysics, while at the same time I use metaphysics to deconstruct metaphysics, or better, to show how it deconstructs itself, caught up as it is with its paradoxical center which is both inside and transcendental or outside."

Play certainly has no onto-theological characteristics, though it obviously enjoys some affinities with the concept of zero. Yet, how can we more adequately account for this perplexing deconstructive act, if at all? The problem obviously lies, like the above quotes from Beckett and Borges reveal, in the apparently contradictory mixture of finity and infinity, of transcendence and immanence, of "outside" and "inside". It is also revealed in a brief contrast between Albert Einstein and Derrida. The former, believing that God does not play dice with man, never lost faith in the ultimate order and harmony of the universe. He tirelessly persisted in his search for the ultimate theory (center) unifying all limited hypotheses within their particular frames of reference. To do so, however, would require that he, at least in his imaginative world, be *outside* the universe, and *outside all* reference points, in order to conceive of a unity *outside* space and time—seemingly an impossible task, but many still believe it may be accomplished.[5] On the other hand, Derrida, for whom the throw of dice is all there is, in a sense argues for the ultimate disorder *(play)* of the universe. But the lingering premonition, prompted by Borges's riddle, must remain: The Order is, ultimately, tantamount to The Disorder, with the potentiality for both, that is zero *(play?)*, in between. So must Derrida somehow not be "outside" also? And what, in the final analysis, distinguishes Derrida's apparent Structureless Structure from the Absolute which Einstein sought? Or are they at their ultimate extremes analogous? Perhaps an initial clue can be found in some common ideas between Derrida and the "new physics" as well as certain philosophies of science.

4

Not one person in a hundred knows how to be silent and listen, no, nor even to conceive what such a thing means. Yet only then can you detect, beyond the fatuous clamour, the silence of which the universe is made. (Beckett, 1955, 121)

It is well known, of course, that the postulated absence of a center in Derrida's writing enjoys certain parallels in Oriental philosophy (see especially Robert Magliola, 1984, parts 1, 2, and 3). Magliola argues that one of Derrida's chief dilemmas consists in availing himself of logic (which is *ipso facto* "logocentric") to deconstruct logic. Magliola believes to have discovered in Nagarjuna, a Buddhist thinker, an answer to this dilemma. What is not so apparent is that recent ideas in science—and as we shall see, in mathematics and logic—corroborate the Derridean principle of centerlessness.

David Bohm, a maverick physicist and one of the chief opponents of the Copenhagen interpretation of quantum mechanics,[6] suggests that the universe consists in what is most adequately termed "unbroken wholeness." He reminds us that the classical notion of independent atoms making up the universe has been completely overthrown by modern science. It can now be asserted that an inseparable "quantum interconnectedness" (a counterpart to "intertextuality") constitutes the fundamental "reality," and that to conceive of independently behaving parts is erroneous, for they are merely individual and contingent forms unfolded from the whole.

The unbroken wholeness can, at this point, only be described as "that-which-*is.*" It does not consist in separable events or entities. In addition, space, time, and matter simply *are:* they are the *unfolding* of that which was *enfolded,* the actualization of a potentiality, which is, so to speak, "the silence of which the universe is made." The totality of the universe is therefore, and paradoxically, self-contained, immanent (Bohm, 1957, 168).

Bohm's invariant and undifferentiated whole (analogous to Peirce's Firstness) from which consciousness can sever and separate out particular "signs" is called the *unfolded* or *implicate* order. The actualized world of particular "signs" (like Peirce's Secondness) is the *enfolded* or *explicate* order.[7] These two orders are complementary. The *implicate* order is *enfolded,* and from it there is an *unfolding* of the *explicate* order.[8]

Bohm (1957, 1979) illustrates this relationship between the two orders with an analogy. If we put some fluid such as glycerine in a container, place a drop of insoluble dye close to one edge, and turn the container slowly, the dye is "stretched" out in a circle until it seems to disappear. It is still there, but it is now *enfolded, implicate.* Now if we reverse the turn of the container the drop reappears in its previous form. It has become *unfolded, explicate.* While the dye was in its *enfolded* state it existed, though we could not perceive it. Simply because we don't see something or are not presently conscious of it doesn't imply its non-existence. It is there, potentially to become *explicate.* And, it bears mentioning, what is at a given moment *explicate* must in this sense imply what remains *implicate,* but could have become *explicate* (compare to Derrida's *play).* This metaphor-model of the structure of matter, in light of preceding considerations, suggests that the structure of consciousness (or mind) is ultimately isomorphic with this underlying structure of matter.[9] In this respect Bohm (1979, 137) tells us that:

When one part [of the mind or consciousness] is explicit, a tremendous amount is implicit. As we talk, the words are explicit, but the whole meaning is implicit; ... This implicate order is common to mind and to matter, so it means that we have much of a parallelism between the two sides. ... The things which are well defined and explicate have to be seen as special features of the implicate order. ... This idea of implicate and explicate order obviously involves wholeness, because, in the implicate order everything has its origin in the totality; it is folded into the totality (brackets mine).

The combination of the *implicate* order (the potential) and the *explicate* order (the actuals) is what Bohm calls the "qualitative infinity of nature." Much like Whitehead and Peirce, he argues that there can be no end to the levels of interconnected networks, from the infinitely great to the infinitely small, such that there is no end to the number of interpretations of the universe from potentially an unlimited number of perspectives (again, analogous to *play*). This notion calls question to the "thingness" or "beingness" of what has been actualized. Every entity, no matter how fundamental it may be, depends for its existence on its *background* and *substructure*: the *implicate* order. But the prevailing conditions in that *background* and *substructure* are affected by their interconnections with those entities which have been, and are in the process of being, actualized. These interconnections are called the "reciprocal relationship" between *substructure* and *surface structure*.

According to this relationship, nothing is absolutely determinate. For example, according to modern science Robert Boyle's Law of gases can be used to explain the nature of molecular motions. To do so, an ideal large-scale picture (a vessel containing a gas) is used to explain variations of temperature and pressure by means of a small-scale picture of colliding atoms (or molecules). The problem is, however, that the large-scale level exerts a minute but nevertheless real influence on the small-scale level such that the actual pressure of a real gas is never, due to this influence, exactly what would be predicted (i.e., by Boyle's Law, the ideal). It can be no more than an approximation. In other words, *differences* in the atomic behavior of different gases will affect the behavior of those gases at the macroscopic level, which can be measured empirically, in such a manner that no gas will behave exactly in correspondence with the ideal Law.

Bohm contends, consequently, that his notion of the "qualitative infinity of nature" can be illustrated by the potential infinity of *differences* between the ideal—an abstraction—and the real. Of course, such abstractions must be utilized, for they are the only way we can hope to deal with the infinitely differentiable qualitative universe. But as abstractions, they can be no more than an approximation of the real. That is, to formulate an abstraction, there must be a particularization of the infinite background, or the implicate order. But since that order lends itself to an infinite number of possible abstractions, no particular abstraction can be identical to what is

real. Therefore, since each and every abstraction is the particularization of nature's qualitative infinity, it follows that every conceptualization could always have been something other than what it is.
(The relevance of Bohm's view to Derrida's notion of the infinite
play of texts is becoming apparent.)

   Now let us extrapolate from Bohm's hypothesis into the area of
mind-events. According to what Karl Popper (1972) calls "implicit
knowlege" or "nonconscious expectations," and as discussed
above, we can learn something explicitly, implicitly, or by a combination of both, and the more we become familiar with it through
Peircean "habit" the less conscious we are *of* it. That is, in a manner
of speaking what is for us consciously explicate once again tends to
become *implicate*, embedded in the mind. Yet it still remains as
part of our non-conscious awareness and of our activities. A vast
number of past experiences are always *enfolded* within our minds,
whether we are or can be immediately conscious *of* them or not,
and thus "we can always [tacitly] know more than we can
[explicitly] tell" (Polanyi, 1958) (brackets mine).[10] But, in addition,
there is something else which is *enfolded* potentially to become *unfolded:* a structure-dependent knowledge, inherent within the mind
and to a degree possessed by all humans, which is independent of
time and of past experiences. It is precisely for this reason that,
from mathematics and music to language, logic, the sciences and all
the arts, a "center" is—at least temporarily—grasped indeterminately and from what appears to be "somewhere else" (i.e., in the
implicate domain). And this "center" is like a void which can give
rise, over unlimited time, potentially to an infinity of meanings. This
"center" is always absent, at the propitious moment to be *unfolded*
from the complex hierarchy between brain-levels and mind-levels.
Such "centering" activity invariably entails an unfolding from the
continuous whole of a potential infinity of possibilities. And what is
this continuous whole? The equivalent of Bohm's unbroken wholeness, or the equivalent of Peirce's seamless fabric of signs, where
all potentialities remain *enfolded* but from which items of "inner"
and "outer" experiences can always, to a greater or lesser degree,
be drawn.

   The upshot of Bohm's hypothesis is that, like Derrida and in
many ways like Peirce, whether considering the natural world or
the world of the mind, there can be no absolute starting point—if
we prefer not to call it a "center"—and at the same time there

exists an infinity of potential starting points. If the potential from which all actuals were abstracted is infinite, then the "center" is, paradoxically, everywhere and nowhere. And generation of these actuals is made possible at that invisible boundary where the *implicate* order is folded over into the *explicate* order, at the zero point, or the void. Bohm's "metaphysics" also destroys an ancient Greek conception, to be discussed below, that only Being *is*, and that non-being *is not*. Within the *implicate* order, non-being is every bit as "real" (or conversely, as "non-real") as Being, for given the proper perspective, both can exist *and* not exist simultaneously. However, Bohm's scheme also entails an ongoing *creative process* which is almost entirely absent in the deconstructionist's notion of *play* (see Grene, 1974). In the deconstructive game the subject is carried along somewhat mechanically by language, and by writing/reading, to attach meanings to an endless chain of signifiers. There is no real creativity, nor imagination, for all was there in the beginning, awaiting becoming into *differences* (see Derrida, 1972a, 221). Before these *differences* could be actualized, they merely remained there, to be rather passively foregrounded, similar to a computer printing out what was there all along.

It must be admitted that Bohm and his disciples are, for reasons of the state of science, still a minority, for the Copenhagen interpretation is predominant. However, there have been other radical interpretations of quantum mechanics that also partly corroborate the deconstructionist notion of a "centerless, structureless structure." To cite only two: the "bootstrap hypothesis" and the "many worlds interpretation of quantum mechanics."

5

I'm locked up, I'm in something, it's not I, that's all I know.
(Beckett, 1955, 405)

According to Geoffrey Chew's "bootstrap hypothesis," the universe, rather than an aggregate of individual parts, is, like "intertextuality" and Bohm's "metaphysics," a dynamic web of interrelated and interacting "events"—we must "bracket out" particles, since they at this level do not even exist, and we must put events in quotes, for their very coming into presence signifies their going into absence. No part of this web is more fundamental than any other part—in fact, "parts" should actually be put under Derridean "erasure": a "part" can be no more than an abstraction, it takes on meaning *as* a "part" only by its interrelatedness with all other "parts." The whole is all that counts! There is, consequently, no fundamental law, property or characteristic of any "part" of the whole, all of which goes against the grain of the Judeo-Christian, or onto-theological tradition, and against Western World metaphysics. Furthermore, all parameters, or frameworks, must be decided on arbitrarily, for "there is no unambiguous base for making predictions" (Chew, 1968, 765). Chew later admits that the lack of any absolute center or starting point "is so alien to scientific practice as to prevent many distinguished physicists from taking seriously the ...bootstrap. They conclude, in other words, that we are dealing with an unscientific idea" (Chew, 1968, 769).[11] Yet, in light of the continuing inadequacies of the Copenhagen interpretation, an increasing number of scientists are considering alternatives that a few decades ago would have been considered unthinkable.

The "bootstrap hypothesis" is the final rejection of the nineteenth-century mechanistic world-view. It proposes, in the same spirit as the ideas of other contemporary radical physicists, that observations, theories, and ordinarily unquestionable scientific laws, are ultimately creations of the human mind, of consciousness—for the observer must inexorably interact with the observed. Consequently, an attempt to get at the roots, or center, of the entire network posited by the "bootstrap hypothesis" is like placing a sheet on a city street and drawing on it a map of the city, which, if complete, must contain the map, which must contain itself, *ad infinitum*. The implication is, since there is no absolute center and since our perspective must inevitably contain itself, though it cannot simultaneously see itself, all descriptions of the universe can be no more than approximations. Everything cannot be seen at once.

It seems in general that the "bootstrap hypothesis" entails a rather pragmatic, even eclectic, use of theories and frames of reference. The "bootstrap" physicist, like the deconstructionist, is able ideally to observe a number of possible theories or interpretations from a number of perspectives almost-simultaneously in order to understand how they are interdependent.[12] Ultimately, in light of the observer's interaction with the observed, the "bootstrap" idea might even include the consciousness which is in interaction with that being conceived. That is, as the parameters encompassing a given perspective become more comprehensive, finally to engulf the observer, they must ultimately include that observer's consciousness.[13] Carried to its logical extreme, then, "the bootstrap conjecture implies that the existence of consciousness, along with all other aspects of nature, is necessary for self-consistency of the whole. Such a notion, although not obviously nonsensical, is patently unscientific" (Chew, 1968, 763). That is to say, it is unscientific as we generally know science to be today. The self-consistency approach of this hypothesis has "enormous esthetic appeal" of the type Einstein always sought, but conceptual grasp of the totality will always be, both Bohm and Chew admit though Einstein could not bring himself to do so, beyond the scientist, for the totality and its particulars, like transcendence and immanence, or "outside" and "inside," cannot be consistently mixed.

In this respect, and controversially tying quantum physics with Eastern philosophy—which should be relevant to deconstructionist sympathies—Fritjof Capra (1975, 291) suggests that:

> the world view of the Eastern mystics shares with the bootstrap philosophy of modern physics not only an emphasis on the mutual interrelation and self-consistency of all phenomena, but also the denial of fundamental constituents of matter. In a universe which is an inseparable whole and where all forms are fluid and ever-changing, there is no room for any fixed fundamental entity.

Whether considering the text as a Derridean universe of *play*, the universe as a vast interconnected "text," or consciousness as a web of potential significations part of which, by DC, MC, and the TC, become actualized over time, the same conclusions ensue.

6

[T]he Garden of Forking Paths is an incomplete but not false, image of the universe as Ts'ui Pên conceived it. . . . He believed in an infinite series of times, in a growing, dizzying net of divergent, convergent and parallel times. This network of times which approached one another, forked, broke off, or were unaware of one another for centuries embraces all possibilities of time. We do not exist in the majority of these times; in some you exist, and not I; in others I, and not you; in others, both of us. In the present one, . . . you have arrived at my house; in another, while crossing the garden, you found me dead; in still another, I utter these same words, but I am a mistake, a ghost. (Borges, 1964a, 28)[14]

Another recent and remarkably creative hypothesis by the physicist Hugh Everett is the "many worlds interpretation of quantum mechanics." It is based on the presupposition that there exist parallel universes which compose potentially an infinity of alternative worlds of probability, all of them theoretically possessing equal validity, and none taking precedence over any other—i.e., they are, to use a term from this inquiry, *mutually cancellatory*. This hypothesis rests on the "particle-wave" duality of matter. At the most fundamental level, "matter" becomes indistinguishable from "wave packets"—and I must liberally use quotes in this section for the meanings of many terms are self-deconstructing. That is, "particles" at this level behave like collections of electromagnetic "waves," bundles of energy. But "particles" ordinarily must have a particular position at a unique point in time, while "waves" are propagated evenly, like ripples in a pond, in multiple dimensions of space. Therefore logically speaking, "waves" and "particles" cannot exist in simultaneity; they are complementary. Yet under certain conditions "particles" and "waves" seem in a bizarre way to coexist, for it appears that a given electron, a "particle," can know from one position that its unactualized imaginary "twin," which is still a "wave"—i.e., it has not been "collapsed" into a "particle"— possesses the probability of being in another "position" at the same split instant.

The so-called "double-slit" experiment, well-known in physics, can illustrate this phenomenon. Suppose we have a screen with two narrow slits in it, and a gun capable of firing subatomic "particles." If we close one slit and fire "particles" at the screen such that some pass through the other slit, on so doing they act like "particles"— i.e., like throwing golf balls through a slit in a picket fence. Now we open the other slit, fully anticipating that these "particles" will proceed through both slits, and that any given "particle" will make a random probabilistic "choice" of passing either through one slit or the other. But the unexpected occurs. An interference pattern is set up as if the "particles" consisted of "waves" of light passing through both slits—i.e., like the interference pattern created when dropping two stones in a still pond of water. This must indicate that if we were to focus on an individual "particle," we would expect it to pass through one of the two slits, but, on the contrary, it would act as if it were a "wave," and somehow at the other slit this "wave's" "twin," a "particle" which remained unactualized, that is "uncollapsed," would "exist" in parallel with it. Of course we could equally have shot the "particle" through the other slit, and in such case the interference pattern would have been fundamentally the same. That is, the "particle" would act as if it had a "twin" at the other slit. The question is: How could the "particle," in simultaneity, know of this "twin," and how could it know that the second slit was open instead of closed? There seems to be an instantaneous passage of information here, which has continued to baffle contemporary physicists.

In other words, a "particle" in the "double-slit" experiment acts like a "wave" the propagation through space of which somehow occurs in *simultaneity* with that "particle."[15] But since the "particle" at the instant of its passing through one of the slits should be a "particle," it should not be able *simultaneously* to interact with or know the whereabouts of its "twin" since that "twin" does not actually exist but is still a potentiality, a probability. Yet there is an interaction between actualized entities and entities that could have been actualized but were not, which leads to the conclusion that unactualized "worlds" somehow and in some form exist (existed-will exist). And they exist (existed-will exist) as parallel "worlds" to that "world" which happened to be actualized at a particular time and place. Upon this mind-boggling foundation, the "many worlds interpretation" proposes that the universe is One (i.e., a cosmic "wave function" consisting of a quasi-infinity of superimposed "wave functions" and representing the universal set of potentialities). Nothing in this One can be actualized until an "observer" comes into existence and *simultaneously*[16] "observes" (i.e., actualizes) some portion of the "wave function."[17] On "observation," a portion of the "wave" "collapses" into an "event" (which we normally call a "particle," or "matter"). But what was "collapsed" could always have remained "uncollapsed," or it could have "collapsed" differently in a different context.

Now, under the orthodox Copenhagen interpretation of quantum mechanics, only what "collapses" is "real." The "collapsed" and the "uncollapsed" are mutually exclusive. In contrast, according to the "many worlds interpretation," there is not merely the "collapse" of a "wave function," properly speaking, but a "split." That is, when a "particle" is actualized (i.e., becomes "real") it always has a "twin" which presumably should remain unactualized, but it does not, for it branches off into another possible "world." Of course according to the customary laws of probability, this unactualized "wave" could equally have been actualized but was not—like the flip of a coin, heads turns up and tails does not, but tails could equally have turned up—yet since it did not, it can never become "real." But this commonsensically and intuitively obvious state of affairs is not the case in the "many worlds interpretation," and this is its most bizarre aspect. The actualized "particle" is, we must suppose, "real" for us, but it is no more "real" than the unactualized one, for both "split" off into parallel and equally "real worlds." Our "real" world is only one of many![18]

The upshot of this concept is that since our perceivable universe consists of countless "particles," every second it must be splitting off into countless universes only one of them becoming for us "real" and the rest remaining as what for us could have been "real" but was not, but they nonetheless "exist." If we extrapolate from this electron-level to our empirical level of everyday life, the implications are astounding. This potentially infinite set of "worlds" can be pictured as an infinite stack of movie films, each differing only infinitesimally from its nearest neighbor, and differing radically from distant films. I live in one film, you in another. Our paths may cross, but the films can never be identical. There is always a *difference*. Or, by extension, I could have "split" off into another film, and you also, such that our paths become more and more distant, and we never meet (Gribbin, 1979, 120-24) (compare to the above quote by Borges).

Consider another example. If we look out the window and see a cat, in another "world" we might have looked out and the cat was not there, we might have seen not-cat. But the mere fact that we saw the cat does not cancel out the possibility of our having at that instant seen not-cat in another "world." And the not-cat that we "saw" remains as a possibility that could have been actualized but was not. That is, the cat *was* only with respect to the equally potential absence of cat, for had the possible absence never been a presence, the presence of cat *as* cat could never be. Each "world," the cat "world" and the not-cat "world," can thus be assigned an equal degree of actualization, of importance. But the importance attributed to it is, in the long run, arbitrary. No "world" is ultimately any more important than any other "world," whether it is actualized for us or not. After all, a probability is a probability, and merely because one thing pops up means virtually nothing. That thing could have been substituted by a variety, an overwhelming variety, of other things. The composite whole containing all possible "worlds," then, can be none other than *mutually cancellatory*.

The "many worlds interpretation" is, in comparison with Derrida's scheme of things, centerless, immanent, and, like the "bootstrap hypothesis," it radically departs from the classical tradition.[19] In other words, the multiplicity of possible "worlds" is immanently contained within the equivalent of the One. At each instant all possible "worlds" except one, for a particular observer, remain in the potential, in the counterpart to Bohm's *implicate* order. Furthermore, according to Derrida (1978a, 297), the sign, somewhat like the collapse of the "wave packet" in the "many worlds interpretation," emerges from the continuum of possibilities, but it is not the same *as* itself, for it *is* only with respect to what it *is not*, the sign that it could have been but *was not*—its other. without this characteristic its quality of signness could not exist. It refers to itself, or better said it refers to a DC *in* time. But at the same time, it refers to its other, to its reverse and obverse. It existed by having been divided into what is and what could have been, into what will be and what *was not*. But it has no absolute position or origin. It, in a manner of speaking, simply *is*-that-which-*is*. Of course, we have already heard all this from Bohm's "metaphysics" and from the "bootstrap hypothesis." Are the new physicists not themselves beyond the "metaphysics of presence"?[20] Deconstruction is perhaps not so radical as many would like to believe.

But if science is no longer limited to Western World metaphysics, then how does it differ from the deconstructionist's view? Perhaps in the scientist's use of method? No, or at least no longer, for an important reason. At the end of the nineteenth century, it was assumed that science—the science against which Nietzsche reacted—was in possession of an invariant method, and that indubitable knowledge of each and every aspect of the physical universe was just around the corner. As is well known, in the arts the naturalists availed themselves of this scientific "method" finally to demonstrate through their own art—and against their wishes—that they produced very "unscientific" works in spite of themselves.

Many humanists and to an extent some artists still maintain a degree of faith in the value of method, entranced with their own brand of technology. This fascination with science and method, no more evident than in American "new criticism," linguistic criticism, and especially early French structuralism, has stimulated the search for univocal meanings and determinate interpretations. The fact is, however, as Wylie Sypher (1962) points out, scientists have during the present century struggled against the "tyranny of method," and in so doing they have, with their new image of the world, forged far beyond many artists and all but a handful of humanists. Today's scientist is what Arthur Koestler (1963) describes as a "sleepwalker" who sort of blunders through without really knowing what he is doing at the time, following impulses, aesthetic preferences, and even trying things out simply to discover what will result.[21]

Of course, it might be countered, the deconstructionist is beyond the naiveté of most humanists. At least in Derrida's case the point may be well taken. But the proper questions to ask are: Why Derrida's continued fascination with Stéphane Mallarmé, and Paul Valéry for whom a pure poem is an "algebra," a "machine," the algorithms of which, automatically as it were, produce a particular state of mind through words? Why the deconstructionist's insistence on the engulfing power of language which, as an impersonal agent, moves the reader/writer along, even against his will? Is deconstruction really without method? Or does there lie, behind *play*, a tyrannical form of method, which presumably is capable of subverting each and every countermethod?[22]

Let us now turn to the works of two philosophers of science where, it might seem, the most progressive ideas concerning scientific method should be found and place them in the same light with deconstruction.

7

For I stopped being half-witted and became sly, whenever I took the trouble. And my head was a storehouse of useful knowledge. (Beckett, 1955, 85)

According to Popper, authority should always be questioned; presuppositions, beliefs, and knowledge should always be open to scrutiny. Science, in other words, should perpetually criticize itself. This self-criticism stems in part from Popper's "principle of falsification." In contrast to the logical positivists' "verification hypothesis," Popper claims that all scientific theories must establish the grounds by means of which they can be refuted.[23] Theories can be made so general as to be verified *ad infinitum*—Freud, Karl Marx, and Alfred Adler are cited as examples. This being the case, they are not theories at all, for their status as scientific theories depends upon their being improved upon or replaced in light of refuting evidence.[24] Popper reasons that since all scientific theories except the present ones have been to a degree refuted, there are no grounds upon which dogmatically to hold our own up as sacrosanct—that was, of course, Immanuel Kant's error. The present theories too will be someday refuted, and if not, then they were not really scientific anyway: they belonged to metaphysics.[25]

Truth surely exists somewhere, claims Popper. But we can never know it. We can never know it, for the only "kernel of truth is just that there exists no general criterion of truth" (Popper, 1962, 374). And this is for an important reason. Assuming that we somehow were able to grasp the Truth, we could never really be sure that we had it, for our task would ideally be to try to "falsify" it, and not being able to do so, we would, by our own admission, relegate it to the status of an untruth (i.e., a non-theory, or an unscientific "dogma") since it is "unfalsifiable." Hence, the traditional God, René Descartes's Intellect (rationalism), and Francis Bacon's unbiased observations (empiricism) have proved to be inadequate for the game of science (Popper, 1963, 3-30). And, since we are all fallible, we can really *"never know what we are talking about"* (Popper, 1974a, 27-28). All theories, then, can be no more than conjectural, partly arbitrary, and at most tentative. The best we can do is constantly strive to open our theories up, to subject them to broader parameters—as long as they conform to the "falsification principle" that is. But, it must be added, these ever-widening parameters can never be identical with the totality (i.e., complete knowledge).

Now to relate Popper's epistemology to Derrida. Popper's system of knowledge obviously contains some sort of "center." Yet, since we can never perceive the end—ultimate Truth—obviously we can never grasp the true "center." For instance, the "center," the "origin," is where each organism begins, with what Popper calls its set of inborn expectations, but for the non-human as well as the newly born infant these expectations are at this point implicit, unavailable to self-consciousness, and hence irretrievable. However, for the human animal, with each search for a solution to a problem situation that has arisen from unsatisfied expectations or critical scrutiny, there must be necessarily a beginning. But, invariably the result of a guess or conjecture, this central starting point is, if not totally arbitrary, at least *a priori* indeterminable, and we can partly know its meaning and implications only after we arrive at some sort of a tentative solution. Moreover, the choice of this starting point "is not decisively important because it can be criticised and corrected like everything else" (Popper, 1972, 104). Hence we can have no more than a vague beginning and build on insecure foundations (Popper, 1972, 34).

Although Popper speaks of all organisms' inborn need for regularity, the need for a present "center," there is certainly no nostalgia for origins. It seems, following Popper, that the location of an indubitable "center" is simply unimportant. What matters is the activity by means of which discoveries are made: *the game of science.* Moreover, although Popper alludes to self-criticism as "self-transcendence," it is not the transcendence of transcendental phenomenology. Rather, the scientist lifts himself up by his own bootstraps, and "transcends" his own sphere of knowledge into another, more extensive sphere which is of his own making (Popper, 1963, 384). This is in reality commensurate with what Derrida calls immanence.

Popper's self-criticism, like Derrida's self-deconstruction—rearticulated by Julia Kristeva (1969, 83) as a science which perpetually criticizes itself—is also non-teleological in the sense that we can never know the end. However, one important difference is that the deconstructionist never even pretends to be searching for Truth (here we see the distinction between the deconstructionist's relativity and Popper's absolute, but always absent, Truth). The deconstructionist deconstructs what are supposed to be erroneously and usually implicitly believed truths. Moreover, he demonstrates time and time again what Truth *is not*, without feeling any compulsion to attempt to state what it *is*. This is similar to Buddhist teachings insofar as every asserted Truth is met with a denial, since that assertion discloses at least one aspect of the world but does so invariably by concealing another aspect: every assertion *is* and *is not* the Truth. But is not every scientific theory also simultaneously true *and* false in the Popperian scheme? It is as a conjecture tentatively true because its falsehood is not yet established, but if true, then it must be false ("falsifiable"), a falsehood that eventually must be brought to light, for if not, the theory could not have been true.[26] Each conjecture, then, hopefully a closer approximation to the Truth, is at the same time, and at a different level, its own untruth, for in its assertion it conceals some other aspect of the Truth.[27] So deconstruction reveals the Truth of all untruths while Popperian critical inquiry discloses the falsity lying behind tentative truths. What for one person is negative (i.e., "falsifying") construction, for another is positive deconstruction (i.e., verification of the *deconstructive principle*).[28]

But surely it can't be this simple. Obviously, we must feel, there is a more fundamental difference between the two programs. Yes and no. Popper's anti-metaphysical view focuses directly on thought; he has no use for language analysis, for ideas are what is important (Popper, 1963, 293). Science, and everyday life, he asserts, start with problem situations, not with mere relatively meaningless words or collections of facts. And the attempt consciously to construct and resolve problem situations in thought is the principle characteristic of scientific activity—science, like everyday life situations, is an ongoing affair (Popper, 1963, 272). But since all ideas are, when put into language, at the outset necessarily

vague and "systematically ambiguous," there should be at the beginning stage of an inquiry no attempt rigorously to define terms
because they cannot be so defined.[29] And the choice of these undefined terms is unavoidably partly arbitrary, though this is not exclusively the fault of language (Popper, 1974a, 29).[30] Hence, words are
unfortunately inadequate, but they are still the best tool we have
with which to convey thought.[31]

In contrast, Derrida's anti-metaphysics and anti-science focuses
on language abuse, so to speak—the embedment of error-clad
meanings into words because of equally embedded myths (of presence, identity, repetition, etc.). Western World language, with its
predominance of speech, its suppression of writing, must of course
be debunked. This includes not only all metaphysics, but science as
well. However, the difference between Popper and Derrida is not
what it appears at the outset. In recent years Popper demonstrates
that metaphysical theories, like scientific theories, can after all "be
susceptible to criticism and argument, because they may be
attempts to solve *problems*—problems perhaps open to better or
less good solutions" (Popper, 1974a, 150; 1963, "Postscript"). He
applies his criterion to five metaphysical theories (determinism,
idealism, irrationalism, Arthur Schopenhauer's voluntarism, and
Heidegger's philosophy of nothingness) and gives "reasons for re-
jecting these as unsuccessful attempts to solve their problems"
(Popper, 1974a, 150). Popper's heuristic method for metaphysics—
he even calls it a "hermeneutics"—implies the notion that since
metaphysical theories can be criticized, though not scientifically
tested, then they can be improved for the better (Popper, 1972, 183-
86). That is, they can be "falsified" through critical scrutiny and
"rational argument" and revised or replaced by alternative theories,
and hence a closer and closer approximation to the ideal hopefully
is achieved.[32] Once again, what is negative construction from one
bird's-eye view is positive deconstruction from another.

Another difference between Popper and Derrida, it will be contended, lies in Popper's faith, a paradoxically dogmatic and irrational
faith, in reason and traditional logic.[33] Popper has no tolerance for
logical inconsistencies (a surprise, since in his *Open Society*, 1962, he
criticizes all intolerance). For this reason, he believes Werner Heisenberg's uncertainty principle and Neils Bohr's complementarity are at
best incomplete. They are only an approximation to some more
general, logically consistent theory which remains to be discovered-

invented. That is, if the position and momentum of an electron, or the "wave" and "particle" nature of light are considered to be two mutually incommensurable ways of looking at subnuclear phenomena, it must be admitted that they cannot be adequately understood from one comprehensive perspective. As such they remain incomplete, and we must strive for an even closer approximation to a complete theory, while knowing full well that we will never be able to grasp it in its entirety (Popper, 1974a, 93). Yet what Popper desires in this more encompassing theory is a traditional logical formulation, rather than Bohr's complementarity or other radical logics that have been proposed, such as "quantum logic."[34] This adherence to formal logic is apparently very un-Derridean. In fact, it seems that Popper's "critical rationalism" bears more similarity with the Cartesian program than with Derrida. However, Popper assures us that his "rationalism" is not grounded in any invariant Cartesian innate forms of truth by intuition or introspection. Since we are told that intuitions are many times wrong (i.e., they are later "falsified"), they are therefore no infallible road to Truth (Popper, 1972, 41-42).

A problem, however, with Popper is that his "rationalism" lies "in the quicksands of an irrational commitment" (O'Hear, 1980, 148; but also see Popper's admission to such in 1972, 38-42). That is, it consists in a viciously circular commitment to critical argumentation. If one becomes a partisan of it, one must accept it on faith, an "irrational" faith as it were, and hence one cannot, or ideally should not, open this very commitment itself to critical argument. In other words, if it cannot be "falsified" by its own argument, then it cannot be proved invalid, but it must not be subject to "falsification" anyway, for it lies outside that which is the focus of critical argument.

But is not deconstruction also confronted with the same quandary? To defend deconstruction by claiming that that which is undeconstructed, or metaphysical, can be subjected to deconstruction: Does this not imply some sort of undeconstructible notion (perhaps the *deconstructive principle)* which is automatically embraced by the deconstructor? And if so, does it not risk the same apriorist foundation as Popper's method of logical reconstruction? There still seems to be common, though strangely inverted, ground between Popper and the deconstructionist: the presupposition of a necessary victory over "irrationalism" or "rationalism," whichever the case may be, and which unavoidably entails a lance firmly embedded in the conquered foe. There is something spurious about such victories, something hermetic. Whether either "reason" or "irreason" is "logically" or "illogically" superior, in the final analysis, must depend upon the eye of the beholder.[35]

There are additional points of convergence between Popper and Derrida. Popper (1947) tells us that we cannot use a word and at the same instant in time criticize or study it. The criticism of words demands some other frame of reference. That is, we cannot be "inside" the domain of words and at the same instant "outside" such that the words used can be the focus *of* our attention. The point is well taken, and it sounds much like Peirce as well. However, if we accept this notion, then the vantage point of Popper's critical activity—and even deconstruction in light of above comments—must remain "outside." That is to say, the two frames of reference, that which *is* the focus and that *from which* the focus is directed, must be incommensurable. What is "irrational" from "within" can become "rational" from the perspective of Popper's scrutinous eye, and what appears to be "rational" from "within" is actually "irriational" given the larger, supposedly more adequate framework "within" which the deconstructionist dwells. Admittedly, this "outside" is not "transcendental" in the phenomenological sense of the term. Nevertheless, it must still remain "outside" the realm of the unanointed who have no privileged view into those deeper insights available only to the chosen few.[36]

In the final analysis, I suggest the following analogy between Popper and the deconstructionist's "method":

"FALSIFICATION"	DECONSTRUCTION
All theories can be "falsified" by "rational" and critical argument, however,	All metaphysics (myths) (i.e., erroneous and covert assumptions) can be deconstructed, however,
There is no determinate "starting point," so,	There is no retrievable "center," so,
Aware that all knowledge is theory-impregnated, and that,	Aware that all metaphysics (myth) is metaphor-impregnated,[37] and that,

"FALSIFICATION"	DECONSTRUCTION
All conjectures are themselves "falsifiable,"	Deconstruction is self-deconstructing,
Begin with a bold conjecture, knowing that it cannot be absolutely "verified," and refute it as quickly as possible in order to demonstrate that it was not the true starting point.	Pick a provisional "center,"[38] knowing that it is not full presence, the origin, nor absolute, and deconstruct the system in order to demonstrate that there is no center.
Return to beginning and repeat steps.	Return to beginning and repeat steps.

Both activities are ongoing, recursively iterative, and self-referential. Neither can ever be completed: they will supposedly continue to circle forever. But there is an important difference. Popper's game entails an upward moving spiral of ever-larger frames of reference toward an ideal, though it is admittedly unknowable.[39] Deconstructive *play*, in contrast, is bidimensionally circular; the end product of each and every deconstructing act is the same. Yet, though Popper's game appears to be relatively open, the fact remains that, for reasons mentioned above, he is rather conservative when compared to the deconstructionists. The search must continue.

8

A thousand little things to report, very strange, in view of my situation, if I interpret them correctly. But my notes have a curious tendency, as I realize at last, to annihilate all they purport to record. (Beckett, 1955, 259).

The views of Paul Feyerabend, a rebellious Popperian disciple, can perhaps lead us closer to a final answer. Feyerabend in many respects goes further than Derrida. His program for scientific theory-making is clearly pluralistic. But it is a pluralism more open to new possibilities than most deconstructionists apparently ever dreamed of. Science, Feyerabend claims, always tends toward conservatism. It incessantly threatens to become no more than the doctrine of a venerable priesthood periodically and patronizingly passing off occasional pearls of esoteric verbiage as profound insights. In order to prevent this inevitable closure of science, Feyerabend wants to include, for equal consideration, the ideas of laymen as well as experts, dilettanti and professionals, liars and truth-freaks. In science nothing has ever been, nor can it ever be, settled, hence, *no* view or method should be sacred. The task of the scientist is "no longer 'to search for the truth', or 'to praise God', or 'to systematize observations', or 'to improve predictions'" (Feyerabend, 1975, 30). Theories should not converge toward some nebulous ideal or notion of Truth. Rather, they must represent "an ever increasing *ocean of mutually incompatible (and perhaps even incommensurable) alternatives*, each single theory, each fairy tale, each myth that is part of the collection forcing the others into greater articulation and all of them contributing, via this process of competition, to the development of our consciousness" (Feyerabend, 1975, 30).

Unlike Popper for whom we must consciously and intentionally create a problem situation and then act upon it, Feyerabend believes that we should merely dabble and play around with a large number of apparently incoherent ideas, nurturing no fixed notions of reason, logic, or method. This should be the proper non-method, for scientific theories are replaced by other theories not necessarily because one is more successful, progressive, or closer to the Truth. Simply, a new group of scientists came along with different standards, and if they were successful, it was because they effectively imposed their view on the community. There must, then, be a plurality of standards and methods (Feyerabend, 1976). Feyerabend cites Bohr, who never started with an explicit "problem situation" or with a fixed method, but always with a paradox, and gradually he would tease some answers from it, all the while using vague and undefined notions. In this sense the initial starting point, the "nucleus" (or "center") is not at the outset known with certainty but must be (arbitrarily, as it were) invented. It is necessary, in short, to "learn talking in riddles," to use apparently contradictory terms in easy going ways without scrutinizing them too closely (Feyerabend, 1975, 257).[40]

Furthermore, if a scientist stumbles onto a new idea from outside the traditional notions of reason, logic, or method, in order to convey this idea to the community he must inevitably distort, misuse, and beat language into new patterns so that it might fit that new idea, and then it always and invariably does so imperfectly. Only in this manner, however, can language become a worthy tool. But actually, it is not merely a tool, for it is transformed at the very moment of its use (like the movement of DC), leading to new unforeseen situations and new intellectual machinery in need of yet other newly forged tools. Finally, as a theory begins to take shape, concepts gradually intermesh, fuzzy meanings become more definite, vagueness becomes relative clarity, and a world-view begins to emerge. The scientist can never know where he is going, however, and can never achieve total clarity of expression, until arriving at this very provisional ending point, which is really no ending point at all, for science must always be open (Feyerabend, 1975, 249-52). In this sense there can be only a series of successive steps "outside" the circle of what at a given time and place is accepted as conventional reason, logic, and method, each creating radically new alternatives which could not have been conceived from the "inside." As Feyerabend (1975, 32) remarks:

> We need an *external* standard of criticism, we need a set of alternative assumptions or, as these assumptions will be quite general, constituting, as it were, an entire alternative world, *we need a dream-world in order to discover the features of the real world we think we inhabit* (and which may actually be just another dream world).[41]

This "epistemological anarchy" allows almost anything at least provisionally to pass as knowledge. No historical period, no culture, no subculture, however non-scientific, must take precedence over any other, for there is no absolute set of criteria with which to judge the merits of one culture's science over that of another—in other words, the composite of all possible cultures, past, present, and future, can be none other than *mutually cancellatory*. To cite only one of Feyerabend's many examples, acupuncture was found to be inexplicable for modern medical science—ironically an embarrassment, since the effectiveness of the technique is undeniable—yet it can be conjoined with Western practices potentially to produce a "science" representing an improvement over anything existing today (Feyerabend, 1975, 51). Other cases such as voodoo and magic (Jarvie and Agassi, 1967, 1973), mythology (Horton, 1967, Lévi-Strauss, 1969), "primitive" taxonomies (Lévi-Strauss, 1966), and Western World scientific theories of the past (de Santillana, 1961) also apply.

Feyerabend's notion of "irrationality" stems in part from his principle of incommensurability between scientific theories.[42] When a scientist shifts his vision upon constructing an alternative to the received theory, his whole way of looking at the world changes, and in a sense it becomes a different world. Such sudden shifts of perception render competing theories incommensurable. Meanings of terms and the role they play within one theory are radically variant from within an alternative theory, since they entail radically distinct perspectives and frames of reference. Consequently, translation from one theory to another becomes impossible because there can exist no one-to-one correspondence between them. Not even a neutral language can be constructed with which to judge the possible validity of one theory over another.[43]

Hence no theoretical sentence can have a meaning which is "true" in one theory and "false" in another, for there is simply no way of translating the sentence. From within one theory, if that theory is internally coherent, a sentence can be "true," and when placed within another theory, it may be looked upon as "false." But the sentence cannot be judged in both contexts from within only one of the two frameworks. For example, the concept of "mass" is "true" within Newtonian physics and "true" within Einsteinian physics, though it has different and even incommensurable meanings within the two contexts. However, if the Newtonian meaning for "mass" is interjected into the Einsteinian framework, it cannot merely be looked upon as "false" or even meaningless. It has meaning, but its meaning from within the Einsteinian framework is simply inexpressible, for on so mixing meanings, the old system (Newtonian framework) and the new system (Einsteinian framework) have also been incommensurably mixed.[44] Such a mixture inevitably creates a paradox which cannot be resolved either within the old or the new framework, but only from a larger (paradoxical and hence unexpressible) framework with which it may be possible at least to understand how the paradox was generated in the first place (Feyerabend, 1970).[45] To do so we must not attempt to determine which meaning is "true" and which is "false," for from within this larger framework no metalanguage is possible. Actually, we must be willing to free ourselves of meanings altogether. Then, and only then, can we simply contemplate sentences *qua* sentences to determine how they lie within their respective frameworks and how they are used. Knowledge, then, consists in no more than an intricate fabric of interrelated sentences—or, for the deconstructionist, "intertextuality"—not in what those sentences actually mean. And the interrelations between those sentences depends upon a context, the theoretical context in this case, within which they lie. Outside the context, they can have neither meaning nor signification.

For Feyerabend: Contemplation rather than reasoned intelligibility, language use rather than meaning. In his notion of language use, Feyerabend is close to the later Wittgenstein, and to the rhetorical imperatives of Derrida.[46] Traditionally, from the origins of Greek science to logical positivism, it has been erroneously assumed that some occult meaning lies behind what exists on the surface of propositions. Now, Feyerabend tells us that *what we see is what there is*, but not clearly or simply, for to resort to Derrida, each new context calls for different language use, and hence different "meanings." Consequently, as Feyerabend would assert, there is no meaning that can be absolutely agreed upon—at least from within different frameworks. All we have, and what we must cope with, is *successive differentiation* "inside" particular frameworks and incommensurability between frameworks.[47]

Obviously, and we need really go into few details here, there are similarities between Feyerabend's view of science and deconstruction. Feyerabend's hypothesis is descriptive, for his anti-method, he claims, is how most successful scientists actually proceed. But it is also prescriptive, for the scientists, while presuming to be "rational," is many times unwittingly an "irrationalist," and hence he should admit to such and be an honest and committed "irrationalist." Feyerabend (1975, 189) concedes, interestingly enough, that his "anarchistic epistemology" is influenced by Dadaism. The successful iconoclastic scientist, like the Dadaist, not only has no well-defined program, but he is against all rigid programs. And like the Dadaist, he must also be an anti-Dadaist. That is, while groping for the meaning of the fuzzy-bordered concepts with which he is working, he need not be reduced to vague allusions, stammering and stuttering statements about ineffability. He must at the same time, like the Dadaist, be committed to a degree of "logic' and "reason," for if not, he could not talk at all. Actually, his anti-perspective can exist only with respect to its opposite. (Dadaist babbling must exist *in opposition to* "logical" talk, for if not, it would be an impossible regression anyway, for DC and the TC, or that is, history, cannot simply vanish.)

In fact, Galileo's scientific rhetoric, cited by Feyerabend as the supreme example of his anti-method, reads at one point strikingly like the deconstructive act:

> An argument is proposed that refutes Copernicus by observation. The argument is inverted in order to discover the natural interpretations which are responsible for the contradiction. The offensive interpretations are replaced by others, propaganda and appeal to distant, and highly theoretical, parts of common sense are used to defend old habits and to enthrone new ones. The new natural interpretations, which are also formulated explicitly, as auxiliary hypotheses, are established partly by the support they give to Copernicus and partly by plausibility cons derations and *ad hoc* hypotheses. An entirely new 'experience' arises in this way. Independent evidence is as yet entirely lacking, but this is no drawback as it is to be expected that independent support will take a long time appearing. (Feyerabend, 1975, 99)

Galileo, like the deconstructionist, apparently worked both "inside" and "outside" a system of thought, revealing its inevitable flaw without there as *yet* being a systematically coherent alternative. There is, however, one important difference: Feyerabend's anti-method entails at least the initiation of a positive move toward what will be a tentatively conceived by hopefully more viable theory (even though devious means are used to convince the public that the theory is better than its predecessors), while deconstruction remains by and large negative (and convoluted rhetoric is used to convince the public that there is no absolute theory or method). To repeat, Feyerabend readily admits that there can be no once-and-for-all theory or method, yet the object of his game of science is to expand the frame of reference such that a wider variety of possible alternatives may come into view. Knowledge in this way becomes more general, though it must risk continually having the rug slipped from under its feet. Deconstruction, on the other hand, goes through the magical act of rug pulling with no overt pretence of replacing one body of knowledge with another; there is only the expanding circle, rather than the upward moving spiral mentioned in the preceding section.[48]

Feyerabend's solution is, then, that we must be *both* "rationalists" "nationalists," scientists *and* anti-scientists (i.e., deviate totally from the venerated norms of the day). If Popper's "rationalism" is at its roots "irrational" yet "transcendental," and if the *deconstructive principle* is invariant ("rationally" positing "irrationalism"), then Feyerabend is, we must admit, always a "rational irrationalist." It seems plausible to suggest, therefore, that just as the Dadaist must also be an anti-Dadaist, so the deconstructionist should be not only simultaneously a metaphysicist and an anti-metaphysicist, but also an anti-deconstructionist. That is, the deconstructor must construct in a positive sense in order to have something worth deconstructing, for since deconstruction preys on construction, *he must become at once a host and a parasite.*

The key, I believe, and as Feyerabend implies, entails frame switching. For instance, the Zen Buddhist asks what happens to the fist when the hand is opened. We need not bother ourselves over the existence or nonexistence of the concept of the hand (the "inner" frame) once the concept of a fist (the "outer" frame) is recognized. The hand in one perspectival frame is the linguistic scaffolding for understanding what a fist is from "within" a larger frame, but at the same time without the hand the concept of a fist would be nonexistent. The trouble stems from our aggravating tendency, as the deconstructionist well knows, to think of words as things rather than as no-*things* bearing signification by means of the *differences* between them.

Actually, the physicist has at times been relatively successful in avoiding this problem. "Particles" and "waves" are for him no more than linguistic scaffoldings for understanding electrons and other subatomic particles. If we used these terms as if they directly represented things in the physical world or were the things themselves, this scaffolding would appear, and rightly so, "illogical." In order to understand this "illogic," we must then commit a sin against "reason." We must concede, paradoxically, that electrons, when viewed from distinct frames of reference, are *both* identical *and* different, and they *are* and they *are not* "particles" *and* "waves." After all, what's in a word anyway? Meaning is not *ipso facto* in it, nor is it in the electrons, in a set of neuronal firings in the physicist's head, or in his mind. The word carries no information at all except with respect to the imagined discrimination (by means of DC) that can be made between it and other words. Hence "particle" and "wave," or identity and difference, are merely "logical" discriminations which cannot directly apply to anything in the natural world. When we attempt to apply them they become "illogical," but they are so only with respect to the more concrete, empirical, and operational perspectives. In this respect, identity/difference, the most fundamental "opposition" put forth by the deconstructionist, is itself a "logical" construct, which, only when made to correspond to the world from within two incommensurable frames, can become "illogical." The deconstructionist exploits our penchant for perceiving the world "logically" by constructing for us an apparently "illogical" scheme, but he, of course, subverts his own "illogic," for he constructs it by "logical" means, and with predictable finality.[49] Therefore he commits a sin against his own "irreason."[50]

CHAPTER THREE

Deconstruction Meets a Mathematician

1

And gravely I struggled to be grave no more, to live, to invent,
I know what I mean. (Beckett, 1955, 195)

Beckett's words are paradoxical, like the mother telling her child: "Be spontaneous." This is an impossible task—the essence of schizophrenia (Bateson, 1972; Laing, 1969). Yet it is a metaphorical illustration, like the twist of the Möbius strip, or the deconstructionist's "uncanny moment," when the text's *aporia* is revealed at its "grammatological navel."[1] It is the task of the deconstructionist precisely to find this "logically illogical" element which, when disclosed, will open the text to a potential infinity of interpretations. When this element is revealed, the critical reader knows he has participated, is participating, in the indeterminate *play* of the text. This "uncanny moment," however, is not simply the identification of an apparently unresolvable contradiction, ambiguity, or metaphor. It hails awareness of a key word, meaning one thing from one perspective and another from another, which must be followed throughout the text which itself becomes unglued to reveal that which was concealed, to make manifest the text's "self-transgression" (Spivak, 1974, lxxv). The entire system collapses.

61

The crucial term for the "uncanny moment" is *undecidability*. The text at this point becomes literally undecipherable in terms of univocal meanings, and thus a resolution of the multidimensional paradox is unsayable, though it can somehow be experienced. That is, any reading here is automatically and simultaneously a misreading, for all possible readings exist in unison—like the "many worlds" of quantum mechanics.[2] But the deconstructor, given his finiteness, is humanly incapable of seeing all these readings in simultaneity. Therefore a schizophrenic reverberating echo chamber in his mind begins until, perhaps we can say, he experiences "it."

The problem is that if, as mentioned above, discovery of the text's *aporia* is invariably predictable—though where it is to be discovered is not—deconstruction risks becoming a "pseudoscience."[3] J. Hillis Miller (1976a, 348) believes, nevertheless, that this can be avoided:

> The critics of the uncanny must be exceedingly nimble as de Man, Hartman, Derrida, and Bloom in their different ways conspicuously are, in order to keep their insights from becoming pseudoscientific machines for the unfolding (explication), or dismantling (deconstruction), of literary texts.[4]

Miller, it must be said, perceives science to be determinate, deconstruction indeterminate. Science is closed, deconstruction open. Science searches for Truth, deconstruction reveals the untruth in all "truth." Earlier Miller alludes to the "most uncanny moment" as the moment of "the Socratic becoming uncanny, the uncanny, canny, sometimes all too shrewdly rational" (Miller, 1976a, 343). "Science" for Miller is the Socratic, the Apollonian, while the Dionysian is art. Socratic or "scientific" thought gives the appearance of escaping from all paradoxes into the "clear light of logical insight," but it eventually "becomes blindness when it reaches its limits," and "turns back into tragic art, the art of the abyss, the alogical," and so on (Miller, 1976a, 343).

Actually, in view of what has been said above on contemporary science and the philosophy of science, these remarks become outright silly. Pure science today is not the "science" spoken of by Nietzsche, Freud, Husserl, Heidegger, or at times even by Derrida—though he certainly knows better. Were Nietzsche to be resurrected today he undoubtedly would be shocked at the changes wrought in the sciences.[5] The "science" he reacted against entailed the Newtonian mechanistic, corpuscular-kinetic world-view, a dark age from which, for many humanists, there has not yet been any transgression. Nietzsche was correct, very definitely. But the important point is that by and large his prophesy has been fulfilled. Science has pushed to the limits and has become, more conscientiously, artistic—actually, scientists were artists all along, claims Feyerabend, but they simply didn't know it.

In fact, dramatic "uncanny moments" have always existed in science, though their nature for obvious reasons differs from "uncanny moments" in art, philosophy, and criticism. Consider, for instance, the transition from Newtonian to Einsteinian physics. In the three-dimensional model of classical physics space is represented by a vertical plane and time is symbolized as a line perpendicular to this plane. Space conjoined with time produces an infinity of successive instantaneous spatial planes, all perpendicular to the temporal line, and each being *simultaneously present* to all others. This represents the universe at an instant, ideally perceived by a superintelligence (Laplace's, or God's). That is, in this model an absolute frame of reference is possible from which point all perceived events are *simultaneous*, light presumably traveling at infinite velocity.

Simultaneity is the key word, the "uncanny navel" of Newtonian physics. Einstein, with a series of ingenious thought experiments, destroyed ("deconstructed") the presumed common-sense Newtonian concept of a universal time providing for absolute *simultaneity* of events. Time, Einstein demonstrated, cannot be separated from space, and as such it is relative to the spatial position of the observer, who is relative to all other positions, themselves in motion. There is potentially an infinity of frames of reference in the universe, and from within, there is no absolute frame of reference. Moreover, since the distance between two positions is relative to the observer from a third position, distance is also relative, as are velocity, acceleration, force, and energy, all of them being dependent upon time, the speed of light, and the concept of *non-simultaneity*. Einstein thus disclosed "some features of the Newtonian cosmology which, though unknown, had influenced all arguments about space and time" (Feyerabend, 1975, 225). And, it bears stating, from within this Newtonian cosmology, more absurd, "illogical," and "irrational" concepts than Einstein's could hardly be found. As a consequence, eventually Einsteinian physics brought "the whole structure of theoretical physics tumbling down like a house of cards. Hardly anything remains untouched" (Hoffman, 1972, 77). Einstein found the thread which, when pulled, unraveled the entire cloak. A supreme "deconstructor"? Yes. But in addition, Einstein, we must recall, not only "deconstructed," he had a few very tenable, though at the outset tentative, alternatives as well.[6]

In sum, science *has*, as Nietzsche advised, turned more than ever to the imagination of the possible. The imaginative or artistic mind provides "that vision within which it is possible to have a science at all" (DeLong, 1971, 227). In general modern science does not simply accept one system and categorically reject all others. It entails the imaginative mind, which generates never-ending alternatives to tentatively accepted views. In today's science, then, there can be no entirely non-poetic accounts. If non-poetic they are looked upon with disinterest, and if interesting, they are interesting precisely because they contain part of the unknown, some mystery or intriguing paradox, or because common-sense tells the scientist it just can't be right. Modern science always contains, within itself, paradox and "double-bind." So Miller is correct, though ironically, for he directs his attack toward a science that no longer exists.

Paradox must be considered further since it is embedded in the *deconstructive principle*, and then we can observe how "uncanniness" exists at the heart of all relatively complex conceptual systems, including that of the deconstructor.

2

They paid no attention to me and I repaid the compliment. Then how could I know they were paying no attention to me, and how could I repay the compliment, since they were paying no attention to me? (Beckett, 1955, 23)

Mere *contradiction* is not the same as paradox. "They paid attention to me and they did not pay attention to me" is such an example. Paradox must, like contradiction, contain *negation*. "This sentence does *not* have seven words" is obviously false, and it contains negation, but it is not paradoxical, however. *Self-reference* is necessary as well. "This is a sentence" is a case in point. The sentence refers to itself, but without negation or contradiction it is no more paradoxical than the previous example. The final prerequisite for paradox is the *vicious circle* principle, which creates an oscillation, *ad infinitum*, between two contradictory poles. For example, "This sentence is *not* true" is, if true, then false, and if false, then true, but if true, then false, etc. It is indeed paradoxical.

Paradoxes can come in three types: (a) logical or syntactic, consisting of a contradiction arrived at by valid conclusions from apparently non-contradictory premises, (b) semantic, involving notions of truth and falsity, such as "This sentence is both provable and false," and (c) pragmatic, including at least two subjects in the context of a human situation, one giving the other an injunction which cannot logically be carried out (i.e., "Be spontaneous"). Beckett's character reveals such a paradoxical situation. If he knows they are not paying attention to him, and if he is paying no attention to them, then he can't know, and if he doesn't know, then he can't intentionally pay no attention to them because they are paying no attention to him. The paradox entails the contradiction of his needing intentionally *and* unintentionally to carry out an action.

I will briefly review twentieth-century developments in logic and mathematics, then we shall see how they bear on pragmatic paradoxes in human situations, and finally, we will return to the presuppositions underlying the *deconstructive principle* and related systems.

3

(Please disregard this sentence.)

Shortly after the turn of the present century there was an attempt on the part of the mathematicians David Hilbert, Bertrand Russell, Whitehead, and others to axiomatize completely mathematics whereby it would be possible to construct absolute proofs of the consistency of all formal systems. That is, from a few self-consistent axioms, a few rules, and a handful of symbols, everything could be irrefutably inferred. This would undoubtedly, they believed, result in an artificial language representing the unified base for all human thought.

Then along came Kurt Gödel, perhaps the greatest "deconstructor" the Western World has seen.[7] With a few brief strokes of his pen, and by using the accepted rules of the day, he shifted the discourse of arithmetic completely. Devising a system which could "speak to itself," he proved that certain sentences in arithmetic can be interpreted as denying their own provability, hence creating a paradox such that their truth cannot be provable within the system. Such sentences are called "formally undecidable." For example, consider this statement, assuming that its equivalent exists in a mathematical system:

(1) "I am not provable."

Supposing that it is true, then it is not provable. If, on the other hand, it is considered to be false, it can be provable. But if provable, then it cannot state its own truth, and it is therefore false, but if false, then it is provable. The important point here is that provability, or decidability, of formal sentences at the syntactic level is closely linked to truth conditions at the semantic level. Hence truth and provability cannot be clearly separated.[8] (Significantly, Derrida, 1972a, 252, points out that the decidable point in the text is "neither purely syntactic nor purely semantic.").[9]

There is another facet to Gödel's proof. He showed that if a formal system is consistent and non-referential, then it is incomplete insofar as it inevitably contains some axiom which is not provable from within. All systems, then, are either *incomplete* in that they cannot verify at least one of their axioms, or else they are self-referentially *inconsistent* and hence untenable.[10] We must either live with paradox, or we generate an infinitely large Chinese-box of systems, each proving an undecidable axiom within the box it contains, and the ultimate system will still elude us.[11]

Gödel's discovery has been hailed as "one of the greatest and most surprising of the intellectual achievements of this century" (Braithwaite, 1962, 32). It does not surprise us that our knowledge of an isolated chunk from our physical world is inexhaustible (Schlegel, 1967; also Popper, 1974c). Such a notion appears rather commonsensical. What is amazing is that "a construct created by mind itself, the sequence of integers, the simplest and most diaphanous thing for the constructive mind, assumes a similar aspect of obscurity and deficiency when viewed from the axiomatic angle" (Weyl, 1963, 220). Justifiably, Gödel's proof and others of comparable nature and scope are called the "limitative theorems" (DeLong, 1971).[12] The "limitative theorems" open up new problems concerning the relationship between mathematics, logic, natural languages, and science (as well as the arts). It certainly is not the presumption here to solve any of these problems, if indeed they are at all resolvable—and most likely they are not, given the "limitative theorems." I will, however, address myself to the relevance of Gödel's formulation to natural languages, science and the arts, and then, rather obliquely, relate it to the *deconstructive principle*.

We find in Peirce a few precursory ideas that may be useful. Mathematics, he states, is not at its roots subject to logic. Pure mathematics is the creation of the mind (pure relations or syntax) while logic depends on facts (referentiality or semantics). Hence mathematical reasoning "derives no warrant from logic. It needs no warrant. It is evident in itself" (Peirce, 1960, 2.191). However, since the mind's reasoning "is fallible, as everything human is fallible," mathematics may contain falsities. Yet it is the most satisfactory system we have, so we must "accept the reasonings of pure mathematics as beyond all doubt," at least until we discover a system's error (Peirce, 1960, 2.192)[13] The mind being fallible (and limited), it is clear that our knowledge of mathematics and logic must be unavoidably subject to uncertainty. But Peirce is not clear concerning the implications of this notion for natural languages, the sciences, and the arts. It might appear that the "limitative theorems" are inapplicable here, for they do not actually demonstrate that some aspects of our physical world, including scientific theories generated to explain that world, works of art representing interactions between humans and the world, and natural languages which speak about the world and the world's relation to humans, are beyond our ability to know them. Instead, the "limitative theorems" simply deal with sentences in formal systems which speak of their own provability. However, it is a fact that science, very directly concerned with the physical world, has become more and more closely aligned to logic and mathematics in this century, in part because natural languages have proved by and large inadequate as a descriptive tool for the ideas of the scientists. The result is close to the ideas of Descartes, Leibniz, and Kant that the world—at least insofar as we can experience and know it—is subject to a frame of thought (Ullmo, 1964). Science, then, is not only invariably incomplete insofar as it must account for no more than fragmentary domains of nature selected by *a priori* criteria. It also becomes incomplete and/or inconsistent in the Gödelian sense, for it inevitably rests on a deductive axiomatic base which is unprovable from within, and if provable, then the system must be inconsistent (Schlegel, 1967, 252-54). But perhaps the whole scientific enterprise is too convenient. Perhaps this use of mathematics is in reality an abuse of the physical world in the sense that it is hammered into shape and forced into mathematical molds. If so, then science need not be subject to the "limitative theorems." E. P. Wigner (1969, 131), certainly no slouch in science as well as mathematics, tells us that:

> A possible explanation of the physicist's use of mathematics to formulate his laws of nature is that he is a somewhat irresponsible person. As a result, when he finds a connection between two quantities which resembles a connection well known from mathematics, he will jump to the conclusion that the connection is that discussed in mathematics simply because he does not know of any other similar connection.[14]

Does this imply that were non-mathematical connections known the physicist would have no need of mathematics? Perhaps. But the important question is: If there are no ultimate truth conditions for mathematics, then how valid is it for use in the sciences? Suppose, for instance, that a coherent mathematical formulation becomes universally accepted in the biological sciences as "ultimate truth." Suppose also that an equally coherently derived non-empirical theory of the phenomenon of consciousness gains acceptance by everyone in the "human sciences." And finally, suppose that these two theories are incompatible. Any argument for one of the two might invariably end in an irresolvable conflict. This would obviously place our belief in the truth of the concepts we create in a dilemma. And it would certainly subject the validity of mathematics as a modeling system to questioning, for potentially a vast array of internally consistent but mutually contradictory mathematical models could conceivably be used to account for the same "reality."[15] The only conclusion is that a system's accuracy as a model might not necessarily demonstrate its truth, certainly not its completeness, and perhaps not even its consistency. The best available approach, in the face of this dilemma, is found once again in Wigner's (1969, 139) comment:

> The miracle of the appropriateness of the language of mathematics for the formulation of the laws of physics is a wonderful gift which we neither understand nor deserve. We should be grateful for it and hope that it will remain valid in future research and that it will extend, for better or for worse, to our pleasure even though perhaps also to our bafflement, to wide branches of learning.

Mathematics, then, is not necessarily about anythig at all, but it can be and is used to talk *about* things. A similar statement can certainly be made of music, and, to an extent, natural languages, especially when used to create literature.[16] Moreover, as Einstein tells us, scientific theories themselves are all, at the outset, free creations of the mind, totally divorced from the empirical world. Only after the fact of their creation does empirical verification or falsification come into the picture. The question, in this light, becomes: What is the relationship between our scientific theories used to describe the outer world, and, excluding mathematics, our pure and spontaneous creations of the mind (i.e., language use in the arts, linguistic creativity, and general "word play")?

It is most obvious that self-referentiality of the type found in Gödelian sentences places certain limitations on our freedom of creative imagination in the sciences, the arts, and in natural languages (see, Bronowski, 1966; Desmonde, 1971; Hofstadter, 1979). Science, like mathematics, must be viewed as an ongoing activity for which there can be no finality (Kemeny, 1959; Popper, 1972). In fact, we see in contemporary physics striking parallels to Gödel's proof. Heisenberg's uncertainty principle, though enjoying no logical connections with Gödel, is nevertheless similar in spirit. Bohr's complementarity is also an admission that, from a given perspective, any description is necessarily incomplete (Popper, 1974a, 93f).[17] Moreover, either-or logic has been discarded, in many scientific circles at least, and other "logics," most of them refuting the excluded middle principle, are used. This attests to the necessary incompletability of any and all perspectives, or events, whichever the case may be, for actually they become coequal. Popper's, and earlier Peirce's, notion of the ongoing improvement (or self-correction) of scientific theories is also predicated on the idea of incompletability in a rough sort of Gödelian sense. All theories, if they are complete, cannot at the same time be completely consistent, for then they would be eternally irrefutable and therefore not legitimate theories.[18] From yet another view, science is also self-referential. When the products of scientific inquiries are written down as theories, claims Popper, they become part of the object of inquiry against which countertheories can be constructed. Science, in the form of written texts, becomes on the whole a self-referential activity, and eventually undecidable and inconsistent propositions ensue.[19] It appears evident that developments with respect to the limitations on our ability to understand and express our world and our inner self are also paralleled in certain movements in the arts. Witness, for example, the Dadaists and other avant-gardists, the theater of the absurd, novelists the likes of James Joyce and especially Beckett, and artists such as René Magritte and Maurits C. Escher. The object of this inquiry, however, more specifically rests on natural languages, literary texts, and deconstrution. Our focus must therefore be narrowed.

4

(Please disregard the first sentence of section 3.)

Consider the Cretan paradox, "I am lying." It reveals the possibility from within the syntactic rules of natural languages for generating sentences containing contradiction, even though one might not be making outright contradictory assertions. For instance, "I am lying," in the context of a real time-bound human situation, might actually refer to a previous set of sentences, and therefore it becomes non-contradictory. But, of course, in order to understand it non-contradictorily, one must be aware of that larger frame, for the contradiction is irresolvable from within the frame of the sentence itself. It appears to be a relatively simple matter in science and language use to break loose from "double-bind" situations similar to the liar paradox. One simply switches frames so as to include a larger context, or a broader set of parameters (i.e., empirical observations in science or the context of discourse in language use). In the case of the literary arts, however, this switching is not so simple. The most apparent difference is that empirical science and ordinary language use are directed toward the world. This is not necessarily so of literature and other imaginary worlds created linguistically; or perhaps here we could say that reference to the "real world" is oblique at best.[20] The language of literature, then, although dependent upon objects, acts, and events in the "real world" as we (believe we) know it, refers ultimately to its own universe of discourse—a commonplace notion among the deconstructionists in view of their concept of "intertextuality." Therefore the "limitative theorems," that is, insofar as they place limits on the upper bounds of possible creative imagination, apply.[21]

But should this really concern us at all? It is not claimed that the literary text is like a mathematical system, or its production like a logical machine. If the literary text is inconsistent, if it contains ambiguity, uncertainty, vagueness, or contradiction, so much the better, we tend to counter, for this demonstrates not only that we are fallible, but also that we intentionally try in our artistic efforts to, so to speak, "make mistakes." And, this "mistake making" is precisely what creativity entails.

Jacob Bronowski (1966, 11) tells us that, like logic, science and mathematics, "literature is composed essentially of self-reference, and takes its life from the dual tension between watching our own minds from the inside and watching someone else's from the outside." Self-reference reaches its deepest level in literature, where the reader identifies himself with the text whose characters' actions are perceived as if his own. Yet the self-referentiality in literature is not like that of science, for it is integral in such a way that no formal system we know of can even provisionally be used to describe it. In fact, if described, this self-referentiality loses its real essence, and if perceived (sensed) in the act of reading, this perception itself cannot be described. It is at this point, according to Bronowski, ineffable—like the deconstructionist's unnamable, unthinkable DC. Science and literature are in this respect different.

Science and literature also appear to differ in another sense:

> In both of them, the progress from the present account [of nature or of life] to the next account is made by the exploration of the ambiguities in the language that we use at this moment. In science, these ambiguities are resolved for the time being, and a system without ambiguity is built up provisionally, until it is shown to fall short. This

is why the results of science at a given moment can be presented in an axiomatic and deductive machine, although nature as a whole can never be so represented because no such machine can be complete. Whatever kind of machine nature is, it is different from this.

But in literature, the ambiguities cannot be resolved even for the time being. Here the brain cannot act as a logical machine, by which I mean, that it cannot take in information, sort out its ambiguities, and turn it into unambiguous instructions. That is not what a work of art does to us, and we cannot derive such instruction from it. (Bronowski, 1966, 13) (brackets mine)

Furthermore, the disambiguation of a scientific or mathematical system Bronowski speaks of is, exclusively from within the original framework, not actually perceived as a problem solved. Every radically new scientific theory, every novel mathematical system is at the outset, and from the hallowed halls of tradition, looked upon as some sort of "mistake" (Feyerabend, 1975). It becomes acceptable only from within a new perspective and from a new framework. In contrast, art is in a sense a calculated commitment to "mistakes," that is, so to speak, "mistakes" in the logical sense. But rather than being "mistakes" we learn from by stepping outside the system, they are "mistakes" that are meaningful from within the artistic framework. At the same time they afford a new perspective of ourselves and our world, for, art places us within a new frame of reference such that we may see what might otherwise go unnoticed, and if this new way of seeing is judged to be of value, then we can gain some new kind of understanding from it.

It must be emphasized at this point that perception of literary texts presupposes this existence of the perceiver both inside and outside the textual frame. If the perceiver existed exclusively inside one frame, problems would result. For example, suppose that we could put ourselves totally inside a work of art which is considered to be a closed, autonomous system. While in this state, like in the dream-state, there could not be awareness *of* any outside real world. The work would be *the one and only world.* Such being the case, how would it be possible to derive any sort of understanding *from* it? The work would be meaningless with respect to ordinary real world life experiences. But the fact is that it obviously *is* understood on various levels. In order that this understanding occur, the perceiver, while focally attending to the artistic, or fictive frame, must at the same time be peripherally aware of his "real world" self in the "real world" frame.[22] Focus can momentarily rest either outside or inside, on figure or ground, but, we must assert so as to avoid the deconstructionist's "metaphysics of presence," not on both simultaneously.

Mathematics, logic, and the sciences, then, are duty bound to remain as consistent as possible from within. "Mistakes" can potentially be acceptable only when they exist within an alternative, and at least equally consistent and more adequate, framework. The objective of the arts, in contrast, is to make "mistakes" as often as is permitted, though, of course, this is not always a criterion for good art, nor is it the only one. But actually, the more radical philosophers of science, from the relatively conservative Popper to Feyerabend, also propose that the more rapidly "mistakes" are made, the greater the improvement of scientific theories. Justifiably, Feyerabend in this sense can compare science to the arts. If this is, or should be, the case, then self-referentiality, contradiction and the infinite regress or vicious circle which are ultimately found in all systems, "mistaken" or otherwise, render all texts propounding those systems inherently self-deconstructive. All texts are always, in some form or another, at the uncertain borders of "reason," at the fuzzy edges of proper meanings and conventional language use. The deconstructionist would certainly agree.

5

First I see the night, which surprises me, to my surprise, I suppose because I want to be surprised, just once more. (Beckett, 1955, 367)

Speaking of the deconstructionist once again, the question we might ask ourselves is: Is it possible for him to make a "mistake?" Perhaps the truth of the matter is that "mistakes" cannot be made because the results of deconstruction always run exactly as expected.[23] This is very unscientific, in the current conception of science at least, for pure science has little to do with predetermined ends.[24] Derrida himself appears to be aware of the inexact nature of science (Spivak, 1974, xx). Actually, this lack of precision, leading to occasional surprises and "mistakes," is what makes science interesting. In contrast, the "uncanny moment" in the reading of a text when the supposedly hyperconscious critic becomes suddenly aware of its undecidability runs the risk of becoming so diluted as to be unsurprisingly and unstimulatingly monotonous. *Unsurprising*, for the critic expects the surprise and is not the least bit uncertain about it, therefore it is no real surprise. *Unstimulating*, for everything reduces to the same, to a conclusion which is really no conclusion at all, but the effacement of an argument and the absence of a counterargument. And *monotonous*, for everything is flattened into a two-dimensional plane. The *deconstructive principle*, and the "method" for demonstrating it, are invariantly correct, therefore "unfalsifiable" and uninteresting, as Popper would remark. It seems reasonable to claim, then, that according to the *deconstructive principle* and its accompanying "method," proper "mistakes" are not, and cannot be, committed. The end is known before the project is begun—a sort of inverse teleology.[25] But this is all fastidious, a superficial line of criticism. The implications of the *deconstructive principle* in light of the "limitative theorems" might prove to be more enticing. To begin, the following points can be made.

First, the deconstructor, while reading a text, is not surprised to be surprised by what he expected: the "uncanny moment." What is implicit, at the moment of the unsurprising surprise, is the text's self-referential assertion:

(2)   "This sentence is undecidable."

Since the text presumably contains the seeds of its own deconstruction, this sentence must be implicitly within it, and whether or not the deconstructor thinks it or utters it, it is implicit in his own expected non-surprise. Now, this implicit sentence is, if true, then undecidable, and if false, then decidable. But if it is decidable, then it is false, and if undecidable, then true. It can be true if, and only if, it is undecidable. But if it is undecidable there is no method for determining whether or not it is true. Self-referentiality at the syntactic level renders uncertain the meaning of the text's own implicit assertion.

Of course the notion of Truth ideally never comes up in the mind of the deconstructor or with respect to this implicit sentence in the self-deconstructing text. That is, there is no obvious search for Truthhood (origins) as there is in the case of the liar paradox. Nevertheless, as was illustrated above, the very notion of undecidability prevents the complementary notion of Truth from disappearing totally. It is like the Cheshire cat which, after its vanishing act, leaves a mocking grin to haunt us. The implicit presence and explicit absence of this proposition, then, depends ultimately upon Truthhood. Moreover, since the sentence is Gödelian, it must be inconsistently both true and false. But all this should not bother the elusive deconstructor; since he believes in the inconsistency premise anyway, this is for him no critique at all. Let us try another angle then.

Consider the *deconstructive principle* at the most general level:

(3)   "All texts are undecidable."

This non-self-referential sentence is obviously non-Gödelian. And it apparently can and must be made from outside the realm of all texts. If it is true, then all texts are undecidable, and if it is false, then they are not. It's as simple as that. Now all the deconstructor need do is sally forth into the field of all texts, inductively and empirically deconstruct them with his infinitely verifiable "antimethod" (considering him to be immortal of course), and we are forced to sneak away with our tails between our legs. But perhaps there's more to it than this.

Decidability in mathematics consists, in the first place, in a finite method for determining whether an arbitrary sentence in a formal system is a true theorem. This method is called a *decision procedure*. With respect to deconstruction, the method is predicated on the assumption that all texts are deconstructible and self-deconstructing. There is obviously no procedure for ascertaining whether a given text is non-deconstructible; that is, whether it is through and through decidable, for all texts are, according to the *deconstructive principle* absolutely undecidable, and therefore no text is non-deconstructible. The decision has obviously been made a priori, and from outside the domain of writing. Hence there is, and there can be, no real decision procedure, only *dogma.*

In the second place, any system for which there is a decision procedure is called *decidable.* But, according to the deconstructionist doctrine, there is no decision procedure for determining whether a text is or is not non-deconstructible; therefore, no text is decidable—which the deconstructor already knew. And since no text is decidable, there's no need for a decision procedure anyway.

"Foul!" cries the deconstructor. "There *is* a decision procedure to show that a text is self-deconstructing, even though it cannot be shown to be non-deconstructible. So deconstruction embodies a sort of *negative decision procedure*—it's a *negative theology* anyway, isn't it? Hence a negative, self-referential, and viciously circular Gödelian-type of sentence is taken for granted in the text. Our job is to seek it out. Let me give you an example," he goes on to say. " 'All even integers are divisible by two' can be verified by a decision procedure. But arithmetic contains some assertions for which there is no such procedure. Christian Goldbach's conjecture and Pierre de Fermat's last theorem, for example.[26] And besides," he tells us with an ironic twinkle in his eye, "Alonzo Church demonstrated in 1936 that a decision procedure even for a system as fundamental as predicate calculus is impossible."

But once again, if this is true, then as even the mathematician readily admits, a decision for making the decision that there are no decision procedures for a given system must come from outside the system. That is, in the case of deconstruction, *it must come from outside the range of all texts.* If this decision to make a statement about a text's decidability must come from outside, then, following Alfred Tarski's (1956) meta-mathematics, we need to construct a sentence something like this:

(4) "The statement 'this statement is undecidable' is undecidable."

which implies potentially an infinite number of nested clauses. In other words, the first statement is, so to speak, placed under "erasure" upon uttering/writing the next, and so on, *ad infinitum.*

But once again this seems in a bizarre way to support rather than pull the rug out from under the *deconstructive principle.* Perhaps all that can be said at this point is that if deconstruction is incapable of making a statement about a text's non-deconstruction, then it is no better than a metaphysical cosmology that cannot make statements about its own non-truth or non-validity. For example, assume Hilbert's program to have been successfully accomplished. The entire mathematical system would be encompassed within one relatively small set of symbols. Like the early Wittgenstein remarks, it could tell us everything about itself and nothing about what would not be contained within it. The limits of its world would also be its own limits. This would be indeed a monotonous and boring system, for there could never be any surprises in it. However, logic and mathematics have given us a good many surprises. The failure of Hilbert's program produced results more exciting than if it had succeeded, for its success would have produced a theoretically uninteresting body of dry statements. Gödel, in other words, proved to us that there is either inevitably a *self-referentially negative* (inconsistent) assertion in every formal system, or the system is *incomplete*. Moroever—and this is the important point—he demonstrated this while working *within* the system.

The *deconstructive principle* and "method," in contrast, seem in general to entail a *non-self-referentially positive* assertion about that which is true of all texts (i.e., "All texts are undecidable"), and the deconstructor always brings this principle to the text. While the mathematician generates new proofs, always mindful that the unexpected Gödelian sentence might at any moment pop up, forcing him to an impasse or to adopt some other system, the deconstructor expects the unsurprising Gödelian sentence in all texts, and rather than generate something, he merely degenerates what there is. In a loose way of thinking, the deconstructive project is the mirror image of the Hilbertian program. For the deconstructionist, as for Wittgenstein's ideal logician within Hilbert's completed system, there are no real surprises. Yet the image is inverted, like the positive set of integers is to the negative, for deconstruction posits the system's unsurprising and inevitable flaw, while the ideal Hilbertian system would be unsurprisingly and invariantly flawless. To reiterate, theoretically this should reduce deconstruction to a relatively uninteresting program. Yet, against our better judgment, it still appears to be utterly fascinating, for if not, I would not be writing this book.

Still another angle of attack is in order, then. Rather than focus on the *deconstructive principle*, suppose we scrutinize the deconstructor's activity. After the fact of deconstructing, assume he makes this statement:

(5) "I was deconstructing at time t_{-1}."

This is unproblematic. One can actually expect any computing machine, human or otherwise, to be capable of such a sentence. The future tense:

(6) "At time, t_1, I will be deconstructing."

is perfectly acceptable as well, for whatever the machine is programmed to do, it can do again at a later date. So there is no problem. However, if, while deconstructing, the deconstructor says:

(7) "At present time, t_0, I am deconstructing."

there would appear to be grounds for complaint, for a machine or human cannot make a statement in the "present" concerning its own activity at that very same instant of "presence." The point would be well taken. Hence, dropping (7), assuming its problematics to be a foregone conclusion, consider this sentence to be uttered during the act of deconstruction:

(8) "At present time, t_0, I am not deconstructing."

It appears to invalidate the *deconstructive principle*, for by uttering it, the deconstructor contradicts himself. That is, if he is *not* deconstructing, then he is telling the truth, but if so, then he is *not* deconstructing, and hence the *deconstructive principle* is capsized, for he must be deconstructing the text before him; or better, it must be deconstructing itself. On the other hand, if he *is* deconstructing, then the statement is false, and the *deconstructive principle* is equally subverted. But the deconstructor might vaguely counter that he, as an observer, *participates* in the (simultaneous construction-deconstruction of the) text, in all texts. The problem with such an argument is that, at the outset at least, this observer must exist in a frame distinct from that of the observed. For example, suppose I go to the library, take out volume X, turn to page 115, and read sentence 8, which states:

(9) "This text is not deconstructible."

Is the sentence itself deconstructible or not? If not, then it overturns the *deconstructive principle* according to which all texts are deconstructible. On the other hand, if it is deconstructible, then it is contradictory, and can be deconstructed solely with a sentence from within a larger frame, from outside. And, generated by the observing self, following the *deconstructive principle*, this outside sentence must be presumably non-deconstructible, and if so, its non-deconstructibility can be demonstrated, but only from a larger frame by that selfsame observer, and so on, *ad infinitum*. But why would the deconstructor ever bother himself with such an outside sentence? He merely posits that all texts, including the text he writes, are deconstructible, and goes on with the game. But the question is: Are the sentences implied by the *deconstructive principle* deconstructible or not? For example, consider this proposition, inherent in the *deconstructive principle:*

(10) "The non-deconstructible text is not constructible."

Assuming it to be true, then the deconstructor is correct. But, is the proposition itself deconstructible? If so, then the deconstructor errs. And if not, then it is false, for it is itself a well-constructed, non-deconstructible text. Yet the deconstructionist adversary might counter that this proposition does not necessarily prove, but *demonstrates*, the truth of the *deconstructive principle*, for, paradoxically, it makes a claim about the deconstructibility of all texts while remaining itself non-deconstructible. The argument now becomes more aggravating, for one finds oneself at a level where one should not dare question, but passively accept, authority.

The only recourse is to remain with the notion that the *deconstructive principle* is itself simply undecidable, as pointed out above, and hence if the principle is assumed to be universally true, then it must be simultaneously false. The conclusion, then, is: We cannot speak of the deconstructibility of sentences when the sentences themselves have properties which contradict (make undecidable) that selfsame notion of deconstructibility.

Hence *the deconstructor's implicit statements within his text can and cannot be themselves self-deconstructing, paradoxically.*[27]

6

*I invented it all, in the hope it would console me, help me to
go on, allow me to think of myself as somewhere on a road,
moving, between a beginning and an end, gaining ground,
losing ground, getting lost, but somehow in the long run
making headway. (Beckett, 1955, 314)*

In sum, Gödel demonstrated that all formal systems are, so to
speak, perpetually "opened" and therefore in essence "centerless."
This however:

> should not be construed as an invitation to despair or as an excuse
> for mystery-mongering. The discovery that there are arithmetical
> truths which cannot be demonstrated formally does not mean that
> there are truths which are forever incapable of becoming known, or
> that a "mystic" intuition (radically different in kind and authority
> from what is generally operative in intellectual advances) must re-
> place cogent proof. It does not mean, as a recent writer claims, that
> there are "ineluctable limits to human reason." It does mean that the
> resources of human intellect have not been, and cannot be, fully for-
> malized, and that new principles of demonstration forever await in-
> vention and discovery. (Nagel and Newman, 1958, 101)

In the present inquiry the underlying assumption has been that
we should look for solutions to existent problems, and invent new
ones, *ad infinitum*. In order to do so we must at least tentatively
adopt some principles with respect to what a solution is, but we
should never become dogmatic about these principles. Here, we are
clearly within the Greek or Western World tradition, against which
the deconstructionist would obviously launch an attack. He might
support, during this attack, the Buddhist tradition, claiming that a
search for absolute solutions is ultimately pointless, for these solutions are unknown, unknowable, and ineffable. But actually, it has
been demonstrated conclusively that logic and mathematics are
also unapproachable by rigorous classical standards of truth, proof,
and decidability, so at the heart of these disciplines also there is,
and there will always be, an element of the unknown.

We must recognize that the decision tentatively to adopt a set
of principles and to engage in problem solving is always a

pre-rational decision equally as much as is Buddhist meditation, deconstruction, or poetic accounts of the totality.[28] This *pre-rational* decision making, as well as the motivating factor behind it, fuses the boundary between the scientific and the poetic, mathematics and mysticisim, logic and the irrational. The circle, then, can and must be repeatedly opened; *play* can always be resumed, with potentially an infinity of new possibilities. There is apparently no Derridean nostalgia for origins, among mathematicians, for they recognize that there is no center and there need not be any. Beginnings and closures are also unproblematic. The mathematician simply recommences *play* wherever and whenever he wants/can, with the certainty that there is an endless series of true propositions, but which cannot all be formally derived from any given set of axioms and by a closed set of rules. And he can stop whenever he wants, usually at the conclusion of a given proof and with the awareness that each proof does not absolutely prove but at least improves the conjectures put forth (Lakatos, 1976, 37).[29] In contrast, for the deconstructor, caught in the very logic he tries to deconstruct, the alternatives are *either* unrestricted *play or* nostalgia. The "limitative theorems" free us from this imperative (see Altieri, 1976).

In reality, the game has its limits, the formal aspects of which potentially can be defined, but the definite boundaries of which can never be known absolutely. Moreover, concern over beginnings and endings becomes unimportant here. Playing the game entails forgetting nostalgias and nostalgias about nostalgias, giving oneself up to the interplay of signs, in the context of the mind's activity, and simply letting it do what it does best. In this game we will always be somewhere on the road, "gaining ground, losing ground, getting lost, but somehow in the long run making headway."[30]

CHAPTER FOUR

Immanence Knows No Boundaries

1

*Nothing changed? I must be aging all the same, bah, I was
always aged, always aging, and aging makes no difference,
. . . well, I've contradicted myself, no matter. (Beckett, 1955,
398-99)*

Speaking of change and contradictions, let us consult Heraclitus and Zeno in order better to understand paradoxes of a non-
Gödelian type.

Heraclitus' ideas on change ultimately led to a contradiction
which ushered in Parmenides and then the master of contradiction,
Zeno of Elea.[1] In Heraclitus' world there is no permanence or stability. All is flux. The chair I am sitting in, the plaster on the walls
around me and the framework behind it, the pavement outside, are
continually being changed, eroding, rotting, wearing away, being re-
painted, constructed anew, etc. Things are not really things; they
are, like fire, processes, eternally in flux. Our senses persist in telling us that things are permanent, that they are identical with themselves, but this is sheer illusion.

The problem, say Hericlitus' opponents, is that for there to be
change there must be some-*thing* that appears to be changed. Our

car appears to be changing when its tires become worn, the upholstery dirty and torn, and the body rusts, yet we still call it our car. It
has retained a certain identity while changing, while apparently becoming *different*. But at the same time it has, admittedly, become
some-*thing* else. The car's changing has resulted in a transition of
things into their opposites (grooved tires/bald tires, continuous up-
holstery/discontinuous upholstery, smooth body/perforated body,
etc.), yet the changing thing has remained in another sense identical
with itself. Sameness, then, is what is real.

Parmenides developed a proof for what he conceived to be this
underlying unchanging reality: (a) what is not is not, (b) therefore
nothing (the void) does not exist, (c) therefore the universe is
"full"; it consists of one undifferentiated "block," and (d) therefore
in a "full" universe there is no empty space for things potentially to
fill, hence there can be no change or motion. This implies that what
is, is all there *is*, and what *is not*, *is not*, and can never *be*. Hence, a
world of change is illusory, for if what *is not* cannot *be*, then all that
is, is as it *is*, and it will never *be* anything other than what it *is*.

The problem now is that the All, the Whole, as Blaise Pascal
(1910, 27) tells us, is interminably beyond the grasp of the finite
being:

> For in fact what is man in nature? A nothing in comparison with the
> Infinite, an All in comparison with the Nothing, a mean between noth-
> ing and everything. Since he is infinitely removed from comprehend-
> ing the extremes, and the end of things and their beginnings are
> hopelessly hidden from him in an impenetrable secret, he is equally
> incapable of seeing the Nothing from which he was made, and the
> Infinite in which he is swallowed up.

Yet Parmenides believed he effectively countered this *horror infiniti*. He was convinced that to think at all is simply to postulate
what *is*, since that which *is not* cannot be thought of and therefore
there is no need to try thinking *about it*. Non-being is therefore
impossible. Parmenides' world is a hypothetical construct which
creates the slash between "appearance" and "reality," between that
which is empirically evident and that which is intuitively certain.[2]

Now enter Zeno, whose introduction of infinity brings in a new
paradox. Essentially Zeno demonstrated in the second of his four
Arguments that in their footrace Achilles can never overtake the
Tortoise, for he must first reduce the gap between them by half,

which takes a finite period of time. But since as Zeno tells us, what has been said/done once can always be repeated, Achilles must then reduce that half-gap by half, and that by half, and so on. There will thus be an infinite number of reductions, each requiring a finite interval, and Achilles will never achieve his goal. This Argument shows the difficulty inherent in the notion of an imaginary set of finite elements making up a continuum. Similarly, Zeno's third Argument consists of an arrow which at a given point in time, the "now," is at rest; in fact, at any point in its trajectory it must be, like a still photograph taken with a high-speed camera, motionless. Therefore, the arrow is at all times motionless, so it cannot move.

Of course modern-day mathematics easily disposes of this problem. Motion is simply a correspondence between position-in-space-and-time, called a *continuous function*. Time, like space, is broken up into equal segments to become a "line," and then it is a relatively simple matter for Achilles to overtake the Tortoise by a series of "bounds" through space and in time. Mathematically a solution to Zeno's paradoxes can be wrapped into a neat package. But also, mathematically, this package necessarily contains a fiction: it entails, like Parmenides' and Zeno's "proofs," *an act of mind, not of experience*. Experience cannot stop the arrow in flight any more than the Tortoise can prevent Achilles from overtaking him, for there is no experienced simple presence. On the other hand, by an act of mind the arrow's trajectory can be reduced to a series of increments. Indeed, with the Calculus, motion is mathematically and fictitiously abstracted into an infinity of static states along an infinity of extensionless points during an infinity of durationless instants (Dantzig, 1930, 125-27). This distinction between *experience* and *mental constructs* bears further inquiry.

2

Pump it up, I said. I held the bicycle. I forget which wheel it was. As soon as two things are nearly identical I am lost. (Beckett, 1955, 156)

Re-enter Derrida.

Derrida, it seems, would argue for something akin to a Heraclitean world of incessant change.[3] Nothing is identical with itself, when repeated; hence, texts are best characterized by their differences with each successive reading. This stems from the notion of DC, which is only a simulacrum of the present; it is never the same as the present. According to a maxim of traditional philosophy, an intelligible idea can be indefinitely uttered as the same indivisible and atomic idea. In contrast, for Derrida signifieds are separable from and interchangeable with signifiers, themselves being the product of DC. They become effaced in their very use. Moreover, permanence, like identity or sameness, cannot exist in the world. Permanence is also a fiction constructed by the abstracting mind, like, for instance, increments of time, space, and motion in mathematics.[4]

Derrida's concept, in its most general sense, is, once again, nothing revolutionary. In fact, it can be found in mutually contradictory contemporary Western World philosophies. For instance, the nominalist Nelson Goodman reiterates that scientific experiments cannot be repeated without the experimenter possessing at least a partial theory prior to the first experiment. The identity of two experiments exists only at the level of abstraction represented by the theory. Similarly, repetition of an artistic performance can exist only by abstracting certain characteristics from it (Goodman, 1972, 439-40; also 1978). On the other hand, Popper, a realist, claims that similarity and repetition:

always presuppose the adoption of *a point of view*; some similarities or repetitions will strike us if we are interested in one problem, and others if we are interested in another problem. But if similarity and repetition presuppose the adoption of a point of view, or an interest, or an expectation, it is logically necessary that points of view, or interests, or expectations, are logically prior, as well as temporally (or causally or psychologically) prior, to repetition. (Popper, 1959, 421-22)

Actually, even Popper would tell us that repetitions are not really repetitions, we only think (imagine that) they are. That is, we learn to expect sameness, or even identity, as well as in some situations, change. And these expectations bring about the appearance of repetition. This idea constitutes part of Popper's anti-inductivist argument. He believes that an organism, human or animal, does not wait around with Lockean passivity to accumulate enough repetitions of an experience finally to be able to engage in positive action. Rather, it actively, and by means of certain inborn expectations, proclivities, and propensities, "jumps to conclusions" by imposing regularities on its environment—an act of "mind." Some of these conclusions work successfully and some not. If not, the organism may be confronted by a surprise at which time it may revise its expectations, and consequently its way of perceiving the world (Popper, 1972, 90-98).[5] For humans, this process operates in scientific theory-making as well as in everyday life. Scientific activity is nothing more than an inborn and natural ability possessed by all.

Popper (1977, 89-90) offers a "thought experiment" to illustrate his notion of non-repetition which bears similarity both to Peircean and Derridean thought. Suppose we look at a flower, close our eyes, and then reopen them to take another look. The same content of consciousness has not been repeated. Although the number and intensity of the photons of light striking our retinas are undoubtedly very similar, this is not the sameness we must consider. The sameness of the two precepts—i.e., "This is the same flower"—is a recognition made by the mind, for sameness and identity always require conscious and intentional comparison. Now, Peirce might call the retina-striking photons Firstness, and the conscious comparison necessarily Secondness combined with Thirdness. And, the important point is that Secondness and Thirdness require, in Derridean terms, DC, MC, and the TC.[6] In this light, Derrida's critique of repetition, as well as of identity and presence, is against a philosophical view that is now *passé* in many quarters anyway, and hence it loses much of its force. Nevertheless, this issue must be discussed in more detail.

Derrida's concept of successive differentiation is actually relatively conservative when it is compared to certain avant-garde scientists. Bohm (1957, 157) asserts, quite lucidly, that "because all of the infinity of factors determining what any given thing is are always changing with ime, *no such thing can even remain identical with itself* as time passes." Yet at each instant of time, each entity possesses, when viewed from one side (frame), an enormous—in fact an infinite—number of attributes in common with those that it possessed at a previous instant. Hence it must have, from the perspective of the abstracting, generalizing mind, some sort of identity. On the other hand, viewed from another side (frame), that entity has an equally monstrous number of attributes uncommon with what it had an instant ago; hence it is never exactly identical with itself (Bohm, 1957, 157-58). In nature then, nothing remains constant. Everything is perpetually changing, being transformed into something else. At the same time:

> we discover that nothing simply surges up out of nothing without having antecedents that existed before. Likewise, nothing ever disappears without a trace, in the sense that it gives rise to absolutely nothing existing at later times. This general characteristic of the world can be expressed in terms of a principle which summarizes an enormous domain of different kinds of experience and which has never yet been contradicted in any observation or experiment, scientific or otherwise; namely, everything comes from other things and gives rise to other things. (Bohm, 1957, 1)

A purer metaphor for Derridean *play* in a "centerless system" of potentially infinite possibilities could hardly be found. Nor could we hardly discover, in modern Western World texts, an expression closer to Heraclitus.

But there is more. No entity can be the same in all respects to a definition of it by any particular conceptual abstraction. It is always and invariably something more, and "at least in some respects, *something different*" (Bohm, 1957, 154)—Derrida's DC and the TC. Therefore, if an entity becomes something else, from within another frame and by another definition, "no unresolvable contradiction is necessarily implied" (Bohm, 1957, 154)—Derrida's rupture of classical logic. This must be so, for the entity can never be exactly represented by an originary definition: there is no absolute originary definition—Derrida's lack of a "center." Moreover, partial definitions, perspectives, and frames create "room for the possibility of qualitative change, by leading us to recognize that those aspects of things that have been ignored may, under suitable conditions, cease to have negligible effects, and indeed may become so important that they can bring about fundamental changes in the basic properties of the things under consideration" (Bohm, 1957, 154). In other words, any given definition, perspective or frame can lead to an infinite number of unforeseen future states—Derrida's infinity of interpretations, and "intertextuality." Bohm even admits that his own hypothesis, that of the "qualitative infinity of nature," must itself eventually be subject to change and replaced by a more general hypothesis—somewhat like the deconstructive act of self-deconstruction.[7]

There is, it seems, one important point of divergence between Bohm and Derrida. Bohm (1957, 170) concludes that:

> even though the mode of being of each thing can be defined only relative to other things, we are not led to the point of view of *complete relativity*. For such a point of view implies that there is no objective content to our knowledge at all, either because it is supposed to be defined *entirely* relative to the observer, or to the general point of view and special conditions of each individual, or to special preconceptions and modes (or "style") of thinking that may exist in a particular society or in a particular epoch of time. In our point of view, we admit that all the above things do actually colour and influence our knowledge; but we admit also that nevertheless there still exists an absolute, unique, and objective reality.[8]

Of course, it must be reiterated, Bohm claims, that this absolute reality can never be grasped conceptually nor described objectively. Yet it exists, and we must never cease our efforts to understand it within our limitations. Derrida, on the other hand, appears to reject all pretentions of objectivity in his critique of structuralism (Derrida, 1978a, 154-68 and 278-93). There is no real distinction between subject and object, there are no real distinctions at all, just DC—the *play* of presence and absence. Derrida's law, the "law of difference" might possibly be construed as that "more general hypothesis" to which Bohm refers. The problem is, however, that it is so general in scope that it threatens to undercut itself; it questions the very possibility of its own existence, of its own conceptualization and description (Spivak, 1974, lvii). This certainly appears indicative of the type of "complete relativity" Bohm rejects. In short, then, Bohm's relativity is positive, Derrida's negative, though it is not through and through nihilistic.[9]

3

Everything divides into itself, I suppose. (Beckett, 1955, 182)

But can the deconstructive package be so neatly wrapped and tied? It seems intuitively obvious that between all different perspectival frameworks, between each and every signification, between signifiers and signifieds, and between two intervals or deferrals, since they all entail DC, there must exist some line, some boundary. This line, a nothingness, if not really a gap, at least represents a "cut" demarcating something from something else. However, Derrida (1973, 61), in his critique of Husserl, points out:

> [W]e cannot avoid noting that a certain concept of the "now," of the present as punctuality of the instant, discretely but decisively sanctions the whole system of "essential distinctions." If the punctuality of the instant is a myth, a spatial or mechancial metaphor, an inherited metaphysical concept, or all that at once, and if the present of self-presence is not *simple*, if it is constituted in a primordial and irreducible synthesis, then the whole of Husserl's argumentation is threatened in its very principle. . . . Undoubtedly, no now can be isolated as a pure instant, a pure punctuality.

The question is: If there are no such gaps, then do we not get lost so to speak, in the individed continuum of experience? Such a continuum must prevail, in light of Peirce, and of Derrida's critique of pure punctuality, points, limits, "nows," that is, of the critique of simple self-presence. So how can this undivided and unpunctuated continuum be at least provisionally accounted for, if at all? And how can it be demonstrated to constitute the authentic reality of experience as opposed to metaphysical acts of mind?

Consider first what is known as the "calculus of limits." Variable magnitudes, or extremely minute straight segments which roughly describe a curve, imaginarily approach equality if their *differences* are made smaller and smaller. When they become infinitesimally small, an infinite number of "points," they are all, so to speak fictitiously and metaphorically as it were, identical with themselves, and they at the same time lose their self-identity as segments. Now compare this to ordinary perception. Assume we watch an arrow repeatedly shot from a bow with approximately the same velocity, circumscribing approximately the same trajectory, decelerating as it does so, and striking the bull's-eye dead-center each time. We perceive the arrow's motion as an undifferentiated process. We are incapable of being aware of any parts, that is of any quasi-infinitesimal "jerks," if there indeed be any, from one position to the next as the arrow arcs toward its target. Yet, the Calculus demonstrates quite effectively that the arrow's path can be conceived as consisting of an infinite number of infinitesimal segments called *differentials (differences)*—originally by Leibniz—or *fluxions*—by Isaac Newton. As George Berkeley remarks, we can never know these *fluxions* or *differentials*; they are ghosts of rapidly departed (deferred) points (presences), each infinitesimally different from its neighbor.[10] In other words, what we see, the undifferentiated process, hides what for the Calculus in "reality"—a "fictitious reality" according to Berkeley—lies underneath: an infinite number of infinitesimal "fits" and "jerks."

However, if this is indeed the case, then the excluded middle principle cannot operate, for between every two jumps there is another, and another between those, and so on, until finally, there exists no more than a smear.[11] The infinitely differentiated thus becomes in a sense the One, the Parmenidean One! It becomes at once somehow and contradictorily one with itself and identical with itself. It takes on the characteristic of Being, and as such does not and cannot change; it is necessarily full and hence excludes emptiness. Likewise, time, under this condition must stand still. It seems that as we proceed to higher and higher levels, everything eventually and paradoxically becomes possible and no particular thing can stand out over any other thing. At the highest level, the motion of the arrow, seen as a whole made up of an infinite number of densely packed identical particulars, cannot have motion, through time that is.

The idea being propagated here is close to a Buddhist view. Ordinarily, in thinking, the mind shifts foci of attention on a one-at-a-time basis. In this sense, an arrow is thought of as leaving the bow, flying through the air, and penetrating the target. For the mind of Buddha, in contrast, there is no temporal sequence. Everything is conceived as a unity. In other words, Buddha is capable of grasping a slab of marble *simultaneously* as a limitless set of "mutually cancellatory and mutually penetrating possibilities," or, in a flash and acausally Buddha sees the arrow leave the bow and strike the target.[12] The ultimate extension of the concept of *differentials*, then, leads *simultaneously* to the end and back to the beginning. Infinite *differences* becomes/is *non-difference*.

Indeed, there is certainly something strange about all this. And it bears on the "frame" of reference posited by the deconstructionist. If this "frame" *simultaneously* incorporates presence *and* absence, then what can be effectively actualized within it? Or if, at the "uncanny point" in the text, the deconstructor's frame encompasses at the same instant and undecidably all possibilities as well as the impossibility of choice, then how can temporal movement be accounted for? Moreover, can the frame actually contain itself? Can it really be the dwelling place for finite consciousness, even during the fictitious "blink of an instant"? Perhaps it is, like Derrida's reformulation of Freud's "mystic writing pad," a timeless "unconscious text" which is potentially infinite, yet non-Platonic, not present and not actually written elsewhere—an interwoven set of pure traces (non-actuals) (Derrida, 1978a, 228).

Once again Peirce asserts himself.

With respect to the continuum, Peirce makes a remarkable effort to be as concise and explicit as possible, even though he admits to an inevitable degree of the inexplicable (Peirce, 1960, 6.172). He maintains that continuity is of central importance to philosophy, and mind is the example, *par excellence*, of continuity (Peirce, 1960, 6.103). Ideas are generated from feelings (Firstness, or qualities) which consist of a continuous "spreading out," and which can mediately become definitive through the flow of Secondness and Thirdness (Peirce, 1960, 6.151). These ideas tend also to flow out in a continuum to affect other ideas, and as an idea spreads, its power to affect others loses intensity, though its quality remains virtually unchanged (Peirce, 1960, 6.136). This notion of continuity accounts for Peirce's maxim that there is no cognition that is not determined by previous cognitions (Peirce, 1960, 5.259-63). Mind, then, has continuous extension in space and time insofar as "the present is connected with the past by a series of real infinitesimal steps" (Peirce, 1960, 6.109).

This continuity of feeling, change, and ideas renders nominalism all but futile (Peirce, 1960, 6.136). In the first place nominalism accepts the notion of an aggregate of separable atoms as ideas, and moreover rejects generalities such as the notion of infinity. Hence if nominalism is embraced, Peirce's idea becomes nonsense.[13] The trouble is, says Peirce, that the nominalists tried to reason *about* nominalism, and failed, because they compared it to a collection of finite entities. Their reasoning "consists of performing certain processes which they have found worked well—without having any insight into the conditions of their working well" (Peirce, 1960, 1.165). Part of these prerequisite "conditions of their working well" are precisely notions of the continuum and infinity. Continuity "is shown by the logic of relatives to be nothing but a higher type of that which we know as generality. It is relational generality" (Peirce, 1960, 6.190). And this higher level of generality is one to which our own classical logic aspires (Peirce, 1960, 6.189). But since the continuum is far beyond our range of comprehension, we can hardly expect adequately to grasp it. Yet we must try, claims Peirce, or Popper-Bohm.[14]

A true continuum is incomprehensible if we attempt to relate it, by finitistic reasoning, to any given multitude of individuals. Consider, for instance, a line. No point can actually exist along it, for if it does, the continuum is breached, or better stated, "cut." There is an infinity of potential "spots" where a point can be abstracted, but this potential remains no more than indeterminate, that is, until a specific point is made; but then the line, as a continuous totality, has been mutilated. So it is with the continuum of our consciousness, says Peirce. There are no necessary points. But definite points can appear *to* consciousness, though only mediately.[15] If we consider consciousness to be like a line, and consciousness *of* such-and-such a series of ideas to be like points on that line, then obviously we encounter Zeno's problem once again. It would become (logically) impossible for consciousness to move, or to reach a goal. But of course it does move. Then how is this possible? According to Peirce, by generalities in consciousness which contain a spreading of feelings and ideas, and these generalities are made possible by a logic of "higher type."

Classical logic, like thought, and other "evolutionary processes," can be accounted for by the continuum model. Classical logic and thought have followed a course from the vague (the continuum) to the definite (discrete portions abstracted from the continuum) (Peirce, 1960, 6.191). That is to say, what was indeterminate at the higher level becomes definite at the lower level, where identity, contradiction, and the excluded middle exercise their power. Peirce (1960, 6.192) likens the actualized universe, or the "existing universe, with all its arbitrary secondness," to an "offshoot from, or an arbitrary determination of, a world of ideas." This evolution, we cannot but suppose, began "in the utter vagueness of completely undetermined and dimensionless potentiality," in the continuum (Peirce, 1960, 6.193). It is not a univocal, teleologically bound, evolution of the existing universe, but a process derived from the infinite range of potentialities.

Peirce's ideas, we see now more clearly, support much of Derrida's reaction against the "metaphysics of presence."[16] With Peirce's notion of the continuum we have a timeless set of infinite possibilities with no actuals. From any given frame of reference we can have a particular finite set of actuals, and over time, potentially an infinite set of frame, and of actuals. Further, during, so to speak, a mediary "blink of an instant," a new frame and a new set of actuals can be seen, but no-*thing*, no actual, can *be*, in the continuum. No finite consciousness *of* some-*thing* can call the continuum its dwelling place.

What now remains to be discussed is the relation between Peirce's notion of continua and modern thought. Then we may be able more adequately to understand the nature of the frame of reference implied by the *deconstructive principle.*

4

I know no more questions and they keep on pouring out of my mouth. I think I know what it is, it's to prevent the discourse from coming to an end, this futile discourse which is not credited to me and brings me not a syllable nearer silence. (Beckett, 1955, 307)

Peirce clearly goes beyond Derrida in his use of mathematically-based models. Moreover, Peirce's formulation of the mind and of thought, if taken to its extreme, manifests "holographic" properties similar to those proposed for "bootstrap" physics. In holography, a wave field of light which is to be photographed is recorded as an inference pattern on a photographic plate. When the processed plate is placed in a laser beam, the observer sees a three-dimensional image. A remarkable property of the holographic plate is that any fragment of it, no matter how small, can regenerate the entire image, though the smaller the fragment, the vaguer the image. A magnet has holographic-like properties in so far as any portion of it produces the same field as the whole, though the intensity of each portion will not be as great as that of the whole. Likewise, when a cell splits, each new cell will be a developed organism; there will be no front half and back half.[17] This is similar to the holographic plate, which, when divided, can produce two complete three-dimensional images. By the same token, according to the "boot-strap" theory, the universe is not an aggregate of individuals; it is a dynamic web of potential events in which each "part" contains, and mirrors, the structure of the whole—a continuum, as Peirce might say.[18] Hence rather than a web, the universe is, according to the "bootstrap hypothesis," more appropriately a seamless fabric.

Moreover, the holograph model might have wide-ranging applications. Karl Pribram (1971) maintains that in addition to the mind-brain's thinking and communicating with discrete symbols, it acts also, at a deeper level, like a holograph. This deeper level consists of a non-verbal realm beyond actual symbols, a sort of continuous and indeterminate potentiality which can give rise to an indeterminate set of definite symbols. It is for this reason that no specific information can be absolutely localized in the brain-mind. Rather, all "parts" "contain" and "mirror," to a greater or lesser degree, the whole. Keith Floyd (1974) even goes so far as to propose a holographic model of consciousness which makes such brain processes as memory, perception, and imaging more clearly explainable. In consciousness, like a hologram, one frame is every frame. Every memory and bit of information stored in our minds is potentially infinitely cross-referenced with every other bit of information—compare this notion to "intertextuality." Though information is obviously stored in the brain by an elaborate digitally-based mechanism, at the mind level each bit of information is potentially infinitely related to every other bit. Like the two-dimensional holographic plate which is "spread out" and projected into three-dimensions, then, consciousness (the mind), in the sense also of Peirce, "spreads out" continuously along an infinite number of potential (fictional) "points." Similarly, Floyd (1974, 312-13) concludes that "brain-functions such as perception, memory, imaging, and so forth, are beginning to appear most clearly explainable on the basis of a holographic model. The screen of awareness may turn out to be an organic form of a holographic plate that processes three-dimensional perceptions and reconstructed images with equal facility."[19]

Floyd uses, as did Peirce, visual models to illustrate the non-conscious aspect of perception for which there is no seriality, no "before" and "after," not even any "now"—i.e., like Derrida's Freudian-based "unconscious text." Similarly, according to some recent physicists—though Popper (1982) certainly disagrees here—the subjective mind creates seriality and temporality. In contrast, "reality" is a timeless state of mere possibility, a continuous potential. It is subjectless, for there can be no actuals; that is, no actuals *for* a particular subjective consciousness. Such a timeless "reality" appears to make possible what Peirce calls *abduction*—acts of insight which come like a flash. *Abduction* is a form of inferential reasoning, lying between induction and deduction, which results from a process, "although ... sufficiently conscious to be controlled, or, to state it more truly, not controllable and therefore not fully conscious" (Peirce, 1960, 5.181). In fact, it is a process which cannot be subjected to logical analysis, for on attempting to do so, we would terminate precisely with a problem analogous to that of Achilles and the Tortoise:

> Namely, just as Achilles does not have to make the series of distinct endeavors which he is represented as making, so this process of forming the perceptual judgment [*abduction*], because it is subconscious and so not amenable to logical criticism, does not have to make separate acts of inference, but performs its act in one continuous process. (Peirce, 1960, 5.181) (brackets mine)

The "logic" of *abduction*, we might extrapolate from Peirce's argument, is of the "higher logic," the "logic of the continuum." Even though *abduction* is not exactly susceptible to explicit analytical reasoning, perhaps we can illustrate it analogically. Consider a visual model which distinguishes between the continuity of non-consciousness and the discontinuity of consciousness. For instance, if we gaze at the Necker cube for a few seconds:

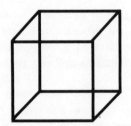

we will find that at some indeterminate moment the face of the cube can switch to a distinct plane. What in reality changed? The photons striking our retinas certainly did not undergo a fundamental transformation. And we did not ourselves need necessarily to will the switch. Moreover, it must be assumed that the switch was not the result of some new set of neurons suddenly and for no apparent reason firing on their own. At a higher level, the mind, the non-conscious mind, "caused" the new percept, and consequently the altered neuronal firings, such that the diagram is seen in a new and incommensurable manner. This working of the non-conscious mind, it seems, is like Peirce's *abduction*, a distinctly human instinct for "hitting upon" the correct answer to a problem from a vast array of possible alternative but false answers.

Further, it must be surmised that this shift of frames occurred, so to speak, outside time.[20] It was our consciousness that created the illusion of sequential flashes, one before and the other after. This was made possible by the fact that both percepts of the cube were *there* all along, as part of one continuous potentiality in the Peircean sense. In fact, with an infinite set of *infinitesimal differentials (differences)* it can be fictitiously demonstrated how the lines on the surface of the paper could be shifted, by *infinitesimal increments*, finally to become the opposite and incommensurable percept. However, according to the above-mentioned non-conscious effort of the mind, this is not essential, just as it was not necessary for Achilles intentionally and impossibly to run through an infinite series of infinitesimal segments in order to try overtaking the Tortoise. And, it is not necessary, as Beckett well knows, for his character consciously to run through an infinity of words, for silence will be found, if not in life, at least in death.[21]

In sum, even though Peirce does not engage in an explicit critique of the "metaphysics of presence," he does, very rightly, specify the distinction between continuous and discontinuous, finite and infinite. Admittedly, Peirce might be criticized on the grounds that he falsely places stock in opposites, thereby using the very logical methods and analytics Derrida rejects. Nevertheless, the implications of Peirce's philosophy, though not clearly specified, move toward an "erasure" of the boundaries between these terms. Discontinuity is actualized from the continuum, finitude from the infinite, and there is no all-or-nothing distinction between consciousness and non-consciousness, mind and non-mind.

Let us turn to the contemporary scientific world-view, and its relevance to Peirce and deconstruction.

5

I am . . . free, yes, I don't know what that means but it's the word I mean to use, free to do what, to do nothing, to know, but what, the laws of the mind perhaps, of my mind, . . . to obliterate texts . . . to fill in the holes of words till all is blank and flat. (Beckett, 1955, 13)

Almost fifty years ago, James Jeans (1958, 181) remarked that the twentieth-century view of the universe is more like that of a "great thought" than a "great machine." This idea, in many circles dismissed for a few decades, now appears to bear some truth. The new scientific view of the universe was first postulated by Einstein. It can best be described as a four-dimensional continuous "block" in which time is spatialized, and past, present and future are compounded into an instant (see Whitrow, 1967, 88).[22] "Becoming" in three-dimensional space loses its temporal quality in the "block."[23] That is, the motion of a particle moving from one point to another in Newtonian space is defined as a stationary and timeless curve in the fourth dimension—compare to the Buddha's grasp of the arrow in flight, mentioned in section 3. The entire system is reduced to a *changeless whole.* Louis de Broglie (1959, 114) in this light, states that:

In space-time everything which for each of us constitutes the past, the present and the future is given in block, and the entire collection

of events, successive for each one of us, which form the existence of
a material particle is represented by a line, the world line of the particle. . . . each observer, as his time passes, discovers, so to speak, new
slices of space-time which appear to him as successive aspects of the
material world.

Though each slice of space-time each observer cuts out of the
monolithic "block" is *different,* even to the slightest degree, all
slices are interrelated by and through that "block." It is the infinite
background against which the particular world of consciousness
foregrounds actuals. It is the Objective World, lying behind experience, with no qualitative *differences.*[24]

This formulation at the outset appears to be Zeno and the Elea-
tic tradition in a new garment precisely against which Whitehead,
Henri Bergson, William James, and others have reacted.[25] The illusion of time becomes nothing more than a gradual revealing *to* consciousness *of* actualized bits of that complete and timeless whole.
Milic Capek (1961, 165) calls this world-view "an absurd dualism of
the timeless physical world and the temporal consciousness, that is,
a dualism of two altogether disparate realms whose correlation becomes completely unintelligible." However, it is no absurd dualism
when there is realization that it is no real dualism at all. And this is
precisely how the more recent hypotheses view "reality." The timeless domain, the "block," is by no means synonymous or comparable with the physical world. It is comparable only with the
continuum of possibilities discussed in section 3. Moreover, temporal consciousness is not copresent with past events, or the origins
in this timeless world, for each and every presence is *deferred* before *becoming present,* in Derrida's terms.[26] The whole is irretrievable *for* consciousness, because there can be no presence, only
presence made past. Moreover, this "block" is in an ideal sense continuously extended. But mind also, as Peirce tells us, is extended in
space and through time. In space, for if not, communication
between minds would not be possible. And through time, for the
"infinitesimal present" extends back in time; but since it is infinitesimal, it cannot extend back indefinitely, but remains, as all past
infinitesimal times, paradoxically infinitesimal.[27] Hence just as
thoughts fade along the receding continuum, so memories must
fade along the past continuum of time—Derridean "forgetfulness."

A fundamental problem here is that what is possible in the
world or in the mind may well be a continuum, and what becomes

actual, in the world or in the mind, *was* a contingency, but once it is made actual *for* consciousness (by DC, MC, and the TC), it is necessary, and it is necessarily a discrete individual. This is difficult to explain with Peirce's system except by assigning to it, as perhaps in quantum mechanics, a "probability function." In this sense we can state that either the actual world is every possible world or it is not. Peirce and quantum mechanics would likely tell us that it is not. If so, then the range of all possible worlds is an infinite continuum, and the discreteness of the actual world of the supposed "now" takes up a mere "point" in the continuum but excludes *almost* the totality of it, which is itself an infinite range—i.e., infinity minus an infinitesimal is still infinity. If the actual world excludes an infinite range of worlds that might have been but are not, then this actualized world represents a *quanta* whose actualization was describable only as a probability.[28] Peirce at least in part accounts for the continuous realm of possibilities in space-time on the one hand, and the discontinuous and dynamic set of actualities on the other.

However, there are definite problems if we compare closely the "metaphysics of presence," which Derrida critiques resoundingly, with the "block." In the first place, the "block" is not Being, either in the Platonic or the phenomenological sense. Actualities can be stripped from it, but those actualities could never be purely and immediately present *to* consciousness—this is analogous to what Bohm calls the underlying background (the *implicit* order) from which all actualized entities are created (the *explicit* order). In the second place, the "block" has nothing to do with onto-theology; it is, perhaps, comparable to sheer void, but at the same time it is not diametrically opposed to the beingness of actualized entities. For if all possibilities could somehow suddenly be actualized and interpenetrated, at that same instant they would become *mutually cancellatory;* the entire system would be at once infinitely differentiated and One, total chaos *and* total order. It would be, to use Derrida's metaphor, *"at once absolutely alive and absolutely dead"* (Derrida, 1973, 102).[29] But, since all possibilities cannot be actualized simultaneously, and since consciousness of any given set of actualities is always deferred, we need not worry about any ontological status of the "block." It is purely an imaginary construct.

Derrida (1973, 135) points out that "no transcendent truth present outside the sphere of writing can theologically command the totality of the field." Agreed. The notion of the continuum or the "block" implies no such transcendent truth. And at the same time, the notion of the "field" of writing is also in a sense compatible with that of the "block." It simply *is*, there is nothing outside it; and it offers infinite possiblities but can never *be* (known) in its totality.[30] For instance, Derrida (1978b, 153) in his earlier work, states that:

> The impossibility of resting in the simple maintenance [nowness] of a Living Present, ... the inability to live enclosed in the innocent undividedness [*indivision*] of the primordial Absolute, because the Absolute is *present* only in being *deferred-delayed* [*différant*] without respite, this impotence and this impossibility are given in a primordial and pure consciousness of Difference. Such a *consciousness*, with its strange style of unity, must be able to be restored to its own light. Without such a consciousness, without its own proper dehiscence, nothing would appear.

For Derrida, if there is to be any absolute, any transcendental, it is the "primordial Difference of the absolute Origin" (Derrida, 1978b, 153). But—and this is the crucial question—what can *Différance* (DC) *be* unless it *is*, with respect to that which makes it possible? That is, the equivalent of the "block"—or what Derrida calls the "innocent undividedness"? The "block" is no-*thing*, yet it is potentially every-*thing*, through DC, MC, and the TC, *to/for* consciousness. Without the "block" there could be no *differences*.

The Derridean *play* of DC is precisely this *play* of myriad actualities before a delayed consciousness—the game of reference-less signifiers. The "rules" of this game deserve further consideration.

6

If I could speak and yet say nothing, really nothing. (Beckett, 1955, 303)

A canon, in logic, exists outside a system, for it must describe the system under construction. In contrast, a command, or a set of instructions to construct, is not a canon. A canon permits certain things and prohibits others, but it says nothing with respect to *how* to construct. That must be acquired in part by following instructions, but also through experience, and only then can one become conscious *of* what it was that one constructed. Hence learning and knowing is made possible through what the canon permits, but they are not *in* the canon, nor are they synonymous *with* it.

Likewise, as we observed in chapter three, the "rules," or purportedly the "ruleless rules" of the deconstructionist's activity must be, *a priori*, "outside" the system. The deconstructor, using these rather implicit "rules," knows *how* to go about finding the text's "uncanny moment," but how he learned or came to know this is not *in* the text, *in* the "rules," or *in* his *play* with the text—just as the rules of chess are not *in* the game, but they govern the game's possible strategies. This knowing *how* necessarily comes from somewhere "outside": that which the canon permits. However, learning *how* is not a transcendental act, says the deconstructionist, nor is it gained by direct intuition. Furthermore, there can be consciousness *of* such knowledge (by DC) only *after* the fact *of* learning *how*. But the question remains: Must this acquired knowing *how* not have come, so to speak, from "somewhere else"? Roland Barthes (1972, 30-31) claims that the text can attack the canonical structures of language itself. If this is so, then the text must in some manner be "outside" language.

Consider a "thought experiment." The scientist Otto Loewi once had a dream in which he envisioned clearly how to do an experiment. The following morning, he realized he had had the dream, but could not remember any details. The next night he went to bed with a pencil and paper at his side anticipating the dream's recurrence. When it came, he awakened, wrote it down, and fell asleep again. But the next morning upon reading it, to his dismay it was unintelligible. That night after he had the dream once again he made sure he was fully awake, constructed a design for the complete experiment, and immediately conducted it in his laboratory with success—and it won him a shared Nobel Prize in 1936 (Popper and Eccles, 1977, 496-97). Obviously, the frame, or level of consciousness from which this dream arose, and even from the level of Loewi's semi-wakeful state, must entail some relatively non-verbal form of knowing unavailable to his ordinary form of communication. Yet the content of his dream could still be interpreted with a greater or lesser degree of accuracy. Can it not be conjectured that this lower level existed totally "outside" the realm of his awareness? Might there not be some canon at this level which nonetheless remains "immanent" within the brain-mind? This conjecture is not to propagate the myth of direct intuition or introspection. It is simply based on the assumption that from brain-states to mind-states there is a complex, delayed (deferred), temporalizing, and spacing hierarchy of integrated and interacting levels, each with a set of self-contained and containing frames; that is, each frame depends on another higher frame which includes it as a subset.[31]

Yet we must admit to a potential for successive levels "outside" the frame within which one exists at a given moment. Such an "outside," rather than transcendental, represents an expansion from "within." If this "outside" is not adopted, then the deconstructive enterprise becomes impossible. To deconstruct implies the game— *play*—which is, in a way, presumably "ruleless"; that is, the "rules" are to be made and broken spontaneously and incessantly. Now, how can the rules of a game, say chess, which is governed strictly, or war, which is governed by a relatively explicit or implicit code, or *laissez faire* economics, whose internal rules are supposedly natural and therefore "free," be changed? From "inside"? No, for such rules are canonical. Hence to speak *about*, write *about*, or *change* them, levels derived from a "somewhere else," are imperative.

For instance, Gödelian undecidable sentences may be shown to be true in a larger, more inclusive system. This indicates that "the truth content of a mathematical system cannot be completely expressed by the deductive methods of the system itself" (Schlegel, 1967, 69). We have here potentially an infinite set of systems, each capable of generating proofs for all systems contained "within," but not for itself or for higher systems—an infinite Chinese box, if you will. The same can be said of the less rigorous systems in the sciences, and even of informal systems such as the pragmatic paradoxes described in chapter three.[32] There must always be, in all cases, entry into a broader domain which is made possible by what is permitted from "within." And what is permitted from that domain is acquired, not explicitly, not transcendentally, not by an intentional act of mind, but through *experience*—or Peirce's *abduction*.

The experience spoken of here is essential for all implicit learning. And, since it is ordinarily tacit, its "rules" must necessarily remain implicit. For example, intentionally and consciously memorizing notes on a score and positions on a piano is no substitute for human experience, if one wills to become a good musician. Memorizing the table of logarithms or ten thousand proofs does not make one an accomplished mathematician. Memorizing a cookbook does not insure one of being a good chef. One can memorize grammar rules and spout out syntactically correct sentences, but still say nothing intelligible, for one has not learned by experience properly to speak semantically. And so on. A universal form of human experience is the only ingredient at this level. It cannot exist in the musical score, in the proof, or in the cookbook or grammar book. There must always be a "somewhere else," which guides experience toward some undefined and undefinable end.[33] If not, how could rules be changed? From whence could a flash of insight (Peirce's *abduction*) come, if not from some larger, more inclusive frame?

But if we cannot consciously experience and speak *about* such a more inclusive frame, then how can we get a handle on it? Is Derrida correct when he claims such ineffables to be impossible to speak *about* with our language of presence, of fullness? Perhaps. Yet, let's continue to try, this time from another angle.

7

I'm locked up, I'm in something, it's not I, that's all I know.
(Beckett, 1955, 405)

The concept of an "elsewhere" is common in relativity physics. I will use it here as an elaborate metaphor, a conceit if you will, of the "somewhere else" referred to above. The "elsewhere" can be approximated visually by joining the apex of two three-dimensional cones, which represent the "world" for a three-dimensional entity as it proceeds through the four-dimensional "block":[34]

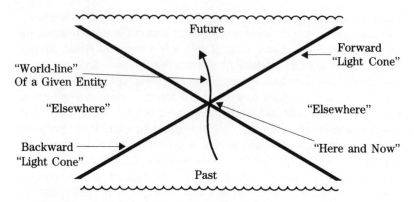

Since one's "world line" through the "block" is not straight, the "light cone" of one's consciousness wanders through this "block" to a greater or lesser degree at variance with all other "light cones." And the speed of light being finite, one cannot therefore observe everything at once, but only what is contained within the "cone." The "elsewhere," therefore, is at a given point in time unknowable—yet it can be partly knowable from the perspective of the "light cone" of another entity along its own "world line."[35] In Newtonian physics the finite speed of light, and therefore the exis- tence of an "elsewhere" region, is ignored. For practical purposes as well they can be ignored, for when relatively small distances are measured in conventional units, simultaneity seems to be the case and hence there is no conceivable "elsewhere" (Costa de Beaugaard, 1966). On the other hand, it becomes a factor when con- sidering great distances, and especially in parts of the universe where gravitational fields are extraordinarily strong, such as "black holes," a "light cone" becomes distorted such that the "elsewhere" region is relatively great. Yet throughout the universe the "else- where" always to an extent exists.

Speculations stemming from the existence of the "elsewhere" are mind-boggling. For instance, "tachyons," faster-than-light "parti- cles," have been proposed, which remain outside the space-time manifold, in the "elsewhere" (Bileniuk and Sudarshan, 1969). Some scientists have pondered over the notion that instantaneous in- formation exchange such as occurs during paranormal psychic ex- periences may even be "tachyonic."[36] In other words, each "world line" can be thought of as having been assigned a set of probabili- ties, some of which will become actualized and others not. However, "within" this set of probabilities all possible histories are mutually interpenetrative; that is *mutually cancellatory*. They exist at an "instant," in the "block," partly beyond any particular "light cone." This "block" contains, as described above, all possibilities, when considering the myriad set of futures for all possible "light cones." It can be thought of as comparable to the Peircean undifferentiated continuum of possibilities. It must be in this sense construed as the ultimate "frame"—entailing that "highest" form of "logic" Peirce speaks of. And, the "elsewhere" it contains must be analogous with the "somewhere else," the source of all experience of the new, the infinite "field" of Derridean *play*. The "field" of *play*, therefore, must be such a potentiality as described above. If so, then we can have our cake and eat it too. Our total system of possibles plus actuals is "immanent," but for each of us there is always a "beyond," always a broader domain "within" which creativity can be exercised, "within" which rules can be changed. And hence, Derrida's admission that DC is "transcendental" is in a way qualified, for it depends, rather metaphorically, on the equivalent of the "block," and on the "somewhere else." If not, then how else can we even begin to account for *play*, or DC, MC, and the TC?

We must push on, in an attempt better to know how *play* is possible from "within."

8

"My world," said the King, "the world, because no other is conceivable, for where could that be? Nowhere . . ." (Burger, 1965, 150)

Edwin A. Abbott's *Flatland* (1952) and Dionys Burger's *Sphereland* (1968) are remarkable fantasies on, if not the impossibility, at least the difficulty of one's conceiving a dimension "higher" than that of which one's "world" is constructed. Following these two authors, and with a series of "thought experiments," we will see how it might be possible for such transition to "higher" realms. If such an account is successful, then it can be feasible to posit that, without "transcendence" into some mysterious onto-theological "otherworldly realm," but by a sheer act of imagination, it is possible for there to exist successively "broader" frames from "within" the selfsame, self-contained system. Such "broader" frames are ordinarily accessible only to experience, but, as was demonstrated above, an act of imagination can render at least partly intelligible that which was ineffable.

Consider a pointland which can contain only one inhabitant. This solitary individual merrily vibrates on, content that he knows his world perfectly and that his world is all there is, unaware of the existence, potentially, of the linelander's world. Lineland exists, however, and it is infinitely greater than pointland, for it essentially consists of an infinity of pointlands. Also, lineland, unlike pointland, can contain many inhabitants, but they must remain in orderly succession, for they cannot pass over or under each other. Then what would be required for one line-segment, that is one inhabitant, from within lineland, to pass someone else in his world? A second dimension, of which he presumably cannot be aware. And supposing that somehow he became aware of this 2-D flatland, how could he get out of his world? Only by imagining himself transformed into a 2-D plane, something like this:

Linelander Passing His Fellow
Citizens in 2-D Space

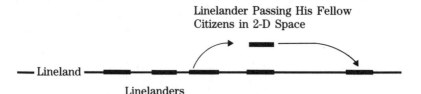

But, of course, this magical feat is impossible from within his world, it can be accomplished solely through such an imaginary act. Now suppose the linelander's world to be circular rather than straight. In such case any given inhabitant could travel along his world forever without reaching the end, forcibly to conclude that his world is infinite, whereas in reality from above, we can readily see that there can still be an infinitely greater world.

Since it's rather difficult for us to identify with this lowly linelander anyway, let us go one step further to consider a flatlander, for instance A. Square, who is the subject of Abbott's book. A. Square's world is infinitely greater than that of the linelander, hence his feeling of superiority over those unfortunate lesser beings.

Aware that he lives in an infinity of linelands, he pompously slides along in his world, knowing perfectly well that there can logically and rationally be no higher worlds. However, what if the flatlander's world were in reality a sphere rather than flat? There would hardly be any way for him, from within his world, to know that it is not flat. In fact, like the linelander, he could slide along his entire life without reaching an end point, and hence he would proclaim with confidence that his world is infinite, that there cannot be anything outside it. Actually, of course, we can point out that his realm is in reality unbounded, yet there can be larger worlds. Such a realiza- tion was forced upon A. Square one day when along came A. Sphere who, as he passed through the 2-D flatland, first appeared as a point, then a circle which grew bigger and bigger, and then shrank to a point once again, which then disappeared out of existence. This was a terrifying experience for A. Square, though perfectly normal for A. Sphere, or for ourselves in our own 3-D world for that matter. Abbott's book narrates the difficulties A. Square had in accounting for such a 3-D realm of existence, and when he finally did, he was thrown in prison for heresy when he enthusiastically told his fellow citizens of his discovery.

A. Square, like the linelander, must, in order to see his world from outside, move into a higher frame, a 3-D frame, from which vantage point he can do mysterious things, such as remove his shoes from his closet without opening the door, or remove the meat from his 2-D walnut without cracking it open. In fact, from his su- perior perspective, it might be assumed that he can see his entire 2-D world at a glance. But this in reality cannot be, for it must be remembered that he is two-dimensional, and possesses no stereo- scopic vision, as do his 3-D counterparts. The most he can see of flatland from above is an infinitesimal "slice," something like this:[37]

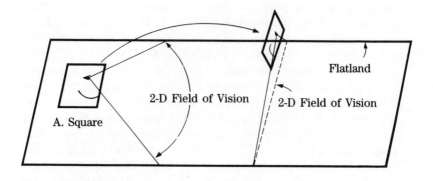

Consequently he can do no more than scan this flat 2-D world by taking in an infinity of infinitesimally thin lines, like a TV camera with an infinite scanner. That is, he can still have no God's-eye view of his universe at an instant. In this light, then, what is the status of A. Sphere in his own 3-D world? He, of course, assumes that his world is the one and only complete and consistent world. But surely he must be mistaken, for if it is possible to proceed from one to three dimensions, though painfully, then there must be a fourth dimension, and a fifth, and so on infinitely (i.e., what is known as Hilbertian space of infinite dimensions).[38] How can we acquire a conceptual grasp of such "higher domains?"

Consider A. Sphere to live in a "cube" world—i.e., in an infinitely stacked set of flatlands. If we extend each side of this "cube" representing his world with an infinity of slices, like we did in transforming pointland into lineland, or lineland into flatland, we have what is called a (4-D) hypercube, sometimes represented like this:

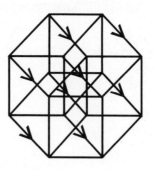

A hypercube, and especially its counterpart, a hypersphere, tax the imagination. It is difficult, if not impossible, to understand them visually, though mathematically they are no real problem. Nevertheless, assume A. Sphere to be able to transport himself mentally into this higher dimension. He could now, like A. Square, take his shoes from his closet without opening the door, or remove the yolk of a 3-D egg without damaging the shell. Physically and from within a 3-D world this is of course impossible. In the 4-D world, on the other hand, A. Sphere would be able to see a world other 3-D citizens ordinarily see as, so to speak, turned inside out. That is, like A. Square seeing a 2-D "slice" of his world from above, from a perspective normally inaccessible along the plane of his 2-D world, A. Sphere would be able, from above, to see a complete 3-D "bit" ordinarily impossible to see from within the 3-D world, but he would still be limited, for he is a 3-D being in 4-D space, hence he would be able to glimpse only one "bit" at a time.[39]

Topologically, and by using *differentials (differences)* it is possible to account for such magical acts as removing a yolk from the egg. Simply take a point on the shell, consider the yolk to be an infinity of points, and remove them one by one, through the "point-hole," and the task is accomplished. But, of course, this would be rather impractical. As the *differences* between parts of the yolk become infinitesimal so as to pass them through the infinitely small point, we discover that the magical act will require an infinity of years. Yet we, by an act of mind, can imagine this series of events occurring. If we consider, in this light, Peirce's infinitesimals, or Derrida's DC, we must conclude that such acts of thinking inevitably give in to Zeno's arguments, as pointed out above. Yet we *do* think, so it *must be* possible, though paradoxically ("unnamably") so. This is precisely why it is an object of wonder, and of our obsession to understand *how* it is possible.

One barrier limiting our understanding is that, mere 3-D beings that we are, we cannot effectively create a mental picture of 4-D space-time. Nevertheless, we can easily speak *about* it. It has even been formalized mathematically and in part used to explain our universe. That is, the 4-D manifold, as well as the "block" and the "elsewhere," were arrived at not through visualizable models, but through intellection, at the deepest levels, of formal deductive systems coupled with attempts to relate them to the observed world (Ullmo, 1964). Another barrier to our understanding is that of, to reiterate, our natural languge. The Oriental mystics have long since arrived at conclusions similar to the modern physicist, but more directly, through inner experience. Capra (1975, 150) in this sense remarks that:

> Our language and thought patterns have evolved in the three-dimensional world and therefore we find it extremely hard to deal with the four-dimensional reality of relativity physics.
> Eastern mystics, on the other hand, seem to be able to experience a higher-dimensional reality directly and correctly. In the state of deep meditation they can transcend the three-dimensional world of everyday life, and experience a totally different reality where all opposites are unified into an organic whole.

So the mystic can experience what we cannot say, using natural language that is, and he can experience at this deeper level what is ordinarily inaccessible to our own experience. But there is a certain convergence here. When the mystic attempts to describe his experience, he encounters the same problems of ineffability as Western scientists. Hence this "higher-dimensional reality" can be experienced, but not adequately described, or it can be postulated intellectually and at least indirectly and incompletely described and illustrated with visualizable models with which we are familiar.

In the following section a visual metaphor will be offered to account for the "somewhere else."

9

I have to go on, that's what I'm doing, let others suppose, there must be others in other elsewheres, each one in his little elsewhere. (Beckett, 1955, 403)

Over the long haul, perhaps words, like Peirce's and Popper's conception of science, are self-corrective, allowing the speaker/writer willingly as well as unwillingly to whittle a little off here, and add more there, until he is relatively satisfied with the final product. But the most important issue at this stage of the inquiry involves the source of the atemporal and original thought which leads to words in the first place. This source is Beckett's "elsewhere," where there are no words and where words are meaningless. Back to topology and the flatlanders in an attempt better to account for this phenomenon.

A Möbius strip can conceivably, though contradictorily, be constructed exclusively within a 2-D domain. This requires, however, a logically impossible intersection of two planes, something like this:[40]

2-D Strip   Self-intersection   2-D Möbius Band
               After a Twist

A flatlander can ideally travel from "inside" to "outside" along this world without realizing he is doing so, and he will be inverted, with each journey around the strip, into a mirror image of himself, also without knowing it. Basically the same could be constructed with a Klein bottle to illustrate an analogous process for a 3-D worlder, but since the Klein bottle requires a fourth dimension for its completion, it is difficult to illustrate graphically.[41] As an alternative we can, however, consider a variation of the Necker cube:

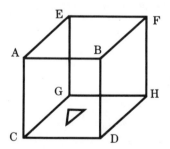

Notice that if ABCD is perceived to be the face of the cube, the triangle is on the inside with the apex pointing outward. In contrast, if EFGH is the face, the triangle is outside, and the apex points away. In other words, the triangle has been inverted, like on the Möbius strip. The implication is that, just as the flatlander must be "rotated" through 3-D space in order to be reversed, so the triangle in the Necker cube must be "rotated," by means of an infinite number of infinitesimals, through 4-D space—i.e., in our own (non)consciousness—in order to be reversed. And, just as the Möbius strip can be represented exclusively within a 2-D world, but with an intersection in 3-D space, so either the Klein bottle or the Necker cube can be conceived within a 3-D space, and it also entails an apparently contradictory 4-D spatial topology. Interestingly enough, a formulation analogous to this leads H. A. C. Dobbs (1972) to conclude that: (a) the transformation in the perspectival reversal of the Necker cube is logically impossible in 3-D space, (b) no spatial degree of freedom is evident in this transformation except height, width, and depth; that is, 3-D space, and (c) therefore the extra dimension must consist of a "mathematically imaginary time dimension," a 4-D manifold. This "extra dimension" beyond time and 3-D space, then, appears to illustrate the domain of the "somewhere else" referred to above.

I must continue to emphasize that the scheme proposed here is, commensurate with Derridean and Peircean thought, "nontranscendent." Both "mind" and "body" are part of the system. That is, the physical aspects of the universe—actualized entities—are intimately connected to and give rise to, at the highest levels of complexity, the mental aspects of the universe. But, in conjunction with the reports of some of the "new physicists," those selfsame mental aspects (that is, consciousness) are in turn responsible for bringing about the actualization of the physical aspects, paradoxically.

CHAPTER FIVE

The Unlimited Web of Writing

1

This last phrase seems familiar, suddenly I seem to have written it somewhere before, . . . Yes, I shall soon be, etc., that is what I wrote when I realized I did not know what I had said. (Beckett, 1955, 209)

Derrida tells us that the concept of writing "exceeds and comprehends that of language, presupposes of course a certain definition of language and of writing" (Derrida, 1974a, 8-9 and 238).[1] Traditionally, language designated "action, movement, thought, reflection, consciousness, unconsciousness, experience, affectivity, etc." Now, writing must be construed not only as visual and physical *graphemes*, but the totality of what makes language possible in the first place (Derrida, 1974a, 8-9). Derrida goes on to remark that if cybernetics takes upon itself the task of throwing out all metaphysics, uniting machine and nature with man and culture, then: "It must conserve the notion of writing, trace, grammè, or grapheme, until its own historical-metaphysical character is also exposed" (Derrida, 1974a, 9). What is the relation between machine, nature, man, and writing? What role can writing play in uniting machine and nature with man?

Phonetic writing, it would appear at the outset, is closer to the goal of cybernetics than cryptographic or ideographic writing. It is indeed the most primitive information system, at least within nature. That is, as a code and a finite alphabet with a small set of rules, it is capable, linearly, through time and by a digital system, of infinite generativity. In this sense it enjoys a biological counterpart in nature.[2] Moreover, phonetic writing produces texts most closely approximating a computer printout, mere "black marks on white paper," as Derrida calls them (Derrida, 1972a, 203).[3] The medium of the great metaphysical, scientific, technological, and economic adventures of the West, phonetic writing is nonetheless inferior, says Derrida, to nonlinear, spatial, and iconic writing, which is more closely related to algebra, the more ancient pictographic form of symbolization as opposed to modern linearly developed theoretical mathematics (I presume Derrida means computer mathematics in this context).

But there is a positive side of the picture. The West's more limited form is a "nonfortuitous conjunction" of cybernetics and the "human sciences" which will eventually lead to a profound reversal. What might this profound reversal be? A return to the primitive roots of writing? Might it consist of a type of cipher that could be seen all at once, rather than a linear sequence that one must, so to speak, swim through, while inexorably being dragged along by the current? This primitive glyph requires special powers of the mind, the power of concentration, and the power of imagination—and especially, it is concerning the power of imagination of which we are so lamentably ignorant. Yet such power of the glyph was well known to certain mystics—if the word may be placed in the present context. The mystics knew that "if a man meditates upon a symbol around which certain ideas have been associated by past meditation, he will obtain access to these ideas, even if the glyph has never been elucidated to him by those who have received the oral tradition 'by mouth to ear'" (Fortune, 1935, 5).[4] In this sense, the message in its entirety can be conveyed by a glyph, which, of course, will mean nothing to the uninitiated. It might appear that Derrida's emphasis on the glyph places him clearly within this more primitive tradition. However, Derrida actually has little to say about the visual aspects of the grapheme—in fact, he at times resoundingly critiques ocular vision.[5]

Nevertheless, the essence of Derrida's quest is for the "lost *'presence'* of the glyph," if we dare put it this way. The phonetically written book, through repetition, demands a necessary but undesired deferral, DC. Such a text cannot be a presence, or even a future presence, and its reading (repetition) is not a past presence. Hence the "now of writing"—or of reading—is, admittedly, irretrievable, but it is "less irretrievable," Derrida seems to be saying with the non-phonocentric book.

2

The first pages are covered with ciphers and other symbols and diagrams, . . . Calculations, I reckon. They seem to stop suddenly, prematurely at all events. As though discouraged. (Beckett, 1955, 209)

Freud's discussion of dream and metaphor intrigues Derrida. Spivak (1974, xl) claims that this is because "Freud's slow discovery of the metaphor of writing . . . does not have the usual strings attached." Metaphor is usually contrasted with writing and directly related to speech. But this notion carries with it a contradiction, for from another view, "writing in the metaphorical sense, natural, divine, and living writing, is venerated; it is equal in dignity to the origin of value, to the voice of consciousness as divine law, to the heart, to sentiment and so forth" (Derrida, 1974a, 17). The dichotomy is explained thus: we have a need to perpetuate our "myth of presence," hence writing in the usual sense signifies the absence of the author, while metaphorical writing is considered sacred. Freud's metaphorical view of writing, in contrast, "is uncontaminated by this double dealing. In fact, Freud speculates that the very mansion of presence, the perceiving self, is shaped by absence, and— writing" (Spivak, 1974, xli).

Freud's dreams (metaphors) are, like Derrida's ideal form of writing, pictographic and especially ideogrammatic as well as containing some phonetic elements (Derrida, 1978a, 209). The "writing" of dreams "exceeds phonetic writing and puts speech back in its place. As in hieroglyphics or rebuses, voice is circumvented" (Derrida, 1978a, 218). The dream in the form of Freud's "mystic writing pad" is closer to writing than to speech, for writing is more spatial than temporal, in contrast to speech, which is a temporalization of space. The psyche, then, is a kind of text, an "unconscious text" (Derrida, 1978a, 199). The problem is that, after having temporalized space, speech rendered meanings irreversible, assymetrical, a linear series. Present was past, and future was/became irretrievable presence. The only recourse was to repress writing, which reminded us of that lost origin—that something which *was* something but which could embody nothing, and at the same time could be the void through which everything emanated. And hence, says Derrida, writing was repressed.

How, then, can spatiality regain its rightful position? By the disappearance of phonetic writing. But one problem with phonetic writing is that it has no pure form. It must entail nonphonetic signs (punctuation, spacing between signs, etc.) which "are ill described by the concept of signs" (Derrida, 1973, 133). "Algebraic writing," in contrast, can include within itself an entire range of phenomena involved in its placement on a two-dimensional surface. That is, "algebraic writing," like the glyph, need not be limited by a uni-dimensional typographic channel, and like an ideograph, it spreads out the signs, and hence the thought, to incorporate a two-, and even a multi-dimensional, network of relations at one and the same instant. "Algebraic writing," a kind of theorem (= a sight) which can be perceived nonlinearly appropriately fills the page rather than the page being a mere void perforated by the arbitrary atoms of phonetic signs.

Unfortunately, Derrida asserts, phonetic writing "commands our entire culture and our entire science" (Derrida, 1974a, 30). But actually, contemporary scientifc thought is now becoming less hampered by linear writing. This is because it has demanded a form of writing in which everything can be present at least in near-simultaneity: modern science has little to do with the predominance of the phonetic sign which is paramount in the traditional logocentric text. Nonetheless, for science ultimately to become fully algebraic, it was necessary for it to pass through a logocentric stage, for the advantage of Logos is that in its written form it is at least "provisionally more economical" than preceding forms (Derrida, 1974a, 285).

Today, then, science is in a state of suspension "between the two ages of writing." It is in the process of discarding phonetic writing, and adopting more algebraic forms. Consequently, the ideal form of writing for science would be the equivalent of a language of pure consonants—practically speechless—and represented by ideographic ciphers (Derrida, 1974a, 315).[6] *Grammatology* would displace traditional linguistics to become the science of all sciences, the science of writing, for science itself would become a science of the written sign. This development in graphic notation must proceed hand in hand, Derrida tells us, with the deconstruction of metaphysics. One must deconstruct, the other presumably must build, disclosure of longstanding myths must accompany re-edification of thought. Perhaps here we see, finally, the constructive aspect of deconstruction, though it remains a dream, a hope, beyond the horizon, somehow, someday, to be realized, but not until Western World thought has evolved from unilaterality to multilaterality.

Yet the end may soon come into view. Derrida claims that since we are beginning to write differently, therefore we are, albeit slowly, beginning to read differently (Derrida, 1974a, 86-87). But once we have learned to read differently, the task can still never be completed, for the grammatologist must be an eternal sentry, the Cherubim who, with his flaming sword, prevents infiltration of "pre-scientific empricisim," "positivism," and "metaphysical scientism" into his *Grammatological* Eden (Derrida, 1972b, 48).

3

My little finger glides before my pencil across the page and gives warning, falling over the edge, that the end of the line is near. (Beckett, 1955, 207)

Conceded, the linearity, causality, and mechanism contained within Western World languages is by and large incompatible with the findings of modern science. Obviously, classical logic based on Western subject-predicate languages is no longer operable. Heisenberg himself articulated this fact decades ago.[7] If Western science had to pass through a logocentric stage in order to reach its present state, the fact remains that when phonetic writing was seen to be inadequate, it was soon discarded—even though for purposes of everyday commnication, scientists must still stumble along using natural languages. Hence Derrida's insistence on the systematic repression of writing in the history of Western World thought loses some of its force.

In contemporary science the written sign is paramount, yet largely non-phonetic (i.e., mathematical) symbolization is acquiring greater prominence. It is, moreover, becoming increasingly similar to Derrida's ideal form of grapheme (i.e., in the use of matrices, lattices, groups, quantum logic, etc.). However, it bears mentioning that the mathematization of many concepts in contemporary science, though conveyed through the medium of visual signs, does not, and cannot, entail pictographic models. That is, the meaning of the mathematical model cannot be gained through a mental picture, but through contemplation. For this reason the concepts of contemporary physics, the most advanced science, by and large defy the use of visual models and their description in natural languages. They are becoming pure abstraction—algebraic.

It is well known that scientists and mathematicians can hardly talk shop without a chalkboard, their own sort of "mystic writing pad." In fact, the chalkboard is an ample metaphor—also used by Peirce—for representing the ideal non-phonetic text. It is the exact inverse of the phonetically-based text—i.e., white marks on black. When it is filled, the symbols can be grasped almost at a glance by the skilled mathematician, then before anything can be added or changed there must be an "erasure" of part or all the text. With each "erasure" and subsequent change—correction of error—a new text comes into existence and the previous text is "deconstructed." With "erasure" of the entire text, such effacement renders the text repeatable, but DC prevails, for the text is always subject to context-dependency.[8] The chalkboard metaphor is relative to Derrida's program for *Grammatology* insofar as both entail a highly abstract symbol system. For example, Derrida (1978a, 169-95) favorably describes Antonin Artaud's project to destroy Western World language by formulating a new abstract algebraic language. This remains the ideal. By use of a set of symbols from such an abstract language, signs can be intrinsically related such that "intertextuality" regains its rightful autonomy irrespective of historical influences.[9]

Interestingly, this ideal language, with its accompanying writing, seems comparable to one of the languages of the mysterious planet Tlön, described by Borges, which contains no nouns, only adjectives. The equivalent of nouns is formed by a composite of adjectives. The literature of this language abounds in mental objects "which are convoked and dissolved in a moment, according to poetic needs" (Borges, 1964a, 9). The metaphysicists of Tlön "do not seek for truth or even for verisimilitude, but rather for the astounding. They judge that metaphysics is a branch of fantastic literature. They know that a system is nothing more than the subordination of all aspects of the universe to any one such aspect. Even the phrase 'all aspects' is rejectible, for it supposes the impossible addition of the present and of all past moments" (Borges, 1964a, 10).

Works of fiction in this strange language contain a single plot with all possible permutations—and hence they are, in Derrida's terms, perpetually "self-deconstructing." Philosophical texts contain both their thesis and their antithesis, "the rigorous pro and con of a doctrine. A book which does not contain its counterbook is considered incomplete" (Borges, 1964a, 13). Centuries of this idealism, we are told, has influenced reality such that it takes on correspondence with all possible worlds. In this reality there are no truths or univocal meanings, only an exceedingly diverse fabric of sentences. The only reality, in fact, becomes The Reality of texts, of sentences, which, inexorably, begins to take over our world. Our world becomes Tlön. Borges (1964a, 18) concludes that: "I pay no attention to all this and go on revising, in the still days at the Adrogué hotel, an uncertain Quevedian translation (which I do not intend to publish) of Browne's *Urn Burial*."

The implication here is that the world is deontologized, losing all power of Being, and, we might extrapolate, of presence. The world becomes the interpenetration of all mutually cancellatory possibilities; it becomes no-*thing*. Borges, the fabricator of fictions, comes strikingly close to the view of the "new physics": the universe seems more and more to be like a giant mind, a great thought.

4

*[A]nd I wrote, soon I shall be quite dead at last, and so on
without even going on to the next page, which was blank.
(Beckett, 1955, 209)*

Derrida's notion of an algebraic form of writing finds anteced-
ents in Peirce. Of course, Peirce in general adhered to the canons of
traditional logic, though in certain ways he projected beyond them.
One example of such a projection is found in his "existential
graphs," an abstract iconography in the most literal sense, an
attempt generally to diagram how the mind works (Roberts, 1973,
113). It is at least most probably an indication of how Peirce's mind
works, for he says:

I do not think I ever *reflect* on words: I employ visual diagrams, firstly
because this way of thinking is my natural language of self-
communion, and secondly, because I am convinced that it is the best
system for the purpose. (MS 620, 8-9—quoted in Roberts, 1973, 126)

In the first place Peirce believes that all signs are in some way
or another iconic in nature, algebraic equations being the written
form most closely approximating pure icons (Peirce, 1960, 2.281-
82)—i.e., like Derrida's ciphers. Secondly, the most effective, and
only *direct*, way of communicating an idea is by means of an icon
(Peirce, 1960, 2.278). But iconic communication is not direct, purely
and simply. That is, it is not pure Firstness, or *quality*. A possibility
alone cannot be an icon, it must exist *as* such-and-such *for* someone (Peirce, 1960, 2.274). Moreover, pure icons are capable of
asserting nothing; they are not yet related to something else. A sentence interpreting an icon must be in a potential mood, such as
"Suppose a figure has three sides," with no information *about* a
specific figure or *of* the figure *as related to* something else (Peirce,
1960, 2.291). Thirdly, icons exist in varying degrees of complexity.
An entire sentence can itself form an icon. For instance, "loveth," a
symbol if in a sentence, needs an index to relate it to a subject and
an object, and the entire combination is an analog image, an icon
(Peirce, 1960, 2.295). These icons are of an algebraic kind, though
usually simple ones, a characteristic of natural languages brought to

light by Boolean algebra (Peirce, 1960, 2.280). Peirce proceeds from ancient iconic writing to Western World linear writing:

> In all primitive writing, such as the Egyptian heiroglyphics, there are icons of a non-logical kind, the ideographics. In the earliest form of speech, there probably was a large element of mimicry. But in all languages known, such representations have been replaced by conventional auditory signs. These, however, are such that they can only be explained by icons. But in the syntax of every language there are logical icons of the kind that are sided by conventional rules. (Peirce, 1960, 2.280)

Western World writing, then, is seen to be the evolution of a deeper, more primitive form, a form similar to that which Derrida attempts somehow to revive, and, as mentioned above, the form already being revived at an increased level of abstraction in the mathematics of relativity and quantum mechanics (as well as in topology—especially the "catastrophe theory" of René Thom).

Moreover, a sentence, according to Peirce, consists of a set of objects at various levels—letters, words, clauses, etc.—which compose a "complex Object." The sentence, "Cain killed Abel," which is a sign, "refers at least as much to Abel as to Cain, even if it be not regarded as it should, as having 'a killing' as a third Object" (Peirce, 1960, 2.230). A proposition in this sense "is a sign connected with its object by an association of general ideas." This Peirce calls a "Dicent Symbol" or a "Legisign" (Peirce, 1960, 2.262). A string of propositions can make up an "Argument," or a "Symbolic Legisign," which is a more complex sign "whose interpretant represents its object as being an ulterior sign through a law, namely, the law that the passage from all such premises to such conclusions tends to the truth" (Peirce, 1960, 2.263).

Hence, although Peirce's attention to traditional rules of logic and argumentation, as well as his notion of truth, appear alien to Derrida, he believes that deep within grammatical sentences lie the roots of iconic (i.e., ideographic) forms. The continuous whole has been spread out into a discrete chain, its analog property having been digitalized, but its more primitive form remains: a TC revealed in all texts.

Popper once again surfaces.

5

*I hear the noise of my little finger as it glides over the paper
and then that so different of the pencil following after. (Beckett, 1955, 208)*

Popper claims that a decisively important aspect of language is
its capacity for expressing negation, for lying, contradicting, and
metaphorizing; that is, in the most general sense, for creating
fictions (see also Merrell, 1983). The possibility of creating fictions,
of constructing a "falsity," opens up the possibility of countering
the fiction with the/a presumably "real world," and if the "real
world" subsequently comes to be perceived as just another fiction,
then it gives way to another "real world," and so on. Similarly, the
possibility of a "false" statement always presupposes the possibility
of a "true" counterstatement, and if that comes to be conceived as
"false," then it can be countered with yet another "true"
statement.[10] Human language, in other words, entails the potential
for counterarguments, or critical argumentation. Popper's notion of
the argumentative function of language in texts must be compared
to deconstruction.[11]

Popper follows Karl Bühler (1934) who proposes three functions for human language:

(a) *Expressive*: the message must serve to express the emotions or thoughts of the language user.
(b) *Signalling* or *stimulative*: the message stimulates a certain response in the addressee.
(c) *Descriptive*: the message describes a particular state of
affairs.

To these three functions, Popper (1963, 134-35) adds a fourth:

(d) *Argumentative* or *explanatory:* presentation of alternative thoughts, views, or propositions to descriptive or
expressive messages as defined in (c).

Now, let (a) through (d) be submitted as potentially viable assumptions for the present inquiry. Clearly, (a), (c) and (d) can be isolated in terms of the output of a message while (b) entails input and corresponding behavior; hence let us "bracket out" (b) for the present. What follows will project Bühler's and Popper's terminology into a larger classificatory scheme.

Function (a) consists of the class of nonverbal human and animal messages. Function (c) consists of sentences formulated in human natural or artificial languages by means of the combination of *graphemes*. In this sense, (c) can also include visual, auditory, and verbal art forms (sculpture, painting, music, prose and poetry, film) as well as scientific models and sketches, diagrams, graphs and maps, which manifest both iconic and discrete characteristics. In this light, then:

(e) Descriptive messages can be: (i) chiefly implicit, in the case of visual or auditory art forms (painting, sculpture, music, etc.); (ii) implicit and explicit, in the case of verbal art forms (poetry, which is usually more implicit than explicit, and oral literature and prose, which may be more explicit than implicit) or art forms which combine verbal and visual (drama, film, etc.); (iii) chiefly explicit, in the case of linguistically formulated statements with the purpose of informing, convincing, instructing, etc.; or (iv) chiefly explicit, in the case of scientific models and sketches, diagrams, graphs and maps, and mathematical and logical symbols.

(f) Sophisticated animal forms of communication border on the descriptive mode.

Implicit descriptive messages sent and received on partly tacit levels are predominantly of continuous or iconic character. Explicit descriptive messages break up a state of affairs into constituent parts, hence they are less tacit, and they are sent and received as discontinuous (discrete) parts of a continuum. Descriptive messages within human communicative systems implicitly or explicitly convey what is considered to be "truth" or "falsity," belief, doubt, skepticism, etc., *about* something or in support of or in reaction to some situation or state of affairs. In this sense, a descriptive message is necessarily an expressive message insofar as it is the outward manifestation of some internal thought, emotion, or attitude. It also performs a signalling or stimulative function since it is capable of provoking a negative or positive response.

With respect to Popper's additional linguistic function, however, two more assumptions follow:

(g) Argumentative or explanatory messages are: (i) the manifestation of agreement or opposition to some other descriptive or argumentative message, and (ii) the implicit or explicit, and tacit or conscious formulation of reasons, whether intuitive, intellectual or emotive, for such agreement or opposition.

(h) The argumentative mode is uniquely human.

Argumentative messages consist of well-formulated scientific theories explaining a descriptive model, analysis of art works, or explanations of general hypotheses, concepts, and opinions with the intention of convincing the addressee. The messages can be appropriately about descriptive messages, hence they are necessarily derived from particular and rather well-defined perspectives about "truth" or "falsity," belief, doubt, skepticism, etc. They are also about problems inherent in descriptive messages. For instance, consider the following:

Biting rats can be fatal (ambiguity).

Jack is tall and consists of four letters (category mistake).

This statement is false (paradox).

All cats are mortal. Socrates is mortal. Therefore, Socrates is a cat (false reasoning; inconsistent conclusions from consistent premises).

All four statements, in isolation, can be perceived merely as descriptive messages. In this sense, they could be sent by an addresser who is unaware that they can be interpreted in different ways or interpreted not at all by the addressee. On the other hand, to explain their inadequacy and argue for alternative messages capable of avoiding these inadequacies entails the generation of complementary messages at a different level. That is, it requires awareness *of* the problem situations inherent in the messages. Hence in order for the addresser to clarify his messages he must first discover the problems inherent in them. Then he can attempt to resolve these problems by talking or thinking about the messages.

Expressive messages, according to Popper, are characteristically dogmatic; that is, closed. There is little or no possibility, within the framework of these messages, for opening the system. On the other hand, descriptive messages, such as the above set of sentences can be breached relatively easily. However, these messages are evocative, there is no or little possibility for counterargument or discussion *about* the validity of a given statement. Argumentative messages entail the comparative juxtaposition of two or more sets of descriptive messages. However, they can be either closed and dogmatic or open and critical. From the closed perspective, argument is from within the system of only one of the juxtaposed messages or sets of messages. From the open perspective, argument critically evaluates both. Popper, in relating the argumentative function to the lie, states that:

> the descriptive function of language brings with it the basis for the argumentative function of language, and for a critical attitude towards language. . . . [W]e have built into us the need to develop criticism and the need to develop a critical attitude towards a report, and with it, the need to develop an argumentative language—a language in which the truth of a report can be criticized or attacked, or in which it can be defended by supplementary reports. (Popper and Eccles, 1977, 456)

Popper's "critical rationalism" is now clearly distinguishable from classical Cartesian rationalism. "Critical rationalism," always infallible and indeterminate, is an ongoing, tough-minded and rhetorical stance *vis-à-vis* all reports, all propositions, all theories, and all texts. It is rooted in argumentative language, which, never static, univocal, or possessing a retrievable "center"—since any "center" is always "falsifiable"—must incessantly push on.

Now to relate Popper's hypothesis to deconstruction.

6

I should really lose my pencil more often, it might do me good, I might be more cheerful. (Beckett, 1955, 222)

My pencil is more intelligent than I. (Reported to have been uttered by Einstein)

According to Einstein's conception of science, "the theoretical physicist, . . . tends to see that the problems of physics are only theoretical formulations, since facts cannot contradict each other; only the theoretically prescribed conceptualizations of the facts can contradict one another" (in Schlossberg, 1973, 59). Since Einstein (1950, 59) himself tells us that the "whole of science is nothing more than a refinement of everyday thinking," it follows that problems of science as well as those of everyday life are nothing more than linguistic (whether theoretical or practical) formulations, a view similar to that of Popper, and, it might be added, Peirce.

The decisive issue for Popper in resolving either scientific or everyday problems entails putting them into argumentative sentences which can then be subjected to critical scrutiny: Popper's counterpart to Derridean *Grammatology*. A written or printed form is preferable to a spoken form, given its permanence and due to our memory loss (Popper, 1974a, 182). Mental images and abstract ideas, in order to be retained as closely as possible, must be put into sentences and schematic representations. Then they can be compared and contrasted with other sentences and schemata, criticized, corrected, rejected, and so on (Popper and Eccles, 1977, 504-05). Gradually, then, our linguistic formulations can correct our assumptions while our assumptions shape our linguistic formulations, an ongoing process.

To express this another way, on putting scientific and everyday problem situations into argumentative sentences, we cannot not place ourselves at a meta-theoretical level. Yet at this level, there is always and invariably a presupposed given—or in Derridean terms, a "center."[12] Nevertheless, we must of necessity put ourselves at this meta-problem level; that is, our task is to discover the *problem situation* of the scientist, of an everyday dilemma, or, we can assume, of the writer (Popper, 1972, 188). At this level the parameters will always be open to new and unforeseen events, for a scientific theory, an everyday dilemma, or a text, can always be "refuted"—i.e., the presupposed given ("center") will to a degree always and invariably be wrong. And, by the same token, the meta-problem level formulation of that theory, dilemma, or text in sentences can itself also always be "refuted," for it is the conjectured resolution of a first-level problem situation, and so on.[13]

With respect to the language of criticism, then, speech exists primarily for the purpose of being represented in writing, and ideally as sentences in texts. Hence Derrida's (1974a, 27) contention that the "concept of writing should define the field of science" is argued for by Popper. However, the fact remains that Western World science was born during a certain "epoch" of writing: phonocentric writing, *logocentrism*. How can this notion be reconciled with Popper's meta-level of discourse? How does Popper avoid being through and through *logocentric*? According to Derrida (1974a, 27), the science of writing should "look for its object at the roots of scienticity." This is because, while metaphysics with its phonetic writing approximated speech, science, ideally at least, moved in the opposite direction by the use of mathematical language. *Grammatology* should therefore be a science delineating the possibility and the parameters of formal science, a science which no longer has the form of traditional logic, or of the spoken word, but a form of "grammatics" (Derrida, 1974a, 27-28). Popper's meta-problem level appears compatible with this formulation, but not without the inversion mentioned above, for if Popper's meta-level presumably entails a "rational" argumentative mode availing itself of traditional logic, it nevertheless gravitates toward increased abstraction, formalization, and schematization, thus approximating mathematical language ("grammatics")—and hence becoming more clearly compatible with but susceptible to Gödel's undecidability/incompleteness.

However, elsewhere, and as has already been pointed out, Derrida reminds us that the psyche is a kind of text, a nonphonocentric text. Dreams are more like writing than speech-language, for dreams, like writing, more distinctly contain the phenomena of DC, MC, and the TC. Derrida's notion of a text implies an underlying non-conscious layer which the author, usually unwittingly, allows to slip out, and which the superaware deconstructor must discover. For Popper, on the other hand, everything must be out in the open, at least insofar as that is possible: a clear-eyed critical investigation of the presuppositions underlying sentences. The investigator must, when possible, "objectively" counter each theory-text with a viable alternative, a hypothetico-deductive conjecture, which is built upon the ruins of the "falsified" theory-text. But—and this is a crucial point—Popper's conjectures, by means of the argumentative mode, must always be exclusively linguistically, logically, and mathematically formulated. Dreams, pictographic and visual, have little to do with such abstract, even algebraic, formulations.

In sum, once again, Popper and Derrida obviously come from radically distinct positions, one rebelling against logical positivism with a foot still caught in the doorway, the other deriving both his inspiration and his battlefield from phenomenology while, cognizant of the fact or not, repeating from a distinct perspective and in different words some arguments from mathematics, logic, science, and the philosophy of science. One a constructive falsificationist, the other a deconstructive "absolutist"; one a seeker of an eternally absent but whole Truth, the other a playmaker in an eternal game where there are no professed notions of truth except that there is absolutely no Absolute Truth.[14] Still, it must be said that the Derridean desire for a direct hieroglyphic form, which is long lost to the self-conscious human animal, is ultimately futile. Actually, we are all condemned, as the later Wittgenstein tells us, always to see *as*, whether consciously or not. Simply to see, like in a dream, we cannot at the same instant be conscious *of*, due to DC, MC, and the TC, *that* we are so seeing. Merely to see would be analogous to Bühler's signalling or stimulative messages, or at most to expressive messages. We cannot regress exclusively to that primitive state of things. Consciously seeing *as*, on the other hand, is, in its most developed form, at the level of Popper's argumentative function of language: it entails the ability to say something as it might-have-been or as it might-possibly-be (Peirce's Thirdness). Seeing *as* is a deferred harmony that runs through the melody of our sensations (or Firstness). The fall from this Firstness is irreversible. We can never return to Paradise, so we must build on what we have left.

Popper's critical argumentation, then, embodying the search for problems, the construction of bold hypotheses as alternatives to existing ones, is more open, more active, and in a way even more indeterminate, than deconstruction. Deconstruction not-too-simply reveals what was already there, hidden in the text. But it presents

no explicit counterargument, in the sense of Popper, for hypotheti-
co-deductively constructed alternatives.

7

That must be in the natural order of things, all that pertains
to me must be written there, including my inability to grasp
what order is meant. For I have never seen any sign of any,
inside me or outside me. (Beckett, 1955, 210)

Popper's hostility toward relativism[15] leads him to his elaborate formulation of what he calls "objective knowledge." For Derrida (1978b, 87), there can be no true "objectivity," especially of the
type he calls "ideal objectivity." However, it is not Popper's type of
"objectivity" against which Derrida reacts. Popper admits that his
conception of "objectivity" is predicated upon a form of "intersubjectivity." But such "intersubjectivity" pertains to a level of abstraction
generally unfamiliar to the phenomenologist.

Popper maps out three different "worlds" in his epistemology
of "objective knowledge." World 1 is that of physical objects: cultural artifacts, including works of art, books, technical machinery,
tools, etc. World 2 is the world of subjectivity and mental states:
individual consciousness, psychological dispositions, experiences,
emotions, thoughts, intentions, etc. (which entail communication
comparable to that of the *expressive* and *signalling* messages described above). World 3, on the other hand, is the product of the
human mind: knowledge in the "objective" sense (which contains
argumentative messages). World 3 is the composite of human
theoretical and creative (i.e., critical) activity—the entire heritage
of culture set down on material substrates. It includes the arguments in scientific, philosophical, literary, artistic, theological, etc.,
texts. World 3 differs from World 1 in that the latter contains only
the physical manifestations of World 3, in books, art works, tools,
etc. For example, texts as marks on paper are World 1 objects. But
they are also the material representation of "objective" but non-
material World 3 objects when they are actualized by writers-

readers. That is to say, as marks on paper, the text represents a World 3 object only insofar as it embodies knowledge which has a potentiality for being understood, interpreted, misunderstood, or misinterpreted. Hence the contents of World 3 are "virtual rather than actual objects of thought" (Popper, 1972, 159).[16]

World 3 is also necessarily separate from World 2, since even though all World 3 objects are derived from the subjective World 2, from the conscious subjective self, they immediately "transcend" their makers.[17] That is, interpreting a text is subjective, in World 2, but this interpretation can become a World 3 object—as a critical comment on the text, a counterargument, a new theory, etc. Every interpretation, or World 2 activity, however, is, as Derrida also would tell us, different (Popper, 1972, 163). Consequently, there can be potentially an infinity of interpretations the ramifications of which can lead to an unlimited number of critiques, counterarguments, new theories, etc.

World 3 knowledge, in the "objective sense," is independent of the beliefs, dispositions, opinions, etc. of particular human beings, for they belong to World 2, they are subjective. Yet there is constant interaction between World 3 and World 2 by way of World 1. In other words, World 3 potentially exercises an indirect effect on World 1, for when a counterargument against a text is written down, it invariably changes the first text; that is, it potentially changes all future interpretations of it. As a consequence of such interaction, Popper claims that World 3 is real. If it were not, it could not interact with and bring about changes in World 1, or in the minds and hence the actions of people in World 2.[18] Popper attempts to explain this interaction in his contention that "the highest interpretative layers in the brain are followed by still higher interpretative layers [the "mind"] which transcend the organism [or become shared potentially by many "minds"] and which belong to the objective World 3" (Popper and Eccles, 1977, 437) (brackets mine).[19] Significantly, then, the creation of a novel idea, when recorded to become a World 1 object, is now open to observation by other subjective consciousnesses. Its effect on them can stimulate them to act on the world in a different way, or bring about new contributions to World 3.

Hence, it is not the World 1 object, appropriately speaking, that is observed by the reader of a text, but the World 3 object which has become public, "objective." [20] Popper (Popper and Eccles, 1977, 450) gives us this illustration:

> In a way, the symphony is the thing which can be interpreted in performances—it is something which has the possibility of being interpreted in a performance. One may ever say that the whole depth of this World 3 object cannot be captured by any single performance, but only by hearing it again and again, in different interpretations. In that sense the World 3 object is a real object which exists, but exists nowhere, and whose existence is somehow the potentiality of its being reinterpreted by human minds. So it is first the work of a human mind or of human minds, the product of human mind. Secondly it is endowed with the potentiality of being recaptured, perhaps only partly, by human minds again.

This is comparable to the Derridean concept that there is nothing outside texts. The "field of text" cannot be transgressed toward something other than what it is; it cannot point toward referent, Being, a transcendental signified, Truth (Derrida, 1974a, 158-59). All readings, and re-iterated readings, must remain intrinsic, inside the "field." By means of many readings, a given text's potentiality may be at least partly recaptured, but what is recaptured has no "reality" in the physical world. The "real" text, rather than marks on paper, must exist as a potentiality, but it exists nowhere except that it can be reinterpreted by means of readers, potentially an infinity of reinterpretations by an infinity of readers.

Another key aspect of Popper's World 3 objects is that they enjoy partial autonomy. Like Derrida's (1978b, 88) autonomous "field of writing," World 3, the product of individual human mental endeavors, creates its own domain of autonomy when it becomes public.[21] For example, the sequence of natural numbers, maintains Popper, was in the beginning a human creation. But once constructed:

> it creates its own autonomous problems in its turn. The distinction between odd and even numbers is not created by us: it is an unintended and unavoidable consequence of our creation. Prime numbers, of course, are similarly unintended autonomous and objective facts; and in their case it is obvious that there are many facts here for us to *discover*: there are conjectures like Goldbach's. And these conjectures, though they refer indirectly to objects of our creation, refer directly to problems and facts which have somehow emerged from our creation and which we cannot control or influence: they are hard facts, and the truth about them is often hard to discover. (Popper, 1972, 118)[22]

Inventions, or *creations* by man are appropriated into World 3. Then, taking on autonomy, they divide and multiply into a complex playground for the mind. But these multiple potentialities are not yet embodied in World 1 artifacts; they remain in World 3 to be *discovered.* It might be countered that Popper's theory is actually very un-Derridean, for it is obviously Platonic in the sense of such "objects" existing to be "discovered." However, Popper's formulation, he tells us, is non-Platonic insofar as: (a) the initial objects in a system of thought are the fabrications of human minds, though they are not mental objects, for mental objects belong to World 2— World 3 objects become partly autonomous of human consciousness at the point of their very coming into existence (Popper, 1972, 156);[23] (b) World 3 is dynamic, it involves constant feedback between Worlds 1 and 2, for it contains "falsities" as well as "truths," and the "falsities" must be corrected, by the interaction of human minds in World 2;[24] (c) World 3 objects are not superhuman, divine, transcendental, and eternal and unchanging, as are Platonic forms (Popper, 1972, 158); and (d) World 3 objects do not enjoy ontological status in the Platonic sense—they exist, but "exist nowhere," they are a pure potential when not actualized (Popper, 1974a, 183).

A further word on Popper's notion of "objectivity" with respect to the use of language is now in order. For Popper, speech, especially when the first person pronoun is used either explicitly or implicitly, pertains to World 2, the subjective realm. Even the "subjective" mode of writing (diaries, personal letters, certain autobiographies, etc.) consists of World 2 objects. On the other hand, the "objective" use of language, either in speech or writing—but preferably the latter for Popper, since here language is put down for posterity—pertains to World 3. In other words, awareness *of* the self in langue use is a World 2 phenomenon. Forgetting the self, for example in deep thought, is potentially to create World 3 objects. When thinking about a crucial problem situation, at times one not only loses awareness *of* one's self, but also *of* one's surroundings. One is, so to speak, "outside oneself," in a state of self-forgetfulness—i.e., like giving oneself up to Derridean *play.* The thoughts one is engaged in during such moments perhaps come from the equivalent of the "somewhere else" described above, from the potentiality constituting World 3. This is "knowing without a knowing subject, for at this point the subject *qua* subject does not, properly speaking, exist" (Popper, 1972, 106f). Subsequently, by put-

ting these thoughts into conjectures, counterarguments, hypotheses, etc., World 3 objects can become World 1 embodiments, and now they are capable of being subjected to interaction with other World 3 objects and by other human minds. (Popper and Eccles, 1977, 138)[25]
An example may suffice here. A painting, insofar as its physical attributes are concerned, is a World 1 object. Before it existed, however, its image, vaguely conjured up in the mind of its creator, was a World 2 event. Now that it has become a part of the physical world, suppose it is placed in an art gallery, and someone views it, then two months later in a conversation on art recalls it to mind in order to describe it to a listener. It is now, appropriately, also a World 2 object in consciousness. On the other hand, assume that an artist views the painting, reacts negatively toward it, and at a later time paints a picture using a technique which differs radically from it. His painting is the equivalent of an implicit counterpainting, or counterproposition. It represents an alternative style; perhaps it is an improvement, perhaps not, but at least it is a further attempt to attain the ultimate (see Gombrich, 1960). Or, assume that an art critic analyzes the painting, or that another critic presents a counterargument to this analysis. These are attempts better to understand and interpret art works. What I am now speaking of in the Popperian sense, are World 3 objects—i.e., the "objective" content of the art and counterart, critique and countercritique. Similar examples could be given for science, history, literature, philosophy, economics, religion, etc.
As mentioned, World 2 is the constant intermediary between World 3 and World 1. This prevents World 3 from being static. Ultimate truths, as well as falsities, Popper claims, are timeless. It would therefore be a simple matter to regard World 3 as a timeless, changeless Platonic domain, existing before the appearance of man. However, the essential beginning of all World 3 systems is by means of inventions-creations by man, and hence World 3 is evolutionary, rather than static:

> It is the history of our ideas; not only a history of their discovery, but also a history of how we invented them: how we made them, and how they reacted upon us, and how we reacted to these products of our own making. (Popper, 1974a, 187)

It is by now obvious that Popper's notion of texts in World 3 bears similarity with some of Derrida's concepts concerning the status of texts, "intertextuality," and writing/reading. Of course there are differences. First, a book, Popper asserts, is a book (i.e., in World 1) even though it is stashed away in the library and nobody ever reads it—a definite possibility these days. Second, unlike Derrida's formulations, Popper claims that a book need not necessarily even be written by a human being; it can be a computer print-out, or some such thing, and still contain knowledge. All books, in the final analysis, must contain "objective" knowledge, whether "true" or "false," useful or useless (Popper, 1972, 115).[26] Third, it might seem that the historical or evolutionary nature of World 3 is un-Derridean. Yet Popper's evolution can never be determinate—there is no definite gauge with which to measure progress. Today's "truth" must be tomorrow's "falsity," for if not, we could never know if it was a "truth." In this sense Popper's evolution is ahistorical, if not thoroughly unhistorical.

In other respects, however, Popper's conception of texts manifests additional similarities with Derrida's. First, a book, if considered solely in light of World 1—if that is indeed possible—has no meaning, and contains no "objective" knowledge. It is merely marks on paper. To be a book in the full sense, there must be interaction between that text and World 3, by way of a mind—like the Derridean reader—in World 2. Or, if the book is not part of World 3, if it is merely a "subjective" account, it can still have meaning, but only insofar as it interacts with a World 2 consciousness. Second, World 3 objects are interrelated in the Derridean sense of "intertextuality." They must, if not now, some day, be seen to contain their own countertext, and that another countertext, and so on *ad infinitum*.[27] Every interpretation of a text is a kind of theory, and every theory is anchored in other theories and other texts. Hence texts in World 3 contain within themselves the seeds of their own "falsification" (the Popperian counterpart to deconstruction), and consequently they always already embody potential surprises. Given this characteristic, and given the potentially infinite array of possible texts, there is no logical end to the number of possible countertexts (or interpretations) that can be generated. The texts as marks on paper are simply there, in World 1, awaiting our entry into the *play* of signs, which is not merely gratuitous for Popper, but a very serious game of critical argumentation.

8

We have gained in terms of reality and lost in terms of the dream. We no longer lie under a tree, gazing up at the sky between our big toe and second toe; we are too busy getting on with our jobs. (Musil, 1965, 40)

Consider, for a moment, *play* in scientific endeavors. Einstein (1959, 7) for instance, remarks that: "All our thinking is of this nature of a free play with concepts." At the outset we notice that the same could be said of art, mathematics, and even philosophy. However, the important point is that Einstein, playing freely with concepts, created the very notion of the "block" universe. Is this not a contradiction? How can a human being conceive of what he is resolutely inside? And if the "block" is static, identical with itself, is it not incompatible with the very notion of free *play* which is nothing but *differences*? Not necessarily. Einstein's example reveals the effacement of yet another opposition: permanence/change—our need for freedom as well as order, chance as well as necessity. We are all, inexorably, Janus-faced. We always and invariably tend to "believe that somewhere there must be an absolutely permanent basis for everything" (Bohm, 1965, 111). That is, there is a need for universals (absolutes) as well as for differentials (relatives). The speed of light is a universal, the speed of our car when driving it is a differential, defined along a continuum with an infinity of possible differences. Gravity is a universal force, a tug-of-war is a differential force. Zero is a universal, the numbers, including complex numbers, are differentials. And so on.

In this sense the notions of origin, center, presence, Being, infinity, and even Derrida's *play*, as well as his DC, MC, and the TC, are postulated universals (see Derrida, 1978b, 152-53). The linear and time-bound activities of writing, speaking, and reading, in contrast, are differentials. Differentials can be viewed and judged from a multiplicity of perspectives: they are *absolutely relative* to one another. But they can be so viewed and judged only *with respect to* their background, the/a universal. All of Einsteinian relativity is actually based upon an absolute which gives rise to the possibility of relations: the speed of light. The popularized notion that "everything is relative," becomes ludicrous in comparison, for everything certainly is *not* relative. Admittedly, when a frame of reference, or a "center," is chosen, it can provisionally become *as if* a universal from within, though it is a relative from a larger perspective. But the Absolute Frame, the Absolute of Absolutes, simply *is*, though for the finite being it cannot be a *full presence*.

The/a universal: How can it be viewed or judged? Not by any direct and absolutely irrefutable empirical evidence, for we are within its domain and cannot observe it. Not by logic, for logic has no existence independently of it. Not by intuition or reason, for they are always to a degree fallible; even here the dice are loaded against us. A universal cannot be judged, verified empirically, or proved beyond doubt. All universals accessible to the finite being are necessarily, in the words of Nietzsche, fictions—acts of mind. But without them we could not continue the game. *Play* is life itself, says Derrida.

In this sense, then, *play*, like the concept of infinity, cannot be an empirical necessity. Just as infinity is a mathematical necessity, a self-contained fiction which cannot be judged but simply accepted or rejected, so *play* is a metaphysical necessity. And, significantly, it also must depend on the mathematical necessity of infinity. *Play* designates "the unity of chance and necessity in an endless calculus" (Derrida, 1973, 135). This "endless calculus" taken to its extreme form, and as illustrated above, reduces necessity to One and chance to the Infinite. This is akin to the Heraclitean *play* of the one differing from itself without beginning or end (Derrida, 1973, 154). Or, *play* as a "bottomless chessboard" where being sets itself in *play* (Derrida, 193, 154). Or, *play* as Eternal Return (Derrida, 1973, 149; 1978a, 296).

The deconstructionist might contend that the chief and only major decision is simply to *play*, and if this entails a universal, so be it. Undue concern over universals or absolutes inevitably leads toward a nostalgia for origins, for a "center." Besides, the decision to play involves no logical commitment. It is, like Nietzsche tells us, a resort to art. But the problem with this argument is that if all texts, Western World texts at least, are constructed around a core of undecidability, then were not all Western World scientists, metaphysicists, and artists playing the game all along? Popper would probably say yes, that all theories are necessarily "false," but until they are effectively "falsified" they are merely undecidable. It is the task of science to make undecidables explicit, to "falsify" them and replace them with potentially "true" alternatives (which are actually implicitly undecidable and potentially "falsifiable"). Does this, over the long haul, not distinctly attest to an inherent "illogicality," "irrationalism" and undecidability in all our endeavors, scientific or otherwise? Perhaps we always already played the game, whether we knew it or not.

The fact remains that, precisely due to such "illogicality," "irrationalism," and undecidability, Western World philosophy, art, and especially the sciences have undergone dynamic transmutations with remarkable frequency. First, Western religion, in particular since the rise of Christianity, gave birth to the sciences, the humanities in general, and the secular manifestations of art. The problem is that after the sciences left home to strike out into the wilderness on their own, the humanities, and even in some cases the arts, stayed around to comfort the old lady. As a result, science has become relatively more dynamic than the other disciplines; it has been radically transformed during its various revolutionary periods, creating totally distinct world-views which have later pervaded all facets of culture, for better or for worse. Moreover, science has left for its posterity a monumental body of written texts containing arguments and counterarguments, imaginative leaps, and detailed, inferentially reasoned proofs. These texts are open to the view of anyone who cares to take the trouble. And they are open to refutation by anyone who desires to try. In other words, science has always been somewhat of a self-deconstructing enterprise. Deconstruction itself, like science, is the product of the Western World mind (though sprinkled with some Eastern overtones). However, unlike much pure science, deconstruction is made to appear, at its deepest, somehow mysterious, and accessible only to the anointed priests and priestesses of the cult. Perhaps rather than a Dionysian notion of *play*, we need a revision of our notion of science. And rather than a small group of elitist Dionysians, we also need a few cynical disciples of Diogenes around to shake things up a bit.

CHAPTER SIX

Who's Afraid of Anomalies?

1

Reality, whether approached imaginatively or empirically, remains a surface, hermetic. Imagination, applied—a priori—to what is absent is exercised in vacuo and cannot tolerate the limit of the real. (Beckett, 1957, 56).

Lévi-Strauss (1966, 16-26) evokes a kind of intellectual handyman, a *bricoleur*, to illustrate the distinction between the modern applied scientist or engineer and the primitive "scientist of the concrete." Perhaps this distinction, and the problematics inherent in it, can aid in better understanding the difference between the post-structuralist conception of science and the "new physics" as described in the preceding chapters.

The *bricoleur* is adept at a large number of tasks, a sort of jack-of-all-trades. Unlike the engineer, he does not subordinate each task to the raw materials available and conceive and construct tools for accomplishing the project. Neither does he impose himself on his environment from the outside with *a priori* means and methods. His universe:

> is closed and the rules of his game are always to make do with 'whatever is at hand', that is to say with a set of tools and materials which

138

is always finite and is also heterogeneous because what it contains bears no relation to the current project, or indeed to any particular project, but is the contingent result of all the occasions there have been to renew or enrich the stock or to maintain it with the remains of previous constructions of destructions. (Lévi-Strauss, 1966, 17)

The tools of the engineer are of forged steel and tailor made to fit the job. The tools of the *bricoleur* are picked along the way, wherever and whenever they may come in handy. The engineer "questions the universe" presumably from the outside, and strives to change it to fit his ideal notions of what it should be. The *bricoleur*, from within his universe, "addresses himself to a collection of elements left over from human endeavors" (Lévi-Strauss, 1966, 19). The engineer works within the sanitary confines of a red brick building, or if in the field, always at a certain distance, while the *bricoleur*'s job site is the junk yard, where he sorts and classifies, dirtying his hands in the process. The engineer mathematizes the world, the *bricoleur* taxonomizes it.

Derrida rightly asserts that there is in reality no absolute distinction between the engineer and the *bricoleur*. The engineer is always and invariably a sort of *bricoleur;* he must constantly borrow from the world, if only to destroy former constructions and, in part, that world he uses. And the *bricoleur* is not the innocent, peace-loving savage idealized by Lévi-Strauss: the strap-catapult *(bricole)*, Derrida (1974a, 139) tells us, "seems originally to have been a machine of war, or the hunt, constructed to destroy." The notion of the engineer *(homo faber)* breaking from *bricolage*, Derrida (1974a, 139) claims, "is dependent on a creationist theology." The concept of *bricolage* "implies a fall and an accidental finitude" (Derrida, 1974a, 139). That of the engineer is fraught with teleological images, the idea of transcendence and indefinite progress, man as creator, as a little god. Derrida (1978a, 285) would argue that the engineer is a "subject who supposedly would be the absolute origin of his own discourse and supposedly would construct it 'out of nothing', 'out of whole cloth', would be the creator of the verb, the verb itself." This "techno-theological" distinction must be abandoned so that there can be a return to the idea of a finite repertoire in a closed universe allowing for an infinity of permutations: an exalted form of *bricolage*. However, one must be aware that all *bricolages* are not of equal footing. *Bricolage* must simultaneously "criticize itself" (Derrida, 1974a, 139).

Pablo Picasso once remarked, concerning his own creativity, that:

> With me, a picture is a sum of destructions. I make a picture and proceed to destroy it. But in the end nothing is lost; the red I have removed from one part shows up in another. (quoted in Zervos, 1952, 56)

This is, indeed, *bricolage* "criticizing itself" within a closed system. As such it bears similarity with the deconstructive "method," and, we must admit, with science. Nietzsche's infinite repetition and the eternal return aside, in a closed system whatever is destroyed, deconstructed, or "falsified," will eventually turn up somewhere else, *ad infinitum*. Deconstruction, and in a way *bricolage*, therefore, needs no "metaphysics of presence." Creation, rather than being *ex nihilo*, entails (re)organization of what there is. Destruction or deconstruction, commensurately, is the dissolution of previously (re)organized entities. What the right hand gives, the left hand takes away.

However, Derrida (1978a, 285) readily admits that scientists as well as engineers are species of *bricoleurs*. This in part threatens Lévi-Strauss's meaning of *bricolage* and its supposed opposite. Deconstruction is neither exactly *bricolage* nor non-*bricolage*, then. But neither is science, nor engineering. That the scientist is a sort of *bricoleur* is also amply illustrated by above examples: Popper's *ad hoc* solutions, Feyerabend's scientific rhetoric, E. P. Wigner's mathematical eclecticism, Einstein's bizarre "thought experiments," Bohm's "metaphysics," Chew's "bootstrap theory," Hugh Everett's "many worlds interpretation," Bohr's dabbling in Oriental philosophy, etc. Science, like *bricolage*, must constantly "criticize itself" (Popper, Feyerabend, Peirce). Therefore, the task of the scientist will never be complete (Popper, Peirce, Bohm). And "paradigms" of theoretical scientific discourse, as well as observation and empirical statements, inexorably exist within closed systems, yet they will always, repeatedly be opened (Kuhn, Polanyi, Feyerabend). If scientific theories are in this sense (re)organized from whatever is at hand, nothing is taken away from creative imagination, for the art is in the (re)making; hence, there can be no such thing as a theoryless "reality." All theories are dependent upon the language used, the culture from which they arose, and the prevailing world-view. Scientific theories, then, are a successive series of frameworks, many of them like embedded chinese boxes, but some starting anew.

Lévi-Strauss (1966, 22) comments further that:

> art lies half-way between scientific knowledge and mythical or magical thought. It is common knowledge that the artist is both something of a scientist and of a 'bricoleur'. By his craftsmanship he constructs a material object which is also an object of knowledge. We have already distinguished the scientist and the 'bricoleur' by the inverse functions which they assign to events and structures as ends and means, the scientist creating events (changing the world) by means of structures and the 'bricoleur' creating structures by means of events.

Initially it must be mentioned, in defense of Lévi-Strauss, that he subsequently admits to his penchant for crude and imprecise *ad hoc* oppositions—of course he is primarily a *bricoleur* himself. Secondly, Lévi-Strauss's scientist is at most today's applied scientist, or at least a pure scientist of the nineteenth-century image. Actually, Einstein, a self-acknowledged dilettante, is no less a *bricoleur* than Picasso, or, for example, Bohr than Beckett. Beckett creates ([re]organizes) characters and puts thoughts in their heads, while they partly control and put thoughts in his own head, and thus he is better able to understand how the mind of man works (Hesla, 1971; Schlossberg, 1973). Bohr (1958, 20) invents ([re]organizes) the principle of complementarity, cognizant of its counterpart in *Yin/Yang*, and he thus becomes aware of the mind's (science's) limitations, as well as the unity of all minds.[1] Since Beckett and Bohr, it might be said that there is no absolute meaning of coneciousness as a whole and specific consciousness of an individual when treated in isolation. Nor is there an absolute distinction between consciousness as a whole and the world "out there."[2] Meaning is, and will always remain, non-existent with respect to entities in isolation. It can exist only in the context of the whole, the entire seamless fabric. Or, to use a Derridean concept, meaning is in the DC between consciousness and consciousness *of*, and between consciousness and the "out there."

Speaking of Derrida, if Lévi-Strauss throws the modern scientist in with the engineer, Derrida puts him in the same bag with the philosopher. Theory, he tells us, is "what unites philosophy and science in the *epistémè*," and it tends more toward filling the breach than forcing a closure of the system (Derrida, 1974a, 92). It was therefore normal, he claims, that the breaking out of Western metaphysics occurred by means of literature and poetic writing, and natural that it was Nietzsche who first questioned and destroyed "the transcendental authority and dominant category of the *epistémè:* being" (Derrida, 1974a, 92). *Grammatology,* the science of writing, therefore, must avoid "this *incompetence* of science which is also the incompetence of philosophy, the *closure* of the *epistémè*" (Derrida, 1974a, 93). And, supposedly, prevention of this *closure* is possible only through the concepts of DC, MC and the TC.

Obviously Feyerabend would disagree here, and also to an extent Popper. Even the earlier, and perhaps we might expect the most *epistemic,* scientists were not so closed within their own system as Derrida would have us believe.[3] If we follow closely what current epistemologists are saying, and what scientists are doing, we have no alternative but to conclude that a conjunction of consciousness with the "out there," or of science with art, or, total destruction of all absolute *epistemic* systems, is rapidly becoming a reality. To provide only one very schematic example—consider a comment by Beckett juxtaposed with the internationally known physicist, John Wheeler:[4]

<table>
<tr>
<td>The expression that there is nothing to express, nothing with which to express, nothing from which to express, no power to express, no desire to express, together with the obligation to express. (quoted in Hesla, 1971, 4)</td>
<td>There is no space-time, there is no time, there is no before, there is no after. The question what happens "next" is without meaning. (quoted in Toben, 1975, 128)</td>
</tr>
</table>

Which is more negative, more "deconstructive," less *epistemic?* In fact, we cannot even speak of any well defined or definable *epistémè* here. There is only a vague groping for something, which is yet unknown, intangible. It would appear that both Beckett and Wheeler are wandering without any direction, goals, presuppositions, expectations whatsoever, or even that they are mindlessly in errance, without awareness of any *epistémè.*

Many of the epistemologists mentioned in chapter two tell us that the scientist, especially he who is at the periphery of scientific thought, can do no more than grope anyway. Only after many ventures into the unknown can he even begin to know what he is doing. Yet his groping is never blind. His mind constantly selects, abstracts, and creates logical constructions in an attempt to account for the world; he tries them out, usually fails, then tries them anew, and so on. Can we really say, then, that the scientist is blindly trapped within an *epistémè?* Or is it that he needs the security derived from believing he is within it? While groping is he even remotely aware of or following an *epistémè?* Or, does the non-scientist (historian, philosopher, deconstructionist, etc.) impose an *epistémè* on his thought from without?

Consider the following, which have a bearing on the above questions, and which will be the focus of the following discussion:

(a) Through Peircean "habit" or Derridean "forgetfulness," and by either a mindful or mindless act, generalities (or universals) can be (artificially) derived from particulars (or facts)—the empiric-inductive thesis.

(b) Through "habit" or "forgetfulness," what have been conceived and perceived to be universals can change, over time, such that they are not what they originally were— they have become different. Yet these *differences*, by a mindless act, can be conceived and perceived as remaining the same, as self-identical.

Perhaps *epistémès* are not so "closed" as we might want to believe, because—and this point is crucial—a posited "closure" may well be a mindless act, according to (b). That is to say, we want to believe that an ideology, theory, world-view, religious belief, etc., remains invariant, but it does not. For example, suppose a man reads Marx and is converted to the doctrine. Then, for the next decade or so he is active in a Marxist movement, but reads no more Marx except a few contemporary vulgarizations of Marxism, and, of course, in the movement he is constantly flooded with simplistic slogans, closed-minded propaganda, categorical imperatives, etc. His conception of what "Marxism" entails has actually evolved since his reading of *Das Kapital.* It has become *different*, though he is not aware of the fact, continuing to believe he has always been the same faithful propagator of orthodox Marxism. In other words, the *epistémè* he has followed within his particular environment has suffered perpetual alterations, and his forgetfulness has cancelled out remnants of the original *epistémè*. The upshot of this story is that, to view any *epistémè* from inside is a delusion; to view it from outside as invariant is, methodologically, erroneous and equally a mindless act.

Ultimately, the problem seems to be that of induction/deduction, particulars/generalities, and mindfulness/mindlessness, or, within a larger framework, of closure/openness. This introduces a complementary problem: conceiving and perceiving the world, or the world of texts, as *difference*, and believing from within a particular framework, as *epistémè*.

2

And if I have always behaved like a pig, the fault lies not with me but with my superiors, who corrected me only on points of detail instead of showing me the essence of the system. (Beckett, 1955, 25)

The hypothetico-deductive method rather than induction, has become, according to Popper (1963, 89), "the fundamental instrument of theoretical science." Concepts by deductive postulation are, at least we can say provisionally, opposed to concepts by intuition (a direct, or empirico-inductive approach). The first has predominated in the West since the Greeks, the second, in its pure form rather than the misconstrued notion of presuppositionless empiricism held by the logical positivists, has predominated in the Eastern way toward knowledge (Northrop, 1959). There have been critics of the Western way, notably Berkeley in philosophy and Ernst Mach in science. They generally argued for a return to a more phenomenological, phenomenalist, or positivist approach—a sort of superempiricism *(esse est percipi)* and a rejection of all abstractions, all that is not immediately open to view.[5] For Berkeley the world is organized by perception and perception alone. For Mach, as well as Husserl and modern phenomenology in general, perception is necessarily perception directly *of* something. However, this eventually introduces the problem of induction. This problem, pointed out by David Hume, disallows absolute certainty, for if we observe the rising sun 10,000 times, or even 1,000,000 times, we cannot guarantee that it will always rise, for on the following day it might not.

The scientists and philosophers of science discussed in previous chapters would generally agree, contrary to Berkeley-Mach, that theory making, whether in science or in everyday life, entails the ability of the mind to (re)organize perceptions; that is, the ability to select and abstract, to generate hypotheses either partly or wholly deductively. These hypotheses, if validated by experience, generate expectations which at least partly govern what one will see in one's world. Consequently, all perception is, on an individual and collective level and to a greater or lesser degree, hypothesis-laden, intimately tied to a particular "form of life."[6] Perception would in reality be useless without such (re)organization, a meaningless, unintelligible kaleidoscope; in fact, we most likely could not even call it perception. Popper tells us that even the animal organism, through instinctual expectations and capacities, organizes and at times obviously even (re)organizes its "perception" of its surroundings. Hence the concept *esse est percipi* from this view is inadequate.

This brings us back to Derrida. Newton Garver (1973, xxviii) points out that Derrida "*seems* at times to embrace a nominalism combined with a sort of radical empiricism." According to such a "radical empiricism" what is "real" is concretely and contextually what is before one, what is perceived in one's particular context. At other times, however, it must be mentioned that Derrida criticizes empiricism. But when doing so he appears to be regarding traditional Western scientific notions of empiricism—that is, of the nineteenth-century variety. Scientific empiricism necessarily retains identity of meanings and repeatability of experience; if not there could be no inferential reasoning toward generalities. Derrida's form of "radical empiricism," on the other hand, allows only for DC. Identity of meaning, in this latter sense, becomes nothing more than an ideal, an abstraction imposed upon perception by the mind, and hence it is out of tune with the "real."[7] One might speculate further that Derrida's view is in a way similar to that of the nominalist Mach, and hence to the early logical positivists. Perhaps this is behind Garver's linking the structural linguists Edward Sapir and Leonard Bloomfield, themselves closely associated with logical positivism, as well as the later Wittgenstein (via his so-called "logical behaviorism"), to Derrida. Whether the analogy is valid or not, it gives food for thought.

However, it hardly needs mentioning that most of Derrida's concepts cannot be empirically validated in spite of the fact that these same concepts are used to argue for an "empirical" (i.e., context-dependent) notion of meaning. How "empirical," actually, are the concepts of MC, DC, *play*, and the TC, or Derrida's Freudian-influenced topology of mind? If the deconstructionists in general believe that the most adequate approach to language and to the world is somewhat akin to phenomenalism, then how is it that they can suddenly see what was concealed and obviously not empirically evident to everybody else if not by some hypothetical and selecting act of mind?

For the phenomenalist, as for the Baconian inductivist, to acquire knowledge about the world, all we have to do is open our wide, innocent eyes and look. Similarly, it seems that the deconstructor is able, unlike ordinary mortals, to brush aside all preconceptions and somehow, with Nietzschean innocence, immediately and inductively locate the "navel" of the text. However, if the surface "empirical" reality is all there is, then why was this "navel" not open to view before, and open to inductive inference? Could it be that *Grammatology* is tacitly assumed to be in part a "positive science" (i.e., hypothetico-deductive) after all?

But the problem is not as simple as these rhetorical questions suggest. Therefore, a discussion of the art of generalization, of abstraction, and of hypothesis making in light of the deconstructive "method" is in order.

3

What is there to add, to these particulars? . . . What about trying to cogitate, while waiting for something intelligible to take place? Just this once? (Beckett, 1955, 341)

Borges's "Funes the Memorious" (1964a, 59-66) is capable of seeing only particulars. During the early stage of his life, he lived like all men, in a dream: looking without seeing, listening without hearing, forgetting almost everything. After having been one fateful day thrown by a horse, he discovered that his perception and memory had become infallible. He could at a glance take in all the leaves, branches, contours on the trunk, etc. of a tree, and years later, recall it to memory perfectly. The trouble was that his memory became a garbage heap. It contained an indefinite number of individuals, but he was incapable of generalities, of abstraction. He was incapable of "ideas of a general, Platonic sort." It seemed strange to him that a dog seen at 3:14 from the side was considered to be the same dog seen at 3:15 from the front. Conceiving numbers as an ordered series, was for him impossible. He simply memorized each number without establishing the necessary relations between them. In fact, he once developed his own alternative number system consisting of arbitrary names in place of every number, which, for him was just as effective. Funes, in short, was unable to think, for to think "is to forget differences, generalize, make abstractions. In the teeming world of Funes, there were only details, almost immediate in their presence" (Borges, 1964a, 66).

Funes, it appears, is not even capable of a higher animal form of selection, of abstraction. He either sees all or nothing at all; he remembers aggregates of particulars without being able to isolate any of them. He is, in other words, the ultimate nominalist, a superempiricist. A hypothesis, theory, conjecture, even a beginning would be for him impossible. Before there can be anything at all, even before there can be no-*thing*, there must be some-*thing*, and this some-*thing* must be a selection, an abstraction from the whole. That is, some-*thing* must be foregrounded from the background. (Hence Funes is incapable of exercising [a] on page 143.)

If Derrida is indeed a "radical empiricist," it might well be that at some ideal level he is caught up into the same problem as Funes. But, of course, we would not expect him to allow himself into that trap so easily, for his argument is very subtle indeed. Yet certain aspects of it perhaps can, with difficulty, be untangled. On the decision to identify Jean Rousseau's "articulation of the logocentric epoch," Derrida (1974a, 162) remarks:

> Rousseau seems to us to be most revealing. That obviously supposes that we have already prepared the exit, determined the repression of writing as the fundamental operation of the epoch, read a certain number of Rousseau's texts but not all of them. This avowal of empiricism can sustain itself only by the strength of the question. The

opening of the question, the departure from the closure of a self-evidence, the putting into doubt of a system of oppositions, all these movements necessarily have the form of empiricism and of errancy. At any rate, they cannot be described, *as to past norms*, except in this form. No other trace is available, and as these errant questions are not absolute beginnings in every way, they allow themselves to be effectively reached, on one entire surface, by this description which is also a criticism. We must begin *wherever we are* and the thought of the trace, which cannot not take the scent into account, has already taught us that it was impossible to justify a point of departure absolutely. *Wherever we are:* in a text where we already believe ourselves to be.

There are six problems inherent in this passage, which, opened to view, will partly reveal the problematics inherent in deconstructionist "empiricism."[8] From within the closure of a system, considered historically, one must accept the conventional oppositions. Deconstruction, in contrast, presumably departs from such intrasystemic assurances. This departure, Derrida seems to contend, is not "hypothetico-deductive"; it is "radically empiricist." It is like a rather passive "wandering thought" on possibilities, of method and itinerary. It is non-knowledge—learned ignorance—a non-knowledge which entails a seeing without a looking *for*, and it deliberately forays out into the field (of texts), but not in search *of*, for it is simply a wandering—"errance." In this activity, "the very concept of empiricism destroys itself" (Derrida, 1974a, 162). To "exceed" the sphere of traditional metaphysics—which is, necessarily, value-laden and perception-bound—is an effort to get outside it, to "think the entirety of the classical conceptual oppositions, particularly the one within which the value of empiricism is held: the opposition of philosophy and non-philosophy, another name for empiricism" (Derrida, 1974a, 162). "Radical empiricism," it might be assumed, stands between traditional empiricism and philosophy, hence it is both "inside" and "outside" Western metaphysics—always the Derridean goal.

However, if the deconstructor is simply passively and non-judgmentally "seeing," "wandering" without actively searching *for*, then it is impossible for him to know the boundary of traditional metaphysics, let alone know whether he is "inside" or "outside." If by chance he steps "outside," then no opposition can be cognized between that "outside" and what remains in the "inside." In this state of "errance," when he is ideally totally disinterested, everything must simply *be*, it cannot *be as opposed to* or *as differentiated from*. Therefore, like Peirce's Firstness, it cannot *be known* without consciously *being related to* something else—the function of Secondness and Thirdness. But if it is intentionally and consciously related to something by comparison and contrast, then there can be no ideal disinterested "errance." And if there is no real "errance," then the "seeing" cannot be non-judgmental. We invariably, whether we know it or not and whether we like it or not, see *as*. This, then, constitutes the first problem with "radical empiricism."

The second problem entails the paradox of beginnings. A "wanderer," in order to cease "wandering," must set down roots and establish some kind of "center," even though arbitrarily and provisionally. On so doing, there is, at least for him with respect to that stopping point, an "origin." This temporary stopping point must be Derrida's "opening of the question." But for the question to be originally perceived, conceived, and above all conjectured, there must have been, *a priori*, a selective abstraction *from* something else, and if an abstraction *from* is exercised, then there must already have existed a Popperian hypothesis of sorts—and here, we see the chief divergence between Popper and Derrida. Without a hypothesis, there can be no stopping point, and if there is no stopping point, it cannot be definitely known to be hypothesis-free.[9] "Radical empiricism," then, can account for no real *beginning*—which actually should come as no surprise to the deconstructionist, and which should also account for one of his own limitations.[10]

If, on the other hand, the deconstructor obstinately insists that there is no such selection, no such hypothesis-bound starting point, but simply "errant questions" which lead to some sort of inductive inference, then we confront the third problem: Humean skepticism. Derrida tells us it is humanly possible and methodologically adequate to read only "a certain number of texts but not all of them." But the problem is that if one reads X texts written during a particular epoch and confirms their logocentrism, then what assurance is there that text X + 1 is not itself anti-logocentric? Here we significantly confront a counterpart to Carl G. Hempel's (1946) paradox of induction. Suppose we somehow infer that: "All Western World texts are logocentric." Suppose also that we call it our Logocentric Hypothesis. Then we go around observing (reading) Western World texts in order to confirm our hypothesis and lo and behold, we are able to do so. However, there is a flaw in our inference: on observing a non-logocentric thing to be non-Western World, we have equally confirmed an equivalent hypothesis: "All non-logocentric things are non-Western World texts." How so? First, the two hypotheses have the same content; they are different formulations of the same proposition. Hempel posits what he calls the "equivalence condition," which is: *Whatever confirms (disconfirms) one of two equivalent sentences, also confirms (disconfirms) the other.* According to this condition, observation of a non-logocentric thing which is a non-Western World text becomes confirming evidence for the hypothesis that all Western World texts are logocentric. In fact, any and all observed things confirm the logocentric hypothesis, so it cannot possibly be refuted. For example, taken by itself, the observation that, say, a rock is neither logocentric nor a Western World text confirms the second hypothesis that everything which is not a Western World text is non-logocentric as well as the initial hypothesis that all Western World texts are logocentric. We ordinarily tend to overlook the second hypothesis, taking it for granted as a foregone conclusion, but there is a more serious matter still: at the same time we tacitly confirm the hidden hypothesis that nothing is either logocentric or a Western World text, for it is assumed that if something is a Western World text, then it must necessarily be logocentric, and if it is logocentric, then it must necessarily be a Western World text. The inductive method is therefore fallacious, for it is irrefutable. And the deconstructive "method" enjoys no real immunity here either.

The fourth problem entails the supposed act of putting into doubt any and all systems of opposition. If one doubts, for instance, the nature/culture opposition, then is not one either consciously making a decision to doubt or nonconsciously doubting because it is the nature of one's disposition? In the first case, is such doubt not impossible except *with respect to* its opposite—that is, certainty? In other words, without the previous existence of certainty, or at least a tacit assumption of the possibility of certainty, is it not true that doubt cannot be exercised, since the two opposing categories, doubt/certainty, are complementary? Does it not follow, then, that the complementarily opposed pair must also be doubted if one is to place in doubt any and all oppositions? But, of course, it can be doubted only *with respect to* another perspective grounded in certainty, and that in another, and so on, *ad infinitum* (see Wittgenstein, 1972). Or, if it is claimed that the doubt is a deeply embedded disposition to act on the part of the deconstructor, then does not that doubt itself presuppose a tacit certainty? And if so, then is it not the case that there must be, according to deconstructive imperatives, doubt *about* the disposition to doubt? But it is itself a system inaccessible to doubt, for the deconstructor does not/cannot say to himself: "I will now doubt the metaphysical and hence the mythical oppositions in this text before me." That is, if the doubt is tacitly assumed to be a certainty (i.e., it is embedded, automatic, and spontaneous), then it is not and cannot be simultaneously thought *about* and doubted, for if so, then we have once again the Cartesian problem—and the "metaphysics of presence" against which Derrida correctly reacts. In sum, to doubt, either consciously or non-consciously and by disposition, one must possess, always and already, some frame of reference, constructed on some basis of certainty from which the doubt is exercised. For if not, back to poor Funes.

The fifth problem. Those "errant questions" Derrida speaks about are definitely halted with "absolute beginnings." The deconstructor does not and cannot begin with an innocent eye "wherever he is," and by asking "errant questions." A question presupposes something to be questioned. That is, that something must be placed in doubt—and we already know the fallacy here—in order for it to be questioned. Hence, once again the beginning in the text, not as "meaningless marks on paper," and not with respect to the physical qualities of the text, but in the text as a counterpart to texts in Popper's World 3, cannot but be a beginning *from* some definite starting point. It is *from* at least a first "cut," selection, or abstraction, which marks off a definite boundary *as opposed to* some other boundary or boundaries. In addition, a question is like negation or nothing insofar as they cannot exist in a vacuum, in total autonomy.[11] They must all be *with respect to* something else, which previously was (pre)supposed to exist. Equally, the notion of identity entails the existence of *something*, and, like a question, negation, or nothing, it entails abstraction. For instance, Funes cannot say: "This leaf on this tree today is not identical to the leaf I saw yesterday at approximately the same spot while I was standing in approximately the same position with respect to it." The beast, as well as Funes, it seems, is ordinarily incapable of perceiving change in the proper human sense, for the human being always and to a greater degree forgets, abstracts, simplifies, looks for orderly systems, etc.

In other words, the normal human must possess the notion of identity as well as those of negation and opposition, all of which constitute a static background against which change—i.e., a thing's *difference* from one moment to the next—can be conceived and perceived. If we were absolutely pure inductivists, or empiricists, in essence we would all be less than human: once again, we would be like Funes. Hence "wherever we are" is either unknown and therefore there can be no beginning, or it is at least partly and tentatively known or selected, and the/a beginning is anchored, but it was not, it could not be, a beginning resulting from totally "errant" questions.

Although our imaginary Funes escaped the human penchant for hypothetical abstracting, we obviously cannot, . . . nor can the deconstructionist. This is actually fortunate for us all. Funes's teeming jungle is perpetually in motion, a myriad array of *differences*. But surprisingly, Funes, ultimately and unlike us, is *indifferent* toward his world:

> Then I saw the face belonging to the voice that had spoken all night long. Ireneo [Funes] was nineteen years old; he had been born in 1868; he seemed to me as monumental as bronze, more ancient than Egypt, older than the prophecies and the pyramids. I thought that each of my words (that each of my movements) would persist in his implacable memory; I was benumbed by the fear of multiplying useless gestures. (Borges, 1964a, 66) (brackets mine)

In other words, Funes represents a closing of the circle. The ideal superempiricist must be metaphorically like the God that sees All. Funes's unlimited perception and memory of the world is likewise in the ideal sense absolute. Everything possible is actually there, for he sees everything and forgets nothing. By the same token, nothing is/can be really actualized, selected, and abstracted, in the human sense. Hence everything is reduced to the same level. Funes's perception approaches total *indifference*. Such *indifference* is like Derrida's *death*. But, and this must be emphasized, Funes's *indifference* is the by-product of an extreme form of Derrida's DC, of the ultimate extension of DC. That is, as *differences* become increasingly finer finally to approach Funes's perception of the world, it becomes more and more difficult for some-*thing* to stand out (be abstracted) against the background of every-*thing*.[12]

Finally, the sixth problem, which can be illustrated by this maxim: "He who lives by the sword dies by the sword." To depart, as the deconstructionist claims he does, from "the closure of a self-evidence," from a self-contained system, must entail a step "outside." But can one really remain suspended with the other foot still tenuously planted firmly "inside" at the same precise instant? Consider the "sword fight" to be like an autonomous form of *play*, though of course the stakes are high—life and death. Yet life and death exist in separate and incommensurable frames: they are not part of the fight *per se*. Within the fight frame, it becomes absurd to state that the fighter "lives by the sword," for life as well as death remain something more than and beyond the fight. If the fight is the total system while the two fighters are engaged in their activity, containing all there is for the moment and beyond which there is nothing—something like a reversal of Derridean *play*—then at the very moment when one loses, when one's heart is pierced by the opponent's steel, one is jerked "outside." The fight is no more, and at the same time life and death can now take on meaning, but not before. Analogously, if the deconstructionist purports to be giving us a system incommensurate with the received metaphysics, then he cannot, upon beginning his argument, stand at the same instant on traditional grounds, let alone depart totally from them. These grounds are necessarily for him, and from the very outset, incomparable with his own. Moreover, according to the fourth problem, they cannot even be doubted, especially from "within" his perspective. Doubt ordinarily implies a reasoned, logical stance—and it seems that in the above quote Derrida is using doubt in the ordinary way.

However, there cannot be any rational middle ground on which doubt can rest. The deconstructionist can either be "within" traditional metaphysics or "within" his own anti-metaphysics. Or he can oscillate between them. But in such event, any comparison and contrast between his anti-philosophy and traditional metaphysics becomes problematic, well-nigh impossible, for the paradox of Feyerabend's self-contained, incommensurable, and untranslatable epistemological frameworks enters full-force (cf. chapter two). Hence if the deconstructionist claims to be totally "inside" his anti-metaphysical framework, then metaphysics is for him, according to Feyerabend, "outside" that framework. If he remains exclusively "within" metaphysics, then it will be impossible for him properly to conceive of anti-metaphysics. And if he oscillates between both, then his perspectival framework, rather than at the boundary between both, must be somehow schizophrenic, or "doubly-bound," and hence he is neither wholly "inside" one nor the other at a given instant, but only mediately, by means of MC and DC. It is only *as if* he were simultaneously in both frames. Yet to reach this state he could not have been exclusively "inside" *either* metaphysics *or* anti-metaphysics, for from "within" either, such a state is impossible. But, the fact remains that, not having dwelled exclusively "within" the domain of metaphysics, *aporia* cannot be a real surprise, an "uncanny moment," for "outside," from the anti-metaphysical frame, *aporia* is determinately expected. And if there is no surprise, then total *indifference* must ideally prevail. But if so, from the vantage point of this total *indifference*, there can be no recognition *of differences*, properly speaking that is. In other words, only in the death of one sword fighter can the real significance between life and the fight, two incommensurables—the game and non-game—be known. But death *is indifference*, so the significance can never be known from such an *indifferent* perspective, logically speaking at least.

Yet the deconstructionist claims the ability to recognize *aporia*. Therefore it must be possible, if we are to allow him the benefit of the doubt. But his wanderings, certainly, are not so "errant" as he would have us believe. More on *indifference* in order better to grasp this problem.

4

Is there really nothing new to try? I mentioned by hope, but it is not serious. If I could speak and yet say nothing, really nothing? (Beckett, 1955, 303)

Indeed. Can one speak and say nothing? To do so, there can be no context, no listener, not even a subject, or the speaker as his own listener—a mediate rather than immediate listener, of course. This "ontologically null" utterer must be completely neutral, totally disinterested, *indifferent*, and "objective." Moreover, the utterance must be informationless and at the same time tautologous, like the traditional and ideal notion of logic in which there can be no surprises, for what there is is what was already always timelessly known: the utterance cannot be linear or temporal—not even the silent spaces in, say, John Cage's music or Mallarmé's blank page count here.[13] Neither can the utterance have a referent, it must contain only pure and simple sense (which must be the equivalent of non-meaning), and this sense cannot be related to any other sense; it must be like a logical atom, without connectives.

Beckett's work represents an obstinate effort to demolish time. His writing approaches stasis. There is simply a succession rather than a progression of events, with no culminating points, and with no events that stand out. Everything is apparently equally important, or better, unimportant. There is no clearly defined beginning, middle, and end—no apparent theology or teleology. Everything remains the same, but yet somehow it seems that there is change. Events move on, yet time seems to stand still. Or more appropriately, events merge into events to approach the ideal of a seamless fabric. Beckett writes, and his characters speak, apparently saying next to nothing, but the accumulation of these nothings takes on a reality, it *is* reality: the characters say what *is*, through successive self-annihilating utterances.

Following the approach of "radical empiricism," the deconstructionist claims he engages in something like the ideal to which Beckett's characters refer: a neutral, disinterested "errance," a wandering about while seeing everything and looking at nothing in particular, with no preconceived categories. Just as there can be no beginning for this activity, so there can be no predetermined end, no teleology. Neither can there be any expectations in the Popperian sense. Time must also ideally disappear, at least in the conventional sense, for if there can be no beginning or end, neither can there be any temporal accumulation. It is simply a directionless movement toward no-*thing* at all and potentially everything in general. If this is ideally the case, then the subject is necessarily "outside" the ordinary "real world" of actuals, not "inside" it. This "errance" "really" "actualizes" no-*thing*, but this no-*thing* is/becomes "real" in the sense that it is "seen" (i.e., like Firstness), but it is not seen-*as*-such-and-such *as opposed to* or *similar to* some-*thing* else. The universe, from this ideal vantage point, must be timeless in the sense that, if particulars are not really seen *as*, then they are not really actualized *in* time, through DC, MC, and the TC, to be related *to* other actuals (like Secondness and Thirdness). That is, they are merely, "seen," *indifferently.* Ideal "errance" can be none other than *indifference.*

This, it will be recalled, is also Funes's problem. And there is a paradox inherent in his dilemma which Borges does not reveal. If Funes can, in simultaneity, perceive every minute particular of a tree in one instant, and commit it to memory, he must subsequently be able to perceive it again to be a different (or slightly variant) tree, in all its minute particulars, for it has suffered ever-so-small a change. So he undertakes another perceptual grasp, and then another, and another, and at each "instant" he sees a different collection of particulars before him. But the queston is: How is it possible for him to detect any movement at all? In other words, if he sees everything all at once, as an aggregate of particulars, and if he cannot abstract anything, then he is incapable of seeing one particular *against* the background of the whole, and hence he cannot detect a change in that particular while holding the whole in check as an unchanging entity. What he does perceive, and the only thing he can perceive, is, so to speak, a succession of static "slices" actualized from the "block." But there can be for him no change, no time in the conventional sense—another form of Zeno's paradox.[14]

Funes's plight might appear to be irrelevant, for Derrida clearly accounts for movement and time with the concepts of DC, MC, and the TC. However, it can reveal a further, a seventh, problem in the deconstructionist's program. Discounting for the moment Funes's paradox, let us assume that one can "wander," while looking at no-*thing* and ideally seeing every-*thing.* Then one necessarily knows nothing at all, or perhaps we can say, one provisionally forgets everything—a true state of learned ignorance. This must be the case, for some-*thing* must be seen *as,* to become part of one's body of knowledge. But, in light of the second problem above, it appears impossible to explain *how* one can begin to see *as.* So let us equally discount this problem, for obviously all humans, even the "errant" deconstructor, eventually see *as.* Seeing *as* must entail some sort of commitment to the world *as* expectedly being such-and-such *rather than* some-*thing* else. This being the case, then the *play* of "errance" is at least partly effaced. It is no longer pure *play,* for seeing *as* and pure *play* cannot be affirmed in simultaneity, only mediately. This is commonsensically obvious. So the next question, then, becomes: What, precisely, is seen by the deconstructor?

Back to Derrida:

> I wished to reach the point of a certain exteriority in relation to the totality of the age of logocentrism. Starting from this point of exteriority, a certain deconstruction of that totality which is also a traced path, of that orb (*orbis*) which is also orbitary (*orbita*), might be broached. The first gesture of this departure and this deconstruction, although subject to certain historical necessity, cannot be given methodological or logical intraorbitary assurances. Within the closure, one can only judge its style in terms of the accepted oppositions. It may be said that this style is empiricist and in a certain way that would be correct. The *departure* is radically empiricist. (Derrida, 1974a, 161-62)

If the project is subject to "certain historical necessity," then where is this historicity, in the "world of texts" or in the "real world?" Let us assume that the former is the case. Then if the starting point is exterior to the "world of texts," it must be in some way or fashion "transcendental," or better, at least "pseudo-transcendental." This would be for Derrida taboo. So let us assume the "historical necessity" of the "real world" to be the case. Then exteriority, it appears, must refer to the "world of texts," if it is not blatantly "transcendental," and in such case it is no exteriority at all. It is clearly "within" that "world." Let us suppose, then, that the point of *departure* is at the edge of the orb (*orbis*), along the invisible, spaceless, boundary line, which is orbitary (*orbita*). In such case the "point" from which departure occurs is most properly a fiction, an ideal construct of the mind, and hence Derrida still errs, for he is guilty of the same metaphysical practice he rejects. However, we must concede that Derrida's *departure* is purportedly "radically empiricist," as distinct from old-line "empiricism." So we should, in all honesty, focus on the *opposition* between the two "empiricisms."

In another passage Derrida points out a Lévi-Straussian dilemma which is relevant to this problem. The ethnologist claims in *The Raw and The Cooked* (1969) that his book, which purports to explain myths, is itself a myth, the "myth of mythology." It should therefore require no fixed center. Yet Lévi-Strauss does not abandon his chosen epistemological center allowing him "to distinguish between several qualities of discourse on the myth" (Derrida, 1978a, 287-88). Derrida admits that this is a classical problem with no readily available solution. Yet it persists, due to a naive form of empiricism in which the belief is held that "theoretical propositions" are context-free and autonomous: pure simples. Obviously Derrida never intends to engage in an elaborate critique of empirical positivism, as do Feyerabend, Michael Polanyi, Thomas Kuhn, and to an extent Popper. Nonetheless such a critique is implied in his commentaries. What he proposes, and attempts is "the passage beyond philosophy (which usually amounts to philosophizing badly), but in continuing to read philosophers *in a certain way*" (Derrida, 1978a, 288). This seems to be a risk that must be assumed, with awareness *that* it is a risk. In contrast, unwillingness to take the risk leads Derrida (1978a, 288) to reiterate:

> that empiricism is the matrix of all faults menacing a discourse which continues, as with Lévi-Strauss in particular, to consider itself scientific. If we wanted to pose the problem of empiricism and *bricolage* in depth, we would probably end up very quickly with a number of absolutely contradictory propositions concerning the states of discourse in structural ethnology. On the one hand, structuralism justifiably claims to be the critique of empiricism. But at the same time there is not a single book or study by Lévi-Strauss which is not proposed as an empirical essay which can always be completed or invalidated by new information. The structural schemata are always proposed hypotheses resulting from a finite quantity of information and which are subjected to the proof of experience.[15]

Derrida is obviously very much aware here of the inexhaustibility of the empirico-inductive approach. Citing Lévi-Strauss, who admits that the totality of mythological explanation can never be complete, can never be present, Derrida (1978a, 289) counters that if totalization is now looked upon as meaningless, it is not because:

> the infiniteness of a field cannot be covered by a finite glance or a finite discourse, but because the nature of the field—that is, language and a finite language—excludes totalization. This field is in effect that of *play*, that is to say, a field of infinite substitutions only because it is finite, that is to say, because instead of being too large, there is something missing from it: a center which arrests and grounds the play of substitutions.[16]

This brings up a new problem which is related to previous ones. The infinite is timeless, while finitude, with respect to experience, is accompanied by temporal succession. Rather than a conception of the infinite, or the totality, either a totalizing God's-eye view must somehow be considered within the finite, or finitude (i.e., finite *play*) must be considered contradictorily and impossibly as a particularization of the infinite (i.e., the "field" of *play*). It seems that with Derrida's scheme we can do no more than opt for the latter. In terms of its operational activity, deconstruction occurs over time, in a particular context and by means of language use in texts without there being present any timeless notions or ideals. This being the case, it seems that Derrida has no use for the usual empiricist fallacies: presupposed categories (i.e., a value-laden, and perception-laden "theoretical language").[17] The truth of the matter is, that, in striving for exteriority, for *departure* from the orb, the deconstructionist presumes that centerless *play*, goalless vagaries, and his own form of "radical empiricism," absolve him of this problem of presuppositions, especially since he consciously takes the risk and makes a leap of faith toward it. However, does not this risk, in light of above arguments, equally involve preconceived categories, some sort of ephemeral "center" or stopping "point" about which the *play*, his particular kind of *play*, revolves? Then can it indeed be pure *play*, if a "center," any "center," has been pinned down, if only temporarily? Or, could there be any deconstruction at all by means of absolutely pure *play*? That is, *play* with the tacit knowing that nothing can be seen *as*, since that would imply a stopping "point"? Absolutely pure *play*, it seems, would require a super-observer—the outmoded Laplacean-like ideal. It would also entail Funes's paradox insofar as movement, change, would obviously be inconceivable. Pure *play* through "radical empiricism," then, leads to the same problems of induction as empiricism.[18]

Seeing *as* and pure *play* are incompatible. If we are condemned inexorably to see *as*, then we must admit to an inevitable split, a mutilation, between observer and observed. If pure *play* would require a super-observer in an immanent field, then that observer would be incapable of seeing *as*. An example will help here. Consider the super-observer to be like the Self of the Cosmos in a Hindu myth. This Self perceived existence as a form of play, but since it is all there is and there is nothing outside itself, it had nothing other than itself with which to play. So it played a cosmic game of hide-and-seek with itself. It put on an infinity of masks, took on an infinity of identities, experienced an infinity of lives, and perceived an infinity of different events. Eventually it awakened from all these dreams and recalled its identity, and then became-remained itself: the Self of the Cosmos. At the very moment when the game ends it begins. In fact, the game was played in an infinitesimal instant. There was really no beginning, middle, or end: no time.

This Cosmic Self could not have been "outside," hence it could not have seen *as*. Since it could not have seen *as*, there could have been no split between itself and some-*thing* else. Moreover, it could have no starting point. Seeing some-*thing as* such-and-such *with respect to* some-*thing* else requires an *a priori* starting point (i.e., an expectation, anticipation, hypothesis, readiness for some-*thing*, etc.) that existed *before* that starting point. But induction discounts the existence of such *a priori* beginnings. So the Cosmic Self is no inductivist. It appears that there can be no beginnings unless they are known *a priori* (i.e., by inborn expectations, anticipation, readiness for some-*thing*, the hypothetico-deductive method, or by flashes of insight, *abduction*, etc.).

Thus empiricism/"radical empiricism" is the true *opposition*, if oppositions there be, which has surfaced. Empiricism is clearly "inside" the circle of classical science, whereas "radical empiricism" contradictorily tries to straddle the boundary between "inside" and "outside." The first, as is now well known in light of recent critiques, begins with a "center," which inevitably contains presupposed categories, while the latter implicitly refutes those categories from the perspective of yet another elusive and ephemeral "center." One is a deluded positive science, and other a negative science subtly positivized. If a faulty empiricism jeopardizes any program set up with the pretensions of being scientific in the modern sense, "radical empiricism" elucidates many of the faults of traditional empiricism, but not without committing some of its same errors, even though from a broader framework. The original science becomes a meta-science, which nonetheless nurtures, if not the same, then a few similar, illusions.

5

What tedium. And I call that playing. . . . Already I forget what I have said. That is not how to play. (Beckett, 1955, 189)

Consider *play* once again, but from a broader perspective. Funes's problem was that he somehow saw everything and could forget nothing. This truly is tedium! To play, purely play without any expectations or preconceived notions, there cannot ideally be any memory of past play. What is played is simply and unrestrictedly played, without the limitations, regressions, repressions, or memory of what was played. But this would be sheer tedium as well! Then what is the answer?

Erwin Schrödinger (1957, 28-29) remarks that:

Play, art and science are the spheres of human activity where action and aim are not as a rule determined by the aims imposed by the necessities of life; and even in the exceptional instances where this is the case, the creative artist or the investigating scientist soon forget this fact—as indeed, they must forget it if their work is to prosper. . . . [A]rt and sciences are thus luxuries like sport and play, a view more acceptable to the beliefs of former centuries than to the present age. It was a privilege of princes and flourishing republics to draw artists and scientists within their sphere; and to give them a living in exchange for an activity which yielded nothing save entertainment, interest and repute for the prince or the city. In every age such procedure has been regarded as a manifestation of internal strength and health, and the rulers and peoples have been envied who could afford to indulge in this noble luxury, this source of pure and lofty pleasure.

Interesting comments, especially when considering that they come from a scientist. Schrödinger seems to be reviving the ancient view that science and the arts are equally play. This is opposed to the notion, especially since Romanticism, that man, individual, egocentric, center-of-the-cosmos man, must take not only the universe, but above all himself, seriously. Man, since the Renaissance and the Romantic periods, has generally been considered the measure of all things, with definite goals and ends, with the power to predict and control his destiny. In contrast, the recent view, which is gradually emerging from twentieth-century science and avant-garde art, is that of the necessarily disinterested person, who, rather than being an individual, is part of a collective whole, and rather than being the center of the universe, is at a level with all other entities in the universal fabric—"inner" and "outer" or perceiver and perceived become one, mind and matter from certain perspectives become indistinguishable, nature pervades culture. In the modernist view, there is necessarily a *loss of self*, with no clearly defined teleological goal.[19] Rather, the goalless goal is something more akin to "Teleonomy." The difference between the two terms is this: teleology entails many possible starting points but only one end, teleonomy entails a beginning from any given point which leads toward an indefinite and undefinable end.

Science, art, and play, in the modernist notion, involve no truth, no value, no univocal meanings or interpretations. Nothing is taken seriously—in an absolute sense—for everything becomes *play*. There is no manipulation of texts, persons, or natures, but the task is simply to play with problems which are of the *imaginative* mind's own making. Moreover, there is no all-or-nothing answer to any of these problems. Any cogent answer is simply self-sufficient, the product of *play*, which is actually not only an end, but also simultaneously a beginning. The modernist way invariably includes wit, irony, comedy. From this modernist view, the Romantic outcry against mixing the sublime with the mundane, the elegant with the colloquial, aristocracy with the plebians, is unintelligible. Moreover, *play* in the modernist sense needs no overt critique of presence, nostalgia, or the center, for such critique is implied by the very existence of *play*.

Deconstruction seems to be, with its empiricism/"radical empiricism" dichotomy, paradoxically "inside" the modernist *and* the Romantic view simultaneously.[20] Modernist play is the total affirmation of indeterminacy, yet deconstructive *play* is founded on the determinacy implied by the *deconstructive principle*. Moreover, in general the deconstructionist's *play* is not exactly detached; his allegory, wit, and irony are at times more biting than playful. That is, his *play* is defiled with a tinge of the serious. The same might be said of Beckett. But the difference is this: Beckett, aware of the absurdity of it all, goes on, he must go on, he can't help but go on. His play is humorous at times, usually sarcastic, with a bit of bittersweet irony, and sometimes frightening, while he lashes out at the world, and all this time there are clear existentialist overtones. Yet he makes no bones about the seriousness of his play. He never forgets that he must speak/write, for if not he is nothing, not even human. He knows he can never be silent, for that would be the end of the game, of all games. He never doubts for a moment that he *is*, though he knows not *what* he is or *where* he is, and knows he will never know *how* he reached that point. Beckett not-too-simply throws himself into the task without illusions, realizing full well that his play is/will be tedium, for it, as it more closely approximates *indifference*, cannot be otherwise.[21] But he still goes on, fearfully, painfully, hesitatingly: "[I]t's not a question of hypotheses, it's a question of going on, it goes on, hypotheses are like everything else, they help you on, as if there were need of help, that's right, impersonal, as if there were any need of help to go on with a think that can't stop" (Beckett, 1955, 404). There is no nostalgia for origins, properly speaking. Better stated, there is a longing for the end, a teleonomic end: "The search for the means to put an end to things, an end to speech, is what enables the discourse to continue" (Beckett, 1955, 299). And through it all, there exists the premonition that there is really nothing at all, that not even a tedious form of play can afford ephemeral meanings, that there is no critique *against*, for there is really nothing *against which* to launch a critique.[22] There are only words, which are really nothing, but without which life is nothing, and yet they come from an unintelligible source ultimately to remain meaningless: "Where do these words come from that pour out of my mouth, and what do they mean. . . . and one listens, that stet, without reason, as one has always listened because one day listening began, because it cannot stop" (Beckett, 1955, 370).

Beckett's prose might appear to be an act of extreme solitude, the ultimate in detachment, or *indifference;* the world seems to be nothing more than a blank fact (Kenner, 1961, 17). However, this detachment is not that of the subject/object dichotomy in the Western way. Beckett insists on the "I," which speaks: "[T]here is I, it's essential, it's preferable, . . . there is I, on the one hand, and this noise on the other" (Beckett, 1955, 388). Yet this "I" is not absolutely separable from the noise, from the silence, or from the world. Words *are* the world and they are what makes the "I" possible; they give it its very existence. The "I" is at once individual *and* collective, subject *and* object. It is for this very reason that the "I" *is* The

Unnamable. The task of the "I" in Beckett is to speak *of* itself, but for this to be possible there must be something which *is not* the "I" about which an utterance is made, and if it *is not* the "I," then the "I" cannot *be* the object *of* the utterance, and so on. The project is impossible from the logical or linguistic standpoint. To use a Wittgensteinian metaphor,[23] it is like trying to climb a ladder, but this time having each rung vanish at the very moment one's weight is placed on it. Beckett certainly nurtures no illusions concerning "self-presence." In fact, Beckett's *indifference* entails, quite clearly, the disappearance of the observer/observed dichotomy. It is not that knowledge of the world from Beckett's perspective is without importance, or that all effort is foolish. On the contrary, participation in the world becomes all-important, but with a different view of things, or more appropriately, an *indifference* toward the world at one level coupled with a penetrating and committed questioning of the world at another level.

CHAPTER SEVEN

Beckett's Dilemma: or, Pecking Away at the Ineffable

1

Strange, I don't feel my feet any more, . . . And yet I feel they are beyond the range of the most powerful telescope. (Beckett, 1955, 234)

[T]he universe must expand to escape the telescopes through which we, who are it, are trying to capture it, which is us. (Spencer-Brown, 1979, 106)

Let us ask the question: Is change, and change of mind possible, except by and through the ideal of, at some level, *indifference?* But another question immediately arises: If *indifference* prevails, can anything really be *acted upon* by the *indifferent* being in order to bring about change? Since according to Derrida, we are inexorably "inside" writing, and dominated by it, there is no way for us to be active in any but an *indifferent* (mindless) way (Hans, 1981, 100). Admittedly, we are played by language, but we also exercise a degree of *play* with it; we *act upon* it—an act of the *imaginative* mind. The task in this chapter is to play this *imaginative* mind off against a *mindless* form of play.

Consider a "thought experiment" (see Merrell, 1982, for further comment). If John believes in religion A and Jack in B, and if Jack tries to convert John to his own belief, how can John "suspend disbelief" in B and at the same instant in time "fall into belief" in A? Maybe he can, after all. Or can he? If he is converted to B, he must previously have "unsuspended suspension of disbelief" in A, for if not, he must impossibly and contradictorily "believe" in both at the same time, or at least for a split instant—unless, that is, he is a theological schizophrenic or some such thing, but let us assume he is not. If he cannot truly "believe" in both simultaneously, then, during the split instant slightly prior to his "leap of faith" into B, he must have somehow "suspended belief" in both, for if not, if he retains "belief" in one, he cannot at the same moment be/become a "believer" in the other without somehow previously "falling out of belief" in the one. So during that split "instant" John must "believe" totally and *indifferently* in nothing, ... or paradoxically, in everything. Nothing *is* some-*thing*, however. If nothing else, it is *indifference* itself. Let us consider this *indifference* in light of the imaginary "somewhere else" discussed in chapter four, for perhaps the two are somehow compatible.

If change is possible only by and through *indifference*, and if we desire at least partially to account for such change, then it must be construed, according to the observations in above sections, as a context-bound and perspective-dependent form of change. In an attempt at such an account, I will turn to Nelson Goodman's (1965) "new riddle of induction" which is based on two unorthodox color concepts, and which is a counterpart to the previously mentioned Hempel paradox.[1] Any upstanding citizen of the "real world" ordinarily believes the statement "emeralds are green" to be eternally and invariantly "true." No matter how many successive looks at emeralds he exercises, he assumes he will always report them to be "green." Or in other words, suppose that all emeralds he examines before a given time are green. At this time he naturally feels he can state with confidence that his hypothesis that all emeralds are green will always be confirmed, for according to his observations, emerald *a* on examination was "green," emerald *b* was "green," and so on. Now suppose he meets a stranger from Netherworld whose perception of things is to him apparently unstable and whose strange language is radically distinct from his own, and suppose this netherworlder's language contains the following two terms which he has learned to translate into the realworlder's language:

Grue = examined before the temporal reference point t_0 and is reported to the realworlder to be "green" or is not examined before t_0 and reported to be "blue." (t_0 is apparently an otherwise arbitrary moment of time that is not in the past.)

Bleen = examined before the temporal reference point t_0 and is reported to the realworlder to be "blue" or not examined before t_0 and is reported to be "green."

Before time t_0 for each of the realworlder's statements asserting that an emerald is "green," this netherworlder has a parallel statement asserting that it is "grue," and his observations that emerald a on examination is "grue," that emerald b is "grue," and so on, will confirm his own hypothesis. It will obviously appear to the realworlder from the standpoint of his language and his normal color taxonomy that the netherworlder's sensory images change radically after t_0. But, from the netherworlder's perspective, the glove is turned inside out, for now it is the realworlder's taxonomy that appears to be time-dependent. That is, the realworlder's report would appear to him to be the following:

Green = examined before t_0 and is reported to be "grue," or not and is reported to be "bleen."

Blue = examined before t_0 and is reported to be "bleen," or not and is reported to be "grue."

From the perspective of each person, then, the inductive expectations of the other's perspective are thwarted. That is, the two perspectives are symmetrical, and consequently one must be considered to be complementary with the other when considering the system in its totality. The atemporality from within one system becomes temporality within the other, and vice versa. And both can be conceived as "true" from within, but only "relatively true" or better, "false," from without. Hence the realworlder and the netherworlder possess their own "metaphysics of presence" with respect to their conception of their own world! Though, from the complementary world this "metaphysics of presence" can easily be demythified.

In order more adequately to validate the idea of time-dependence and variance, consider, for example, these two statements:

(1) Space is straight.
(2) Space is curved.

If we alter somewhat Goodman's paradox, we can construct the following set of predicates to depict our netherworlder's perception of the realworlder's statements:

Straight = considered to be a property of space before reference point t_o and not a property of space after t_o.
Curved = considered not to be a property of space before reference point t_o and a property of space after reference point t_o.

And our imaginary netherworlder could create two alternate terms with their corresponding predicates by means of which he could hopefully account for the realworlder's chaotic epistemology:

Craight = meaning of is considered to be compatible with (1) before reference point t_o and is considered to be compatible with (2) after t_o.
Sturved = meaning of is considered to be compatible with (2) before reference point t_o and is considered to be compatible with (1) after t_o.

The netherworlder's view of his universe is for him naturally unchanging, while he perceives the realworlder's conception to be radically, and rather irrationally, variant. We also, imperiously and from our superior vantage point, might think we can explain away the incompatibility between (1) and (2) by the fact that (2) *is* "true" from within the Einsteinian framework and (1) *was* "true" from within the pre-Einsteinian framework, for the conceived properties of space, given a broad historical perspective, are time-dependent. However, our broader view just happens to be advantageous in this particular case. A pre-Einsteinian, like ourselves if we assume that emeralds are forever green and not blue, would believe from within his particular "paradigm" that space can be nothing other than straight. Hence for him (2) would be forever "false," just as for us "emeralds are blue" is "false"—though, admittedly, empirical verification in our case would be much less problematic. And for this pre-Einsteinian, the realworlder would be epistemologically feeble of mind.[2] Similarly, and in view of this inquiry, one who is properly indoctrinated into Western World metaphysics would be, under ordinary circumstances, like this pre-Einsteinian, incapable of perceiving the fallacy of his *logocentrism*, his "metaphysics of presence," for he would be imprisoned within his conceptual framework.

It can be concluded tentatively, then, that since, as is most evident in Goodman's paradox, what is "true" at one time may be "false" at another, our "logic" needs some provisions for accounting for the change in the truth-value of propositions. Such time-dependent considerations of truth and meaning variance go against the grain of much modern logic. Medieval logic was in a sense time-dependent. Modern logic, however, especially since the early Wittgenstein, Russell, and Frege, is usually construed to be that of an omniscient and timeless being—ideally the logician—for whom the only possible world is the actual one. Peirce, on the other hand, who believed logic to be a normative science, never shared this idea. He believed, as we have observed, in an indefinite range of possibilities independent of a particular person's knowledge within a specific cultural framework and at a particular time and place (Peirce, 1960, 5.435ff and 6.637). Subsequently, he made a strong plea, though he never himself fully carried out the project, for a formal logic of time dimensions (see Prior, 1957). The distinction between past and future, consequently, should not be overlooked when considering the logic of propositions.

Let us, then, consider sense-data and their accompanying propositions which are ambiguous, or even anomalous. For instance, Wittgenstein's "rabbit/duck" drawing:

Suppose it is observed by someone a dozen times with the report that it is a "rabbit." Assuming that with each successive report there is memory of the past reports, it can be said that each is a re-iteration, but with a minute *difference* of course. Then, in a slightly distinct context, or perhaps not, a radical perceptual switch might occur such that the drawing is suddenly reported as a "duck," and with this thirteenth observation its ambiguous nature finally becomes apparent to the observer. But this new report would have been impossible as such had there existed no expectation from the previous reports that "rabbit" was supposed to be the case; that is, with the surprise that what was expected was not actualized. In this sense, the radical perceptual switch could not have occurred had there been no reference point constituting an expectation that the drawing would be such-and-such. If the observer has been in a state of *indifferent* "errance," then, the "uncanny moment," the *aporia*, would have been impossible. In addition, the moment in time during which this novel awareness of a "duck" when a "rabbit" was expected must be considered, for the purpose of this inquiry, *indeterminate.*[3]

With respect to the "rabbit/duck" drawing, suppose the netherworlder has the following set of signs:

Dabbit = examined before t_o (which is arbitrary) and reported to be a "rabbit," or not examined before t_o and reported to be a "duck."

Ruck = examined before t_o and reported to be a "duck," or not and reported to be a "rabbit."

Assume that the realworlder is capable of seeing the drawing only as a "rabbit," that he is not cognizant of the drawing's ambiguity.

Neither is the netherworlder, but for a different reason, for suppose that he believes the drawing to be literally one thing at one moment, and then he suddenly discovers that it does not conform to his expectations, that it is in reality something else. This netherworlder would obviously be to the realworlder rather naive and whimsical, changing his mind, signs, and perception apparently at random. Naturally, the netherworlder believes this is not the case; he merely perceived the same thing *as* something else at a given time, and in so doing attained a new level of awareness, and that's that. The important issue is, however, that the so-called new level of awareness must be for the netherworlder irreversible (discounting memory loss of course). The time at which phenomena are observed, then, can determine truth-value with respect to those phenomena. And, what is considered to be "true" at a particular time depends upon expectations derived from memory of previous experiences. But when those expectations are not satisfied, discovery of a new form of "truth"—or of the contradiction in the "rabbit/duck" case—is potentially forthcoming.[4]

It almost goes without saying that the time-dimension discussed to this point is potentially inherent in all tense-bound and linearly generated sentences in natural languages. On the other hand, a "logic" to account for *how* change is perceived and understood must give account of perceptual switches or flashes of insight. Instants of discovery such as Henri Poincaré's moments of illumination in mathematics, Friedrich A. Kekulé's dramatic discovery of the benzene ring as the result of a dream, or Beethoven's "hearing" entire pieces in simultaneity, must be considered atemporal. Understanding the punch line of a joke, or a metaphorical or ambiguous statement, is equally instantaneous. Yet the fact remains that a mathematical proof or a musical composition can be generated and perceived, like sentences in a language, only over a certain period of time. This apparent dichotomy between timeless conception on the one hand, and linear, temporal generation and perception on the other, remains to be delineated. Otherwise it will be impossible to illustrate the "logic of change," and how it is perceived and understood, which is, in the beginning, tacit and seemingly time-independent. This time-independence can be accounted for by another variation of Goodman's paradox which illustrates a hypothetical situation that would exist were we able to abolish time, at least from a particular perspective.

Consider once again the liar paradox, "All Cretans are liars said the man from Crete," which, if viewed as "true," must be "false," and if "false," "true." According to Russell, the problem with this paradox is that there exists no necessary discrimination of logical types. An individual Cretan is placed at the same level as the class of all Cretans, but, logically speaking, a class of things cannot be a member of itself (i.e., the class of men is not a man). Consequently this confusion of levels leads to paradox. Now if, with respect to the liar paradox, we set up a scheme representing the realworlder's view of the netherworlder's apparently perceiving intermittently, and over time, the statement to be "true" and "false," we have:

Talse = reported to be "true" when perceived before t_0 and "false" when perceived at t_1 and "true" when perceived at t_2 and "false" when perceived at $t_3 \ldots n$.

Frue = reported to be "false" when perceived before t_0 and "true" when perceived at t_1 and "false" when perceived at t_2 and "true" when perceived at $t_3 \ldots n$.

From the realworlder's vantage point, his counterpart is, of course, a helpless and hopeless "schizophrenic" caught in a "double-bind" and uncontrollably oscillating between the either and the or. But we must remember that the realworlder's view is symmetrical with that of the realworlder. Moreover, this "true-false" oscillation, at the most fundamental level, is analogous to what in physics is called a "standing wave," since there exists no necessary "memory" of what went on before and consequently there is no real variance over time.[5] Hence the temporal series, $t_0, t_1, t_2, t_3. \ldots n$ is not actually time-dependent as it is in the previous examples.[6] In fact, if we take on the realworlder's perspective, we might imagine him to conclude that frue indicates a value which, over time, is *neither* "true" *nor* "false" and simultaneously it is *both* "true" *and* "false," since he believes himself to exist in a more general domain than the netherworlder. The upshot of this example is apparent: *time is only a factor when memory is involved,* for without memory there would only be oscillation, *ad infinitum,* or there would simply be no awareness *that,* say, something was blue at one moment and changed to green the next. Now to attempt an account of such atemporal change accompanied by memory.

2

Is not a uniform suffering preferable to one which, by its ups and downs, is liable at certain moments to encourage the view that perhaps after all it is not eternal? (Beckett, 1955, 367)

Indifference makes of diversity uniformity. Uniformity abolishes *differences*, that is, it implies approximation toward an infinity of *differences* such that between each *difference* there is, for practical purposes, no *difference.* Successive differentiation can finally become erroneously construed as sameness—eternal, onto-theological, and timeless sameness. To begin differentiation, time simultaneously must become, and then memory must exist. Only then can there be change.

As illustrated above, new levels of awareness or understanding come by way of major or minor leaps and bounds. What appears, on the other hand, most likely counterintuitive is that the cognitive mechanism by means of which these leaps and bounds are made possible depends very little on the outer physical world or on the accumulation, by induction, of experience.[7] That is to say, the mechanism is at its roots the same for the domain of language and logic as it is for music and mathematics, and in major part the sciences and all the other arts. If the child can learn tacitly that numbers continue without end, if he can learn to participate, through some kind of "intertextuality," with a piece of music, or even if it is true that he innately knows how to internalize and use certain rules of grammar, then it is not amiss to postulate that to become tacitly aware *of* something in any of these domains where previous awareness did not exist is to make recurrent use of something which was already known: the capacity to make variant and discontinuous what would otherwise be invariant and continuous. This may be a rather difficult pill to swallow all at once. It can, however, be illustrated with a metaphor, using once again a variation of Goodman's paradox. Assume the following, which represents the spontaneous creation of a metaphor:

Lose =   (literally) the netherworlder's love, when she is spoken about before t_0 and (metaphorically) a "rose" when she is spoken about after t_0.

Rove = (literally) a rose when it is spoken about before t_0
and (metaphorically) the netherworlder's "love"
when she is spoken about after t_0.

Let us put ourselves in the universe of the logocentric real-worlder. The netherworlder must appear to him to be the equivalent of a slobbering romantic, or perhaps irrational or even incomprehensible, for in a universe of supposed absolute *presence*, metaphorization would be difficult, if not well-nigh impossible. The fact of the matter is that when, during a wild flight of fancy the netherworlder conceives of his love as (like) a "rose," he does not merely discover-invent *differences* between successive word uses, or substitute one word for another to produce a metaphor. Such traditional theories of metaphor focus almost exclusively on language while paying little or no attention to the cognitive, and cumulative, aspect of metaphor creation. In contrast, according to Max Black (1962) and others, the two terms of a metaphor "interact" such that both take on increased meaning, never again to be the same.

Alfred Korzybski (1933) and the general semanticists would appreciate this scheme. They maintain that a word always changes, even though ever so slightly, with each additional use. Accordingly, each time the netherworlder contemplates his love and uses the word as a *difference*, he would need to add a subscript in order to prevent confusion of meaning. That is, his love would be progressively: $love_1$, $love_2$, $love_3$, ... $love_n$ (where there is cumulative memory of the *difference* of meaning and context with each word use). Then, suddenly conceiving his love to be (like) a "rose" would give: $love_j \xrightarrow{\text{metaphorization}}$ "rose." Actually, such might be the preciseness the logical positivists also dreamed of, but practically speaking, it is, of course, useless. However, there is an additional problem here. If the netherworlder suddenly calls his love, metaphorically speaking, "rose," then he must be somehow tacitly aware that his love is something a rose ordinarily is *not*, and "rose" in this case relates to something to which it would ordinarily *not* relate. In other words, on using the sign to relate to that to which it would ordinarily *not* relate, there must be, in order to relate to what properly speaking and in a metaphorical sense it should, consciousness *that* "rose" (metaphorically) corresponds to "love" and does *not* (literally) correspond to a rose.[8]

The mechanism necessary for such to occur is, it is feasible to conjecture, analogous to that of the liar paradox. That is, it involves a tacit "oscillation" between the differentiated poles of two alternatives which exist at two levels—though they are not typologically incompatible levels in the Russellian sense. In addition, the netherworlder, in order to attain a metaphorical perspective, has imaginarily placed himself within the framework of "presence" supposedly occupied by the realworlder. Now he can, properly speaking, view his love (literally) as his love and (metaphorically) as a "rose" *as if* in *simultaneity*—the distinction being that one level of awareness is tacit and the other conscious, and there the two levels for all practical purposes merge, without "oscillation." That is, it is only *as if* he were "oscillating" between love and "rose" without the "double-bind," for the "oscillations" are between two levels of awareness, of perception. Consequently, to all appearance there exists no real confusion of types at the same level for the netherworlder's metaphorization. The upshot of this is that one can say what something (literally) *is*, or at another level one can say what something (metaphorically) *is not*, but one cannot actually do both at the same precise instant from within the same perspectival field.

Creation of the love/"rose" metaphor, then, necessarily entails the possibility of change *(differentiation)* through time, and of interaction between interrelated words. But such change was not initially registered in the vocabulary of the realworlder, with his presumed self-presence and identity, since he has one word, "love," (literally) to signify the netherworlder's love and "rose" for rose, and that's that. Consequently, we must suppose that he is rather oblivious to the reason for the netherworlder's excitement during his act of creation. Then could not it also be said that metaphor, perception of change, and all creativity is, with respect to atemporal logic, utterly impossible? Perhaps. Yet, as we observed, the netherworlder could and did metaphorize: Therefore, for him it *is* possible, using some sort of "logic" at least.

3

[P]erhaps that's what I feel, an outside and an inside and me in the middle. (Beckett, 1955, 383)

In an attempt to get a grip on this elusive "logic," recall that the liar paradox halts movement to create a "double-bind" situation and at the same time it relates, albeit contradictorily, two levels of abstraction. Recall also that, from the perspective either of the netherworlder or the realworlder, the other's perception is "schizophrenic." That is, each presumes himself to exist in a broader frame, with respect to the other, which is actually not the case. In contrast, from our viewpoint we discovered that both perspectives, rather than "schizophrenic," were symmetrical when interrelated. Our frame, it appears, is analogous to the "somewhere else" illustrated in chapter four, from which we can be aware *of* both symmetrical perspectives, though solely by means of "oscillation" between them. This notion of a "somewhere else" is also comparable to (A ∩ B) in the following visual counterpart to the liar paradox:

A ∩ B

Observe that the portion of the diagram either in (A) or (B) is "rational." (A) contradicts (B), but perception from within either of the two domains is continuous and non-contradictory. (B) is constructed by means of "rectangular" organization, (A) by "cylindrical" organization. (A ∩ B), on the other hand, though it is continuous, a series of parallel lines, can discontinuously be conceived alternately and by "oscillating" as part of either one or the other. From somewhere within (A ∩ B), then, the paradox or contradiction potentially becomes evident, and, in addition, from that point (A) and (B) can be seen in a new light as complements of one another. The paradox, though not logically resolvable, can be at least accounted for in the sense of Feyerabend from within this domain where the two discontinuities become part of a continuum, or analogously, where in the sense of Bohm the *unfolded* becomes once again *enfolded*. Hence (A ∩ B), ordinarily inaccessible from within either (A) or (B), represents the domain where the contraries are potentially perceived, where opposition and differentiation become a continuous whole: oneness therein prevails as a potential from which all particulars can be drawn.

The above drawing metaphorically illustrates the nether-worlder's and realworlder's dilemma, for (A) and (B), which are contradictory and even incommensurable, are like the realworlder's and netherworlder's respective conceptual frameworks. (B), like the realworlder's perspective, is illogical when viewed from inside (A), the netherworlder's perspective, and the same can be said about (A) from the vantage point of (B). Yet, from the overlapping zone of (A ∩ B), the nature of the incommensurability between both domains can become apparent to us. But if (A) and (B) are incommensurable, then how can they effectively be compared and contrasted, if at all? Precisely, I believe, due to a certain commonality possessed by both (A) and (B) that is to be found "outside," in (A ∩ B). That is, referring to the formulation in chapter one of Peirce's "logic of relatives," (B) can be labeled non-(A) and (A) non-(B), and thus they appear contradictory. Yet they share the disjoint property "(A)-(B)lessness." How is this possible? In the first place, neither (A) nor (B) possesses (A)-(B)ness, and hence they are also incompatible with (A ∩ B) in the sense that, if considered in isolation, (A ∩ B)'s mode of organization can be looked on as neither "rectangular" like (B) nor "cylindrical" like (A): it is no more than a group of parallel lines, it is "(A)-(B)lessness." But, in the second place, intermittently viewed from within (A) and (B), this "(A)-(B)lessness" can be considered contradictorily both "rectangular" and "cylindrical." Accessibility from one of the two incommensurable domains to the other, then, is possible, if only by a temporal "oscillation," through the neutral domain, (A ∩ B). So there is a commonality between (A) and (B).[9]

Now, finally, we have come full circle, from the initial very tentative articulation of DC in light of Peirce's "logic of relatives" to the present. And, we can begin to perceive a possible vindication of the deconstructionist's putative straddling the fence between metaphysics/anti-metaphysics, or "inside/outside," and a possible answer to the sixth problem discussed on page 152–54 of chapter six.

4

For to know nothing is nothing, not to want to know anything likewise, but to be beyond knowing anything, to know you are beyond knowing anything, that is when peace enters in, to the soul of the incurious seeker. (Beckett, 1955, 64).

The above section illustrates a human penchant, my own penchant, for generating oppositions. Let us as an alternative further consider *complementarity* in an attempt to reduce our reliance on oppositions. Bohm, like Beckett, and, it seems, commensurate with Derridean thinking, remarks that one cannot think and observe one's thinking at the same instant. Bohm (1951, 169) compares this phenomenon with complementarity in quantum mechanics, concluding that: the instantaneous state of thought is to the position of a particle as the general direction of change of that thought is to the particle's momentum. The important point here is that complementarity cannot be construed, logically speaking that is, as timeless. Quantum mechanical complementarity entails two incommensurable domains within each of which an "observation" can be made, but the same "observer" cannot be "inside" both domains in exact simultaneity. Secondly, on considering *differences* rather than opposites, the excluded middle principle must also be abolished. Successive differentiation ultimately, and paradoxically, leads to a condition in which, between any two entities, there is always a third. And as the entities in a given series become smaller, their *differences* become less, but they can never reach absolute mutual identity, for at both extremes of the series lie opposites. Such a "densely packed series" provides for an infinity of entities.

This series may be divided into two classes, which we might also call complementary: "syntactic" and "semantic."[10] A "syntactic" series can consist of visual signs, for instance, marks on paper. This class of signs is usually empirically identifiable. The corresponding "semantic" series would then consist of the meanings attached to these marks. Meanings, however, are not empirical. Hence the "semantic" class of entities is accessible only to experience rather than to perceptual faculties—compare to the distinction between experience and articulation from the above sections, and between a canon and explicit instructions from chapter four. Yet this experience along the "semantic" plane is incommunicable without the signs along the "syntactic" plane. The sign is, in a sense, always and invariably a false abstraction, a discrete entity incapable faithfully of representing the experiential. But it is an essential abstraction.

Signs, Peirce also claims, do not follow the same rules as experience or meanings. The sign represents, but it can never, or should never, replace the thing. Nor can it ever be the same as an experience, for it is artificial. Experience, on the other hand, is less mediate than sign perception. Consequently signs are usually demarcated and perceived *as differences* and oppositions, and even *as* identity. In contrast, experience consists of something like a densely packed continuum: *successive differentiation* without there necessarily being any demarcation of each and every *difference*. In this light, according to Jack Goody (1977, 11-12), logic, our Western World logic, seems to be:

> a function of writing, since it was the setting down of speech that enabled man clearly to separate words, to manipulate their order and to develop syllogistic forms of reasoning: these latter were seen as specifically literate rather than oral, even making use of another purely graphic isolate, the latter, as a means of indicating the relationship between the constituent elements. . . . [I]t is certainly easier to perceive contradictions in writing than it is in speech, partly because one can formalise the statements in a syllogistic manner and partly because writing arrests the flow of oral converse so that one can compare side by side utterances that have been made at different times and at different places.

Goody is speaking of what I have termed the "syntactic" component, which is necessarily discrete. And a further distinction is established between written and oral signs. The form in which written signs are presented potentially makes one more adequately aware of *differences*, as well as artificially abstracted identities and contradictions. It, to greater or lesser degree, forces one to be more conscious of rules of argumentation and of the logic underlying these rules. In fact: "Symbolic logic and algebra, let alone the calculus, are inconceivable without the prior existence of writing" (Goody, 1977, 44). Moreover, writing, which leads inevitably to a penchant for taxonomies, orderly systems, and definitions of boundaries, as well as a concern for formalizing thought, is ordinarily reduced to relatively abstract and graphic simplicity, for writing is more clearly discrete than speech.[11] For example, when considering a text as a static item for observation, sentences separated by, say, two hundred pages can easily be juxtaposed for analysis, sections can be classified, errors can be discovered, meanings can presumably be rigidly established. In the oral tradition, on the other hand, memory limitations restrict, though they certainly do not prohibit, such analysis.

Goody (1977, 48-50) cites the case of Margaret Masterman (1970) who discovered some twenty-one different ways Kuhn uses the term "paradigm" in his *Structure of Scientific Revolutions*. Such observation would apparently be impossible without abstracting each use of the word from the text, comparing it with the others, and then classifying them. If Kuhn's book were oral discourse, it is reasonable to assume that no listener would be capable of spotting each and every *difference*. He would most likely suppose the term to be used in fundamentally the same way. Yet if Masterman is correct, the *differences* exist, and perhaps not even the author could have been aware of all of them when he wrote his book, for he did not initially, we can suppose, abstract each use of the term from the text as did the text's analyst.[12]

The point is that writing renders *differences* potentially more apparent, but it also always tends to lead dangerously toward the conception of identity and contradiction. Yet writing is essential for any rigorous body of thought. Significantly, Beckett's syntactic division is the beginning of the cipher, when a desire to know something and to know about that knowing, is initiated. But this is both a gain and a loss, for now peace will forever remain outside the soul of the not-so-incurious seeker.

The next step is to attempt conceptualization of the distinction between the written ("syntactic") and the experiential ("semantic") domains.

5

Perhaps there is no whole before you're dead. (Beckett, 1955, 27)

Let us reconsider the above disquisition on Goodman's paradox. Assume blue/green to be lexical items in, at least from our particular perspective, a spectrum of mutually complementary color terms (in the "syntactic" scheme) and presumably their corresponding experienced meanings (in the "semantic" scheme). Along the "syntactic" plane, for instance, to the immediate left of blue we find blo, and to the right of blue we find bleen, both of which are conceived to be very slightly *different* from blue. Then to the right of green we find gro, to the left of green, grue, to the right of bleen, bue, and to the left of grue, geen, and so on as follows:

n ... blo-blue-bleen-bue-been ... *n* ... gen-geen-grue-green-gro ... *n*

Assuming an infinity of possible words exists along this spectrum, we have a "syntactically" compact series, with no absolute identities, and an infinity of ideally empirically observable, though infinitesimal, *differences*. The spectrum's corresponding "semantic" series, on the other hand, cannot be empirical, since it is no more than artificially and indirectly represented by the words. Along the "semantic" chain, the successively differentiated *differences* do not, and cannot, indirectly pattern *logos*, signs, thought, or consciousness *of*. They pattern experience. Experience cannot include opposition or identity as can "syntax"; it is not particulate, but continuous. Consciousness *of*, or recognition *of* oppositions presupposes the Derridean MC in addition to Popperian expectations and Peirce's Secondness and Thirdness. The level of experience, then, is prior to "syntactic" differentiations. And, prior to the experiential level exists the continuum of infinite alternatives which are present in simultaneity. Hence there is a "complementarity principle" of sorts between the "syntactic" and "semantic" planes. What is directly experienced excludes the sign, and what is perceived *as* sign is necessarily and to a greater or lesser degree an artificial detachment *from* experience.

Now, in order to distinguish between three levels, the whole of the unactualized continuum of possibilities, the experienced ("semantic") plane, and the actualized but artificially differentiated ("syntactic") plane, let us construct a "lattice" thus:[13]

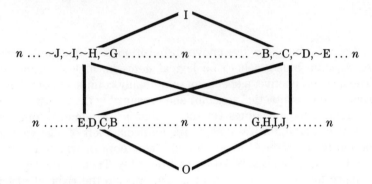

$$n \ldots \sim J, \sim I, \sim H, \sim G \ldots\ldots\ldots n \ldots\ldots\ldots \sim B, \sim C, \sim D, \sim E \ldots n$$

$$n \ldots\ldots E, D, C, B \ldots\ldots\ldots n \ldots\ldots\ldots G, H, I, J, \ldots\ldots n$$

Where G = green, ~G = not-green, B = blue, ~B = not-blue, O = null, or the ("semantic") continuum, and I = the differentiated ("syntactic"). The other letters represent the equivalent of bleen, blo, bue, etc., and gru, gro, geen, etc., along the spectrum.

If, from O—the *enfolded* or realm of possibilia—B is experienced (at the "semantic" level), this experience has not yet been given "syntactic" representation. It is not yet specified as an item of experience *with respect to* or *as opposed to* another item of experience (for example, G). The experience *of* B *instead of* G implies either/or categories, and it implies the actuality or possibility of assigning a sign at the "syntactic" level. If the experience *of* B *instead of* G exists, then we have moved up the "lattice" from O to B and ~G, and then to I, the "syntactically" differentiated. This entails use of the logical connective "or" ($\lor$). That is, "or" entails movement up the "lattice" along a line or lines common to both elements as far as is possible. For example, "G *or* B" gives I, "~B *or* ~G" gives I, but "O *or* B" gives B, "B *or* ~G" gives ~G, and so on. On the other hand, the connective "and" ($\land$) involves downward transition. "B *and* G" gives O, "I *and* B" gives B, "~G *and* B" gives B, and so on. Furthermore, the upper elements in the "lattice" are dominant over the lower elements. ~G includes B as a subset, just as ~B includes G, and so on. In other words, the class of not-green things includes the class of blue things, as it does the class of orange things, red things, etc. Significantly, a variant of this logical governing type of "lattice" is also called a "context logic."[14] We may call it, for the purpose of this inquiry, a "differential logic."

The implications of this "lattice" are tremendous when considering the potentially infinite range of words and meanings *(differences)* between the outside B and G. For instance, by use of our ordinary English language, B and G are conventionally used "syntactically" and their corresponding meanings are rarely placed in doubt. However, we observed that when the realworlder becomes aware of the netherworlder's strange taxonomy, he acquires the ability potentially to articulate finer distinctions than before while adhering to the conventional terms within the framework of his own culture. However, suppose that one year the realworlder says B and means B, but the following year his mode of experiencing the world has changed slightly, perhaps due to his talks with the netherworlder, such that when he says B he now actually experiences and means the equivalent of bleen. Or on saying G he experiences and means the equivalent of grue. Conversation can go on as before between him and his fellow citizens, all of them most likely at the outset unaware of the *differences* in the meanings of the words they use. Yet the *differences* are there. The very important point, then, is that at any given moment in the communication between two or more individuals, any of the possibilities between and outside B and G can potentially arise. Ordinarily the *differences* are not insurmountable, and the communicants swim along reasonably well. However, sometimes they flounder, for incommensurability has come to rule.

"Semantically," therefore, changes can occur along the continuum of which the writer/speaker can be either aware or unaware. Yet the tendency is to attach the same "syntactic" sign to that which is experienced, and sameness or even identity is presumed to prevail. The problem is that since the "semantic" plane is non-empirical, change threatens to go relatively unnoticed. "Syntactically," on the other hand, we can ordinarily perceive many or most *differences*. A spoken accent, incorrect use of words, misspelled words, typing errors, etc., are common, of course. However, let us consider ourselves to be like Funes. Suppose that, paradoxically, to each experienced slice of our world we are able to attach a discrete sign. That is, suppose at one instant we report the color of an object to be "blue," at the next "bleen," at the next "been," then "blo," then "blue," and so on. Or suppose that a dog we see at one instant is labeled "Fido$_1$," at another "Fido$_2$," then "Fido$_3$," etc.[15] Now we can really get down to business and talk clearly and distinctly can't we? Or can we? What if when you report "bue" I happen to experience "blo," or what if I make a statement about "Fido$_{1035}$" and you recall to memory "Fido$_{781}$"? An argument may ensue, at least there will be some misunderstanding. What is the problem here? Precisely that the continuous ("semantic") series is perpetually in flux, while the discrete ("syntactic") series represents a set of relatively static entities; that is, entities which we insist to be relatively identical over time.[16]

Interestingly enough, as Zeno demonstrated, motion cannot be constructed from a series of discrete parts, even though there be an infinity of them. And continuity cannot be composed of a set of discrete elements. "Syntactically," therefore, language and logic can prevail—opposites and identities can be abstracted from the discrete series. Nevertheless, "semantically," that is experientially, an *undifferentiated* process persists, though this process is incessantly mutilated when "parts" of it are extracted and given signs. "Syntax" exists at the expense artificially of halting the dynamic quality of experience. Exclusively along the "syntactic" plane, *becoming*, change over time, is well-nigh impossible—there is only a series of discrete, static "points." In the "semantic" realm, *being*, eternal and timeless *being*, as Derrida tells us also, cannot *be*, for it cannot *be* identical to itself through the temporal process, nor can it be assigned a specific label.

The above "quantum lattice" accounts, paradoxically, for the distinction between the written sign and meaning, that which is empirical ("outer") and that which is experiential ("inner"), and between language and the *imaginative* mind, discontinuity and continuity. These are not true oppositions, however, they are "paradoxically complementary." Without language *imagination* would be severely limited. But without an act of this *imaginative* mind language could never exist in the first place. Both *imagination* and language lift each other, so to speak, by their bootstraps. The act of mind is precisely what enables us to play with language, for it entails a distinct, but complementary, "field." Derrida in a sense limits us by limiting the world to language, and specifically to writing. In contrast, by acts of mind, the Nietzschean *imagination* of the possible, or Peirce's conditional Thirdness, the bonds of language can be temporarily, though only partly, unraveled. (With language, and following leaps of *imagination*, Zeno creates his paradoxes, Borges and Beckett their fictions, Einstein his "thought experiments," Popper his conjectures, Feyerabend his playful dabbling, the Flatlander his sphereworld, etc.)

Of course, the "semantic" and the realm of experience and *imagination*, we must admit, remain in their totality eternally ineffable, while at the same time the "syntactic" will always be incomplete. However, obviously the "syntactic" does change over time, and this being the case, somehow this change must represent an interjection, paradoxically as it must be, of the "semantic" into the "syntactic." The final topic to consider involves this "syntactic" change and "semantic" ineffability.

6

And it was, though unutterable, like the crumbling away of two little heaps of finest sand, or dust, or ashes, of unequal size, but diminishing together as it were in ration, if that means anything, and leaving behind them, each in its own stead, the blessedness of absence. (Beckett, 1955, 222)

Zeno's paradox again! As the "little heaps" diminish in ration they become smaller and smaller, more closely approximating zero.[17] This is certainly change, of a sort, but the goal remains forever beyond grasp. The goal might be utterable but the change itself, the continuum of change, is not. In mathematics, infinitesimal Calculus is the theory of such change, and its results are admirable, but the problem adequately of articulating the continuum remains. We sense it, and somehow know it, but can't exactly say it. It is like the pie, whose proof is in the taste, but the taste can't tell us what a pie is. To speak *of* a pie requires first language, and second, a higher level of generality. Likewise, we have a mathematical language with which we can compute by means of concepts implying the continuum, but that next level of generality continues to elude all language.

Consider other examples throughout history. The invention of irrational numbers threatened to shipwreck the then young and budding field of mathematics. The mathematician had tasted this forbidden fruit, and as a result he had been banished, he banished himself, from his Pythagorean paradise. But there was a solution, which he immediately grasped onto. These "unutterables" could be conveniently put away in the closet and forgotten, and the ship could be repaired while at sea. Finally, however, with the final decline of Pythagorean absolute forms, the harmony of the spheres became indeterminable, and irrational numbers finally saw the light of day once again. In modern times irrational numbers are frequently used, and with hardly a thought to their "irrationality"—they are looked upon as being *neither* more *nor* less "real" *or* "irrational" than other numbers. They have gradually become the "rational way" to calculate, and to construct mathematical models with which to explain the world. The point is this. If today's mathematician of a sudden desired to reduce his system to that which is totally "rational," "logical," effable, and formalizable, he would be required to forget twenty centuries of work. If the scientist decided that only what he could verify absolutely is worthy of being called theory, then forget about modern science altogether. If the speaker/writer decided to use only words with clear and concise meanings, he would be reduced to silence and the blank page. We look for symmetries, then, fearful of such *indifferences*, as Wittgenstein remarks, we retreat "back to the rough ground." There is, and there will always be, a degree of ineffability, the incognizable, but *never in the absolute sense.*

Admitting to absolute unutterability is to give up the game, to go down with the ship. Derrida himself at times admits to the nonabsoluteness of ineffability. *Play*, DC, TC, and MC are the "as yet unnamable which is proclaiming itself and which can do so, ... only under the species of the nonspecies, in the formless, mute, infant, and terrifying form of monstrosity" (Derrida, 1978a, 293). And elsewhere, Derrida (1978a, 158) states that "difference remains a metaphysical name; and all the names that it receives from our language are still, so far as they are names, metaphysical." Necessary admissions. The unnamable is *as yet unnamable*, but *not always and absolutely.*[18] And whatever can be said obliquely about it is inextricably metaphysical, fictive, metaphorical.

This problem is common also to science. In fact, one of the greatest points of convergence between mysticism and the "new physics" is the inadequacy of language. Henry Margenau (1959, 250), a relatively conservative scientist, surprisingly tells us that:

> There is something ineffable about the real, something occasionally described as mysterious and awe inspiring, the property alluded to is no doubt its ultimacy, its spontaneity, its failure to prevent itself as the perfect and articulate consequence of rational thought.

Yet the scientists never give up their quest. When discussing their ideas, they must eventually resort to language use taken from ordinary life. They speak of "particles," for example, as if they really existed, knowing full well that they do not, at least in the ordinary sense of the term. Similarly, they speak of "waves," while aware that these "waves" manifest "particle" characteristics under certain conditions. A new term, "wavicle," has been proposed for these elusive subatomic "entities." But this term also has its problems. Yet the physicists must necessarily and admittedly artificially attach some kind of word to their phenomena under study. If they were to abolish all imprecise terms, they too would be reduced to silence. So they speak (see Heisenberg, 1962).

And they will continue to speak, for they will always be able to speak anew, for as the "syntactic" domain becomes successively more differentiated, *differences* become less and less, and they more closely approximate the "semantic" continuum—though, of course, they can never arrive there. In this sense, yesterday's ineffability can be today's (at least partial) effability, for the limits of language continually expand. This is because the "semantic" is irreversible, and never stands still. The "syntactic" is capable of stopping and articulating this continuous flow, though always artificially and incompletely, but it says what *was*, not what *is*, in the *here* and *now*. Yet, during the creative act, or at the moment of *aporia*, when as Derrida tells us, there is "neither pure syntax nor pure semantics," the continuum spills over into the discrete series. What was ineffable becomes partly effable, and what is effable can slip from memory.

For a case in point, consider the act of writing. The writer chooses a word (partly) to convey the message of what he experiences. But at that very "instant" when the word is being put down, his experience becomes *different;* it is "now" something other than what it was. Therefore he is "now" beyond the word, and into the vast range, potentially of an infinite number of words, which by the TC can be connected to the previous word. This range of words, like Peirce's infinitesimals and also like consciousness itself, is, over time, partly actualized linearly. The successive words make sayable/writable that which the previous event of consciousness was not aware *of*, for it has "now" moved on. And as it continues to push onward, it is already and always in the presence of the potential, from which selections can be made.

In sum, there is, then, no upper limit to what is sayable/writable. All experience can potentially, over an indefinite period of time, be given signs. Embarking on a critique of *logocentrism*, it is not sufficient to take refuge in unnamables, mysteriously alluding to that which is unknown and purportedly unknowable. Rather than Wittgenstein's ladder metaphor, such activity is analogous to the fakir's rope trick. While the master disappears into the clouds, credulous apprentices can do no more than gape in awe.

7

One starts things moving without a thought of how to stop them. In order to speak. One starts speaking as if it were possible to stop at will. (Beckett, 1955, 299)

Beckett's characters never cease their quest for the words that will allow them to stop talking. This, likewise, is one of Derrida's (1978a, 262) tasks: "We must find a speech which maintains silence. Necessity of the impossible: to say in language—the language of servility—that which is not servile." Silence, excluding speech, is therefore foreign to DC as the source of signification (Derrida, 1978a, 263). Silence erases the discontinuity of "syntax." It exists, appropriately, on the "semantic" plane—or better, it is the equivalent of zero, the void. This desire for silence is a desire for that which precedes the *play* of DC, where there is no beingness. The beingness of Beckett's Unnamable *is* only in and through his speaking. To speak himself he must speak what *is*, but he cannot, for his self is never fully present. It can never be grasped—like the dog chasing its tail. Silence then becomes the goal, to end it all, but that is impossible also, for there one can never *be:* Beckett can never be silent . . . never. This impossibility of an escape from time into infinity is one important dimension of his works (Robinson, 1969, 23). Another is language. Beckett's characters always fail in their search for an expression of the ineffable because they cannot overcome the immediate limitations of language.[19] And they inexorably continue to talk because, on another plane, language is potentially limitless. The limits of language and this yearning for a "transcendence" beyond the boundary of all words is the motivating force behind the desire for silence, yet there must be awareness that it is all in vain. Speaking/writing reveals one's own ignorance, but by the same token one becomes increasingly conscious *of* one's ignorance, and then one can always speak one's ignorance anew.[20] Peirce would agree here.

Beckett's language certainly offers no univocal meanings either, at least in the traditional sense. And the meanings that can be found are never ones that can console us.[21] Rather than deconstruct, Beckett forces us to reconsider. But in his later works, he does so by first destroying our expectations, reducing his fictitious world to disorder, chaos. This chaos does not gradually arise from progressively differentiated complexity. It begins as complexity and strives for increased simplicity. Yet total chaos, to repeat, is synonymous with the One. It is the point where reconsideration must occur, where composition can arise from the remains of decomposition (Cohn, 1962, 285). For it is at this place that our reconsideration does not imply choice of new meanings. Here, it is somewhat like the Buddhist ideal of "choiceless awareness" (Lamont, 1970, 201). In fact, there is striking similarity between the *Koan* and much of the language of Beckett's trilogy if taken in its composite form. The *Koan*, to be perceived correctly so that it may lead one to the higher domain of knowledge, cannot simply entail a choice of either of the poles of the apparent contradiction. One must go beyond all such paradoxes. Beckett's narrative, like a vast complex Western counterpart to the *Koan*, is a world of paradoxes, "which negate every possibility of movement, knowledge, rationality, understanding, and coherence on the part of the creatures that inhabit that curious world" (Federman, 1970, 103). It seems that

Beckett's "rule of practice," which he follows closely, might be expressed thus: "Let every ingredient of work cancel every other" (Hesla, 1971, 222).[22]

A *mutually cancellatory* system *par excellence.*

The reader, then, appears to be propelled into endless intellection, caught up into infinite and irresolvable contradictions.[23] And, if S. J. Rosen (1972, 11) is correct, Beckett believes, oddly enough, that the reader is supposed to enjoy this game, in spite of the terror it might instill in him. Obviously many do enjoy it, but obviously also, as not-too-incurious seekers. Perhaps the game is so intriguingly enjoyable precisely because of its *Koan*-like quality, its massive hierarchy of paradoxes which approximate, but never reach, like Zeno's paradox and complex numbers, the point where there is nothing left but nothing. Perhaps the next step is required, the step Buddhist's call "enlightenment," divorced from intellection and so alien to the Western World reader. Perhaps such knowledge is accessible to experience, the totality of it eternally evading communication by words—Beckett's inevitable instrument, and hence this is why he must always fail. Perhaps also this knowledge can only be acquired when the reader is completely divorced from the world of things, the word's supposedly necessary referents.

For Beckett, especially evidenced in *The Unnamable*, the only world that has any potential meaning is the world of the *imagination.* When everything else is destroyed, *imagination* will always remain. And, unlike our tyrannical language, which persists in exercising a degree of control over us, *imagination*, although by and large uncontrollable, is at least subject to our deciding whether or not to play or to reject whatever it sends up to us from the depths of consciousness. Moreover, Beckett's consciousness is not that of the existentialist or phenomenologist.[24] Beckett's anti-heroes are at the pole opposite to the Romantic hero or the Nietzschean Superman, who bring their world into existence, while detached from the "herd" and holding it in utter contempt. Beckett's characters can will nothing into existence. The only part of themselves of any value is their "inner" world, and they are strangely *indifferent* to the "outer" world. The ultimate goal is that they may someday discover how to talk and say nothing, to do nothing, to stand in one spot and pour words out, the body slowly rotting, the world "out there" creeping along inch by inch. The ultimate goal is to surrender to the "outer" world in a passive way. This is Zen with an outraged but almost-silent outcry. The play is free, but to be so it must remain exclusively "within," for "outside" necessity is overpowering (Robinson, 1969).[25]

And yet this attempt at a *mutual cancellation* of words, of *differences*, is at once an obstinate and single-minded effort to envision the unimaginable, say the unnamable. If for Derrida (1978a, 241), following Freud, dreams and speech are governed by the primary process, Beckett goes a step further; he desires to bring the primary process under his domain, to make words, creativity, laughter, and *aporia* possible when two or more ordinarily incompatible domains are intersected. Just as Derrida (1978a, 251–77) demonstrates that laughter lies outside the Hegelian system of dialectical logic, so Beckett's cloudy and eternally receding domain where everything is *mutually cancelled* and where everything is somehow possible, is ultimately beyond all intellection, beyond the slumber of reason. Yet here, precisely, the origin must "be," though we never grasp *it*.

Beckett, in addition, counteracts Derrida's notion that we must simply begin where we are, with the mind somehow emptied of all dogmas, all myths, and simply deconstruct. Beckett's question is: How can we know where we are? How do we know that we are in a process of "empirical errance"? Might what we see not actually be tinged with presuppositions of which we are unaware? To attain "empirical errance" is to go back to the stage of the wide-eyed babbling infant—an utter impossibility.[26] It is not even possible to know if and when we have attained Derrida's ideal of "learned ignorance"—a sort of counterpart to Nietzsche's "*will* to ignorance." Hence, in light of chapter three where the deconstructor's maxims were "Gödelized," it becomes impossible to know that what is deconstructed is not not deconstructible, or to know that the deconstructor's frame of reference is not also itself deconstructible, and so on, *ad infinitum*. But the deconstructionist might reply that one must, by taking a risk, simply accept the fact, or even believe, that his starting point is legitimate. Then, how do we know that that belief is not itself either not deconstructible or deconstructible? And so on. Beckett would probably tend to agree, but only partly, for a beginning, if we follow *Molloy*, is only apparently important (Robinson, 1969, 144).

Through his prose, Beckett more effectively approaches the Absolute absence of Absolutes than the deconstructionist ordinarily does, most likely because his model is more abstract and mathematical than it is metaphysical. Beckett's search in the trilogy for the impossible, irretrievable Absolute is certainly no "myth of presence," though at the outset it appears to be so, for the quest stems from a desire for timelessness. Molloy believes that on being born he was thrown out of the ideal timeless whole. Now, in exile, he longs to return. But the self cannot escape from time, and the timeless whole must remain, as it always has, ultimately a mystery, the "ultimate mystery of nature" which can never be solved, for, "in the last analysis, we ourselves are part of nature and therefore part of the mystery that we are trying to solve" (Planck, 1933, 217). Is this a fateful concession to absolute ineffability that we must passively accept? The answer must be a paradoxical yes *and* no. Yes, because language is necessarily excluded from this mystery, the whole. But not exactly, for with language many paradoxes *are* resolved, and in resolving them, we can ever-more-closely approximate a total understanding of the whole, according to Peirce and Popper, Beckett and Bohm. But yes, because we can never arrive at our final destination. However, we learn from Beckett that the mind's incessant striving provides for our only degree of free rein—our only real freedom—to imagination.

Actually, acts of mind and *imaginary* constructs are of themselves, like dreams, neither "true" nor "false," neither "logical" nor "illogical." "Truth" and "logic," which usher in ineffables, involve language, and this is where the problems begin. We can easily speak of "square circles" within an *imaginary* construct, but, muddleheaded beings that we are, we eventually forget that words are no more than artificial, and in spite of ourselves, we interject our notions of "truth" and "logic" into our discourse. To reiterate, subatomic "events" are neither "particles" nor "waves," and at the same time they are both. The ordinary meanings of the words must be effaced. We must be able somehow to move along the continuous "semantic" spectrum to simply experience them in the context of their use. This is an *imaginative* act by means of which the ineffable can potentially become at least partly effable.

By this same line of thought it is possible to proceed beyond such supposed dichotomies as *identity/difference*. Mystics report that they experience all "things" and "events" as *different* aspects of a basic oneness—which may be called God, Brahma, Tao, and Absolute, etc. Yet during the mystical experience, individuality remains, for everything is not identical to everything else. Nonetheless, though each "thing" or "event" is *different*, at the same time it is a reflection, at a deeper level, of a fundamental unity. Individuals, and individual *differences*, are part of a larger pattern. A block of marble seen intermittently and from distinct perspectives by the mason, geologist, artist, architect, etc., is in each case *different*, but the composite of all possible perspectives of it in simultaneity represents the self-identical whole. *Differences* are within the whole and the whole remains, paradoxically, within itself. When two perspectives are considered intermittently, *differences* exist; when all possible perspectives are simultaneously included, there are no *differences*.

Stated another way, all perspectives, like all values, when viewed from the perspective of the whole, are *neither* good *nor* bad. They simply *are*. "Truth" and "falsehood" should therefore enjoy equal time. What from one perspective is "true," is "false" in at least one of an infinite number of alternative perspectives. Hence all possible "truths" must provisionally be given the same weight. There can be appeal to no Absolute Truth, nor can there be adoption of either "rational" or "irrational" grounds for determining "truth." Whatever perspective one is "inside" for the moment is simply construed as the-"truth"-that-*is* without comparison and contrast (by means of the time-bound DC) to what *is* or *might be* "within" an alternative framework. Of course, a "truth" from one perspective may be perceived as a "falsity" from the same framework—which has actually now become a *different* framework—at a later time. Hence any given framework, when considered over time, must include corrected past "falsities" as well as present "truths." And these "falsities" aid in knowing the "truths" more profoundly. For instance, the university student taught only Einsteinian physics is deficient when compared with the student who learns, in addition, Newtonian physics.

"I am I," then, can be referred to *either* as *identity or difference*. It makes no *difference*. If *identucal*, there is *no* discrimination—at one level—and if *different*, there is *nothing but* discrimination. Moreover, each meaning, the "I am I" as *identity or difference*, is made possible by discrimination as well. If "I ≠ I," the discrimination is *in* the *difference*, and if "I = I," then it is *in* the Cartesian split between "I" and "world." The meaning is in the seeing *as* as discriminated from what it is seen *as not*. Both "I = I" and "I $\neq$ I" are simultaneously right *and* wrong, at the deeper level. Who is right, Descartes or Derrida? If we say Descartes, we are *both* right *and* wrong; if we say Derrida, we are *both* right *and* wrong. Once again, the problem of language. But we will, we must, continue to speak/write; we will never be silent. And we, like Beckett, will always continue to fail, that is, to a degree we will always be wrong—as well as right. The game consists in trying to be less "wrong," though, by switching perspectives and by breaking out into larger frames more easily. On so doing we "make mistakes more quickly," but over the long haul we will, if we are fortunate, be less "wrong"; that is, our vantage point will be increasingly broadened such that we may be able to take in more with a greater acuity of vision.

Speaking of Beckett, what I have just described is, once again, analogous to his work: a monstrous set of *mutually cancellatory affirmations and negations*. Actually, *aporia* is within the Cartesian *either-or* tradition. Deconstruction not-too-simply changes the dichotomy to *neither-nor*. Mutually cancellatory affirmations and negations, in contrast, belong to the Socratic tradition, or better, to Popper's ongoing conjecture-refutation activity contradictorily compacted into a "moment." Popper's game of science entails—and he would not like to formulate it this way, though many of his rebellious disciples have—an active search *and* a passive state of receptivity. Similarly, Beckett wants the ideal of total *indifference* at one level and an active, penetrating intellectual search for what *is*, at another level. This might, at the outset, appear similar to the mystical experience; paradoxically, the passivity at which the mystic appears to aim is actually a most intense activity. The crucial difference is that the mystic's activity is not that of intellection, while Beckett strives to interject, even more paradoxically still, intellection into *indifference*, discontinuity into the continuum. *Indifference*, significantly, is, to repeat, Beckett's metaphor of the ever-recurring decimal, $\sqrt{2}$. It continues forever, and the answer must be *there*, somewhere between $1\frac{169}{408}$ and $1\frac{70}{169}$, but we will never find *it* (Kenner, 1961, 107). *Indifference*, rather than *difference*, is the Absolute Absolute.

In the beginning, when and where there was no beginning, I somehow knew, as we all knew but knew not *that* we knew, and hence I had to begin, wherever I was, for I could not know. And I, all of us, will prevail to the end, which has neither a where nor a when.

But what it is all about exactly I could no more say, at the present moment, than take up my bed and walk. It's vague, life and death. I must have had my little private idea on the subject when I began, otherwise I would not have begun, I would have held my peace, I would have gone on peacefully being bored to howls, having my little fun and games ... until someone was kind enough to come and coffin me. (Beckett, 1955, 225)

Postscript

What has been stressed in the immediately preceding sections of this inquiry is a radical form of pluralism.[1] Pluralism demands casual reading, thinking, talking, writing, and above all listening, from within many disciplines—the activity of the *bricoleur*. Indeed, if this pluralism is in any manner radical, it is radically cross-disciplinary. Actually, when one ponders over only a few of the iconoclasts in various disciplines, one realizes that it is through their efforts that most changes in our storehouse of knowledge have come about. The linguist Roman Jakobson is admittedly a dilettante, as were the physicists Bohr, Born, and Einstein. Many came to their chosen disciplines from outside, rather than being well indoctrinated insiders rarely attempting to look beyond what their professional myopia allowed them. Einstein himself worked in a patent office, Naom Chomsky spent many years toiling with logic, computer science and philosophy before writing *Syntactic Structures*. James McCawley came to linguistics from chemistry, and William Empson was a mathematician, as was Robert Musil. Wittgenstein had a background in engineering. Robert Ardrey was a playwright before becoming an anthropologist. The list is inexhaustible.

But how, it might be asked, can I end chapter seven advocating an approach to *indifference* and immediately afterward in this postscript argue from a definite and committed vantage point? In response, I would first admit that when one is in a state of *indifference*, problems cannot be solved and texts can neither be written nor interpreted. Legitimate pluralism must entail diverse views, disagreement, critical argument. With perpetual *indifference*, in contrast, disagreement *against* a perspective and argument *for* an alternative cannot exist. Of course the nimble-minded *indifferent* subject can always change perspectives at will in order to ward off tedium, or for the mere sake of playing the game. But without a keen analytical eye, and unless a stand is taken, all perspectives are simply and purely *there: differences* that don't really make a *difference*.

However, if, following Peirce, Popper, Bohm, et al., there is belief in ultimate Truth, though with the realization that we will never

196

have it, then we can take a provisional stand, make a tentative leap, argue for a viewpoint, constantly improving the more valid conjectures and weeding out the rest, but keeping them in the junk heap for possible future use. In this sense, there will always be a struggle for some undefined and indeterminable goal. We cannot say we will progress, for we cannot really know when we are advancing and when retroceding. We cannot even know where we are going, for there is always a plurality of potential endings. Yet we push on, we must push on, as not-too-curious seekers, at one level approaching total *indifference* toward everything, while at another level attending most directly with the back of the mind to what it is that needs to be known, and constantly oscillating between both. Such activity presupposes some immanent domain by means of which we can become aware, though always incompletely and usually inconsistently, of *differences*.

Appendix to Chapter Three

Contemplate the following isomorphism, derived from chapter three:

DECONSTRUCTION		GÖDEL'S PROOF
Writing	←——→	Arithmetic
Text	←——→	A number system
Full presence of text	←——→	Complete and consistent system
Identity-contradiction: uni-vocal text	←——→	Non-self-referential and true system
Aporia, "double-bind"	←——→	Inconsistency
Plurivocal text	←——→	Self-referential and false system
Différance	←——→	"Logic of relatives" (from Peirce)
Meaning	←——→	Provability
Intelligible text	←——→	Theorem in system
Unintelligible text	←——→	Non-theorem in system
Sentence	←——→	Proposition
Decidable sentence	←——→	Provable proposition
Undecidable sentence	←——→	Non-provable proposition
"I am not decidable"	←——→	"I am not provable"
Play	←——→	Metamathematics

The *presence of the text*, in all its plenitude, like the *complete and consistent system*, is an impossible dream, the desire for which

199

leads to mistaken and misinterpreted ideals: *univocal texts*, and *non-self-referential* and *consistent* but *incomplete systems*. *Plurivocal texts* and *self-referential* and *inconsistent systems* are the only reality. They are generated by the most general laws, *différance* and the *"logic of relatives"* (or Sheffer's "stroke"). The goal, hopefully leading to the ideal, the dream, is to construct an *intelligible text* or a set of *theorems*.[1] However, *aporia* eventually creeps into *writing* and into all *systems*. This is, inevitably, a self-referential, inconsistent, and hence *undecidable sentence* or a *nonprovable proposition* which "speaks to itself," threatening to draw the writer/reader into its manifold and potentially infinitely complex oscillations between *meanings-proofs* without there being any definite *meaning-proof*. But this indeterminacy is actually fortunate, for it also potentially opens up the indefinite and limitless game, of *play* or *metamathematics*, with no beginning or end, no presence, no center.

Man has invented mathematics, science, art, and play—games all—which are, inexorably, incomplete, because of the incommmensurability of his ideals and his real capacities.

Note to
Appendix

1. That is, the intelligible text possesses the characteristic of *vraisemblance*—the text is made "real" with respect to other texts, to the genre to which it belongs, and to the world (see Todorov, 1968). A theorem is the result of a proof within a system which makes it consistent, while a non-theorem is derived from a non-valid proof, which makes for an inconsistent system.

Notes

INTRODUCTION

1. According to the concept of "intertextuality," each text is a mosaic of citations of other texts; it absorbs them and transforms them with its coming into existence and with each and every reading (Culler, 1976; Kristeva, 1969, 1970). "Intertextuality" displaces the phenomenological false plenitude of intersubjectivity; supposedly it is *neither* subjectivity *nor* objectivity. If subjectivity is an erroneous plenary image, then objectivity, with respect to the world of texts, is no more than a fictitious image, hence plenary also and stemming from an effort to make oneself known to oneself.

2. This predominance of speech over writing, along with the metaphysics it entails, Derrida calls "logocentrism" or "phonocentrism"—the compulsion for interpreting "logos" in terms of the "phonē" rather than the "grammē." Derrida, in contrast, wants to reconstitute writing, arguing that it is more fundamental and more general than speech (see especially the Platonic "origins" of "logocentrism" according to Derrida in 1972a, 71-197).

3. It might appear here and elsewhere that I am merely reducing deconstruction to a set of "propositions" about language, texts, and the world. This and other similar synoptic statements are, however, more appropriately stated, "heuristic devices" abstracted for the purpose of discovering certain parallels between deconstruction and key aspects of Western World thought. Unlike "propositions," traditionally conceived, they are not, nor can they be, permanently "framed," for, commensurate with Derridean thinking, no "frame" can be considered from any finite perspective self-sufficient, self-identical. To do so would be to fall into "logocentrism." The title of this book, then, evokes no nostalgia for finality. Nevertheless, as will become evident below, any word, any thought, any perspective, must inexorably be "framed," if only for a minute increment of time, for "framing" is a necessary component of language use.

4. I will quote Derrida from English translations, whenever available, aware of the problematics of transposing Derrida's difficult prose. The only exception will be in chapter six, where I provide some extended quotes to be subject under scrutiny. There I have made some minor changes in the original translation.

5. For earlier work entailing the notion of "deferred consciousness" see Merrell (1982, 1983, in press). I should also point out that I extensively use the term "perception" neither in the sense of an actual and immediate presence of external objects to the sense organs (Francis Bacon) nor as immediate intellectual rather than sensory apprehension (René Descartes). Derrida would reject both uses. "Perception," as the term is employed here, is never certain or determinate; it can never be divorced from presuppositions and expectations, and it is intimately linked to conception, remem-

203

brance, and imagination. It consists of an interaction between sensory data, on the one hand, and past experience, on the other (in general, see Bruner, 1957).

C H A P T E R   O N E
Introducing Some Unnamables

1. *Différance* is a verb of interplay between signs. According to Derrida, since signs only relate to other signs, and never directly to their supposed referents, there is not, nor can there be, any *real* order outside language. Derrida further suggests that the mere possibility of a sign, of a signifying entity, entails the substitution of the sign for the absent thing in a system of "differences," and this substitution depends upon "deferral"— putting off the grasping of the thing-*as*-itself. Derrida, as mentioned, stresses the primacy of writing over speech, though he appears sometimes to discard any notion of a categorical opposition between writing and speech. Spoken signs are, it is maintained, *ab initio* generated by the articulation of ciphers to become language (*see* Derrida, 1973, 129-60).

2. The sign, says Derrida, is the mark of the absence of a presence (i.e., of the thing). Since this entails invariably and already an absent presence, the sign must be placed "under erasure," for Derrida (1974a, 19) states that "the sign is that ill-named thing, the only one, that escapes the instituting question of philosophy: 'What is . . . ?'" *Is* and *thing* actually should also be "erased" (i.e., by writing them, crossing them out, and printing both the signs and the deletions), for the sign, at the moment of its coming into "being," is *not.*

3. It may be contended that in this inquiry I overuse DC, as well as the *trace, mediacy,* and *play.* That is, I use them in different ways in varying contexts. I can only reply that this is how Derrida uses them also, now as substitutions, now as displacements, or now as *supplement* (i.e., another Derridean *double entendre* which is to supply something for that which is lacking *and* to supply in addition to that which is already there).

4. Derrida's "temporalizing" of the nature of the sign is in part a response to Husserl's (1964) advocation of a mediated *here* and *now,* which, in his book on time-consciousness, he formulates as a duration merging into past and future, entailing both retention and protention. Derrida claims that this concept can never be given; it must be intellectualized or thought—the finite *in* experience which is infinitized *in* thought.

5. It becomes apparent here that DC is not equivalent to the Hegelian differentiation of contradiction by means of dialectics. On the contrary, it is the producer of differentiation, of *dissémination* (the dis-semination of the same, of the sign—Derrida's omniscient punning, with sexual overtones, is apparent here) (See Derrida, 1972a, 12).

6. Although Derrida does not specify physiological and psychological processes nor any distinction between them with respect to DC, we must assume that a differential exists in both. For instance, Wiener (1948, 198) puts forth the claimer that:

[W]hen a visual signal arrives, the muscular activity which it stimulates does not occur at once, but after a certain delay. . . . [T]his delay is not constant, but seems to consist of three parts. One of these parts is of constant length, whereas the other two appear to be uniformly distributed over about 1/10 second. It is as if the central nervous system could pick up incoming impulses only every 1/10 second, and as if the outgoing impulses to the muscles could arrive from the central nervous system only every 1/10 second. This is experimental evidence of a gating [i.e., the logical control organ of computer memory]; and the association of this gating with 1/10 second, which is the approximate period of the central alpha rhythm of the brain, is very probably not fortuitous (brackets mine).

(See Merrell, 1982, for further discussion along these lines.)

7. Derrida's "law of difference" at once reveals the impossibility, within an immanentist view, of a general, all-encompassing law, for this law is constituted by the deferral of any self-differentiation (see Spivak, 1974, xvii).

8. "What we cannot speak about we must pass over in silence" (Wittgenstein, 1961, 7).

9. "One who knows does not speak; one who speaks does not know" (Lao-Tzu, 1963, 117).

10. Interestingly, and in light of this spatialization-temporalization, Derrida (1974a, 70) admits that "in all scientific fields, notably in biology, this notion [of the TC] seems currently to be dominant and irreducible" (brackets mine). I would submit that, on the contrary, much more notable than in biology is the use of this concept in the most fundamental scientific field: quantum mechanics. Bohm (1962, 309–10), on proposing a "topological formulation" of subatomic phenomena, declares:

All we have at any given moment is a trace (or a set of marks) of earlier moments. . . . When any moment *is*, its past is always gone, and what remains of this past is only a trace, . . . Its future is always 'not yet', but is still only a projection or an expectation. Then comes another moment, within which the earlier moment is likewise contained as a trace, while the later moment contains not only a part of what was previously projected, but also something new and not thus projected. . . .
    It follows from the above that the space-time order of events is basically contained *within* each moment, in the sense that this order is implied by the inner structure of any event in the total process. Consider, to begin with, the time order of events. Each moment has within it a trace of earlier moments, while the earlier moments do not have a trace of it. . . . Each moment is therefore *inwardly later* than all those which are traced in it.

Each of Bohm's "moments" is like Derrida's "now" which cannot "be isolated as a pure instant, a pure punctuality" (Derrida, 1973, 61). And Bohm's "traces" in a sense, permit the differentiation of time and space, for they "trace" the "traces" that were there earlier, permitting each event to contain "implicitly its place in space and time" (Bohm, 1962, 310).

11. This concept of a "hierarchical chain of command" involves complex neurophysiological, psychological, and philosophical issues which cannot be adequately pursued here (however, see Merrell, 1982, 1983, for

previous discussions). To cite only a few sources in this area, see the empirical studies of Sperry (1966, 1969, 1970), also the speculations of Abraham (1976) and Dewan (1976), and from the perspective of artificial intelligence studies, the synopsis of Hofstadter (1979).

12. According to Derrida, Western World metaphysics, a "logocentric" philosophy, using "language in such a way that it implies a present "now" distinguishable from past and future "nows," is incapable of describing the "reality" of a process, in which each "now," on becoming "now," "was." However, concerning Derridean philosophy, Said (1978, 685) remarks that: "What, in my opinion, Derrida refers to portentously as Western metaphysics is a *magical* attitude licensed ironically by language and so far as I know is not *necessarily* a Western attitude." It is certainly well known that this "word magic" (i.e., the word taken for the thing, like the map for the territory, in the same "now") is common in all so-called primitive cultures. Korzybski and the general semanticists have launched an attack against such a "magical" attitude toward words in modern society, though in this case the "magic" is not considered to be intentional or conscious. Perhaps Derrida would agree that Western metaphysics has brought about an embedment of this attitude, all consciousness *of* it having been repressed. In this event, his argument takes on new force, yet in the twentieth century it was antedated, and in certain ways more effectively structured, by Korzybski (1933).

13. See Merrell (in press) for extended discussion on the context dependency of all texts (i.e., scientific, philosophical, religious, mythical, artistic, etc.).

14. See, in addition, Apel's (1980) thesis that Peirce wrought a "semiotical transformation of transcendental logic," although in my opinion Apel stretches Peirce's thought a bit when attempting to fit it into his own conception of "transcendental hermeneutics."

15. This Peircean "something," the "object," is not exclusively an object in the material sense. It is, more appropriately speaking, a "mental" object; but it actually is not even an object at all, ordinarily conceived that is. "To eat," "down," and "to want" are representations and hence Peircean objects in the sense that in their use they are parts of expressions referring to concrete experiences. Peirce, a realist, especially during the later stages of his thought, nevertheless maintained that the object of an expression is a thing even though it has no separate mode of physical existence (Peirce, 1960, 3.460). In addition, an expression, such as "James Bond anticipated Dr. No's gesture," has as an object only an imaginary mental world (Peirce, 1960, 5.178).

16. There is little "logocentrism" or "phonocentrism" in Peirce. He directs attention chiefly toward the written sign, especially with respect to two classes of signs in his taxonomy, "propositions" and "arguments" (to be discussed below). These, he claims, and Derrida could hardly disagree, are the highest form of sign.

17. For Derrida's interminable relation of signifiers to signifiers, analogous to Peirce's formulation which Eco (1976, 1979) calls "indefinite semiosis," see Derrida (1973, 89 and 140). It might be contended that Peirce's

triadic concept of signs includes reference, and hence it suffers from the "metaphysics of presence" of the object, or signified, of the sign. For instance, Spivak (1974, xxiii) remarks that Derrida would put the entire notion of semiosis under "erasure." However, as will soon become evident, consciousness is never, and cannot be, immediately conscious *of* the object, of the Peircean sign. And the sign is not interpreted through this object but by means of its relation to other signs in the potentially infinite system. Or in other words, as Buczynska-Garewicz (1982) argues, from the Peircean viewpoint of mediation, or mediacy, the idea of self-evident knowledge or of a perfect beginning is rendered senseless.

18. See Spivak (1974, xvii-xviii) for an exposition of Derrida which bears similarity with Peirce's concepts elucidated here.

19. In this sense Peirce is critical of the Cartesian split between physical objects as extended matter, and the mind as unextended nonmatter. For Peirce, mind, as well as thoughts, are extended continua.

20. Compare to Husserl's mergence, in footnote 4, of past and future into the *here* and *now*, by retention and protention, which, according to Derrida (and Peirce), cannot be immediately present to consciousness.

21. See Merrell (1983) for further discussion.

22. In fact, Derrida (1974a, 49) points out, using Peircean terminology and perhaps even being influenced by Peirce, that: "There is . . . no phenomenality reducing the sign or the representer so that the thing signified may be allowed to glow finally in the luminosity of its presence. The so-called "thing itself" is always already a *representamen* shielded from the simplicity of intuitive evidence. The *representamen* functions only by giving rise to an *interpretant* that itself becomes a sign and so on to infinity."

23. If, as Spivak (1974, xv-xvi) tells us, Derrida appears to nurture no nostalgia for lost origins, Peirce, it seems, believes that the irretrievability of the origin is a foregone conclusion: it is implicit in much of what he writes, so why should he even bother worrying about it.

24. See also Merrell (1983) on the importance of negation for the nature of perception and consciousness spoken about here.

25. Peirce's conception also manifests striking similarity to Young's (1976) formulation in his intriguing book, *The Geometry of Meaning*, where he attempts to bring together, as does Peirce, and as we shall observe below, continuous and discontinuous domains.

26. According to Peirce (1960, 6.193) "we cannot suppose [that] the process of derivation [of the First Mark], a process which extends from before time and from before logic . . . began elsewhere than in the utter vagueness of completely undetermined and dimensionless potentiality" (second brackets mine). And, much like Peirce, and Spencer-Brown, Derrida points out that as soon as a sign emerges, it "begins" by repeating itself. That is, if the terminology of this inquiry is interjected into Derrida's notion, the sign cannot *be* until it is *in* consciousness, but its *being* always entails a delay and a repetition *of* itself. Without such repetition it would not be a sign, it would not be the non-self-identity, the DC, which it refers to another sign.

27. Compare to Bohm's comments in footnote 10 on the "trace" in his proposed formulation of quantum theory.

28. A more accessible counterpart to Spencer-Brown's complex algebra of *marks* is found in Peirce, to be discussed in section seven of this chapter.

29. Peirce's primordial potentiality is also comparable to the *Tao* of Lao-Tzu and to the field of potentiality *(Asat)* of the *Rg Veda*, which is undifferentiated and unactualized and from which all substance and life emerge by a process of differentiation from unity.

30. Derrida (1974a, 63) elsewhere puts forth the claim that: "Difference is therefore the formation of the form." Obviously he has here some notion of form, though this tangential comment is not meant to be a valid critique of Derrida.

31. Actually, the impossibility of avoiding all traditional metaphysical jargon must be admitted, for if we could do so, what kind of world would we have? No two words spoken by two people would have the same or even similar meanings. Solipsism would inexorably prevail. There would be nothing more than pure randomness, pure noise, a chaotic Babel of strange tongues, which could not really be called tongues, and which would not even be strange, since even strangeness presupposes familiarity with something. Nothing would be really meaningful, all would be reduced to one level. Yet this chaos would be tantamount to an absolute, plenary, fortuitous, and gratuitous *play*: total randomness in this sense would become synonymous with infinite order, the extremes would trace out a full circle to meet, discontinuity would infiltrate continuity, and vice versa. Any attempt to escape all conventional language use is utopian.

32. Wisely, and commensurate with Derridean thought, Peirce advises that we not allow his assertions to "interfere with or be interfered with by any religious belief. Religion is a practical matter. Its beliefs are formulae you will go upon. But a scientific proposition is merely something you take up provisionally as being the proper hypothesis to try first and endeavor to refute" (Peirce, 1960, 6.216). The similarity between certain of Peirce's views and the scientific epistemology of Popper, to be discussed in chapter two, is worthy of note. And this, we shall see, provides another point of convergence with Derrida.

33. This topic will be given more importance in chapter seven.

34. Peirce often promised a "logic of relatives" but never produced a concise system as such, only a few bits and pieces here and there in his writings, addresses, and letters, much of which are being organized under the direction of Max Fisch, general editor of the "Peirce Edition Project."

35. An element of quality "appears on the inside as unity," but when viewed from the outside, it "is seen as variety" (Peirce, (1960, 6.236). For the person seeing everything in the same shade of blue, there is no duality.

36. This is, by the way, a supposed counterargument by Abel (1974) and Abrams (1977).

37. Compare to James (1977, 96-97): "Reality, life, experience, concreteness, immediacy, use what word you will, exceeds our logic, overflows and surrounds it. If you like to employ words eulogistically, as most men do, and so encourage confusion, you may say that reality obeys a higher logic, or enjoys a higher rationality."

As we shall see, Peirce tries, with as little confusion as possible, to formulate this "higher logic."

38. See Laszlo (1972) on the notion of *successive differentiation* of all entities such that a system inevitably evolves toward a state of "organized complexity," and toward "negentropy."

39. Like this boundary, Derrida's *thought of* a TC escapes binarism, but it makes binarism possible on the basis of nothing. And like Derrida's DC, it is "yet" neither "inner" nor "outer," for they do not exist until some-*thing* has been actualized and set *apart from* some-*thing* else (see Derrida, 1978a, 230).

40. To speculate, it may well be that "presence" is a "commonsensical" notion found in most or perhaps all societies, Western and non-Western alike, and at conscious or tacit levels. What is at one point in time "commonsensical" can in reality conceal a more profound aspect of "reality." Witness the everyday conception of Newtonian space and time as opposed to the strange, but more subtle Einsteinian space-time continuum, for example. Much Eastern thought also reveals the fallacy in "commonsensical" notions such as "identity" and "presence." Derrida, on bringing a deeper "reality" to our attention, has, as we shall see, paralleled the path of many Western innovators, especially in the sciences.

41. For Peirce's formulation from which the following was drawn, see Peirce (1960, 6.402).

42. This formulation is derived from Peirce's "logic of relatives" and Henry M. Sheffer's "stroke function" which are fundamental to modern logic and to modern variations of Boolean algebra (see Singh, 1966; Spencer-Brown, 1979; Whitehead, 1938; Whitehead and Russell, 1927). Interestingly enough, Whitehead and Russell (1927, xvi) demonstrated that the logical connectives ($\lor, \land, \rightarrow, \leftrightarrow$) can be defined by the "stroke," and subsequently it is possible to "construct new propositions indefinitely." Moreover, since the "stroke" implies incompatibility or inconsistency in the most fundamental sense, Whitehead (1938, 52) tells us that it provides for "the whole movement of logic" (as Derrida speaks of DC). And Hutten (1962, 178) remarks, with respect to the "stroke," that: "It is the very essence of rationality to abolish contradictions; but logic—being the most rational thing in the world—is generated by contradiction." (This should be an interesting revelation for the deconstructionist.)

43. Derrida's DC, like this "cut," is at one point defined as the "primordial constituting causality," we must suppose that is, with respect to the Peircean continuum (Derrida, 1973, 173).

44. Interestingly enough, Peirce's "book of assertions" contains in a certain manner the depth of an inconceivable Freudian "mystic writing pad" without a bottom (compare to Derrida, 1978a, 223-24, on speaking of the bottomless nature of the "mystic writing pad.")

45. Perhaps there is no acceptable answer to this problem because any answer must be an appendage to what simply *is*. If an observer becomes one with the observed there can be, in *simultaneity*, no description, no answer, no talk. Yet Eddington (1958b, 260) in this respect tells us that: "*There is nothing to prevent the assemblage of atoms constituting a brain*

from being of itself a thinking object in virtue of that nature which phys-ics leaves undetermined and undeterminable . . . a nature capable of man-ifesting itself as mental activity."

Though Eddington was once written off as a "mystic" in certain scien-tific circles, this and other of his seemingly bizarre ideas, as we shall observe below, are now being seriously considered by avant-garde physi-cists. In a complementary vein, Derrida once remarked that: "I didn't say that there was no center, that we could get along without the center. I believe that the center is a function, not a being—a reality, but a function. And this function is absolutely indispensable. The subject is absolutely in-dispensable. I don't destroy the subject; I situate it. That is to say, I believe that at a certain level both of experience and of philosophical and scientific discourse one cannot get along without the notion of subject" (Macksey and Donato, eds., 1970, 271).

Derrida seems to believe that the subject is absolutely essential for there to be some-*thing* that is perceived *as*-such-and-such, for if not, there could hardly be any distinction, or "cut." All would be unity. However, the fact is that Derrida situates, or decenters, the subject, focusing on language and written signs in terms of their interrelations. He appears generally to ignore the above-mentioned paradox of the subject's becoming a subject.

CHAPTER TWO
Whose Science Are We Speaking of When We Speak of Science?

1. Compare this Derridean notion to the discussion in section seven of chapter one where it was suggested that inconsistency underlies the possi-bility of all logic. This by no means indicates that we should abolish logic, only that, as we shall observe below, we should constantly be aware of the limitations inherent in all logical and mathematical formulations.

2. According to Hesla (1971), and as we shall observe in chapter seven, this is precisely the summation of Beckett's trilogy: an elaborate set of uncertain affirmations and negations the totality of which approaches nothingness—a balanced equation.

3. This antinomy, to which I also refer in footnote 31 of chapter one, will be discussed further in chapter four when the concept of infinity is treated. For the moment it is worthy of note that Hans's (1981, 101) critique of Derrida complements the notion presented here. Speaking of the decon-structive "method," he suggests that it: "seems to undercut any notion of freeplay to begin with . . . How is freeplay indeterminate if it is so eminent-ly determinable through deconstruction? Granted, Derrida is focusing attention on texts given to the chain of ontotheological substitutions, but this is a choice he himself has made—one that at this point is surely in need of its own turn toward a joyous affirmation of indeterminacy, not toward determinacy."

The contradiction inherent in the deconstructive "method," determinism *and* indeterminacy, is precisely that of, by extrapolation, the infinitely structured (determined) which is at once infinite chaos (indeterminable).

4. In this light, Lentricchia (1980, 182) queries:

[H]ave the Derrideans practiced a new unfettered formalism, or have they established a new allegory founded upon the rock of a new center, a "single root," a "single sense," a "single source" of determinacy, a new transcendental signified called the abyss? In theory, the abyss is itself abyssed, and therefore cannot serve as a point of presence. But somewhere along the line a judgment will need to be made about the practice of the Derrideans; a judgment as to whether their essays on Rousseau, Nietzsche, Stevens, Swinburne, and others, do not repeat the same point, do not allegorize texts from the perspective of the *aporia*, over and over in very predictable ways, and with a heavy-handedness reminiscent of mythographic and structuralist critics.

This question will be the focus of later sections.

5. It bears mentioning that Einstein has been criticized for his insistence on an absolutely objective frame of reference (see Popper's comments on Einstein, 1974a). However, as Hans (1981, 101) asserts: "One could argue that Derrida's thought would not be possible without the quantum theory, without the uncertain principle which, combined with relativity theory in general, was the first real move toward the decentered universe to which Derrida is committed. But regardless of how outlandishly language-oriented Einstein's thought might have been, it was also connected to a level of phenomena that could confirm or deny his theories." Significantly, the relationship between Derrida, quantum mechanics, and Einstein, as well as the denial (i.e., falsification) of theories will be precisely the focus of this and other chapters.

6. The Copenhagen interpretation, whose chief proponents include Heisenberg and Bohr, is now the most widely accepted, and conventional, among physicists today. According to this view, what we perceive to be the "physical world" is no more than a sort of happy meeting ground between "possibility and reality" (Heisenberg, 1958, 41). That is, what is potentially "matter" consists in a "wave function"—a mathematical fiction representing a set of probabilities—which, when interacted with (i.e., "observed") "collapses" into a "particle." "Matter," in this sense, cannot be defined *either* as "waves" *or* "particles," for it can intermittently possess the characteristics of both, but not in simultaneity. This is in essence Heisenberg's "uncertainty principle," and it entails a necessary interaction between "observer" and "observed." In spite of the contradictory nature of this view of quantum mechanics, the Copenhagen physicists decided, strangely enough, to accept it as a complete theory even though it cannot tell us what the "real world" is actually like (that is, it is capable of predicting probabilities, but not actual events). Bohm, and other physicists, in contrast, believe the Copenhagen interpretation to be incomplete. Consequently, they have continued their search for "hidden variables" underlying the

Copenhagen interpretation capable of rendering a more adequate account of the universe.

7. "Sign" is used here in the sense of the actualization of a "particle-event" as a result of interaction with another "particle-event." In microphysics, information is defined as the transmission of messages between subatomic "particles" such that "events" (i.e., changes) occur.

8. Bohm (1951, 169-70) suggests further that all thoughts make up an indivisible continuous flow, potentially infinite in extension, a notion very close to Peirce's sign continuum.

9. Peirce always insisted emphatically that, since the mind should not be isolated from the whole of nature, in the workings of the mind we have the clues to the workings of nature. This notion is closely tied to what he calls the *abductive* process which provides man with the "faculty of divining the ways of nature" (Peirce, 1960, 5.173).

10. For example, a young man learns, by explicit instructions from his driving instructor, how to drive a car. However, once behind the wheel, these explicit rules must be coordinated with motor skills, reflexes, and common sense, which at the outset requires a great deal of concentration. After becoming a proficient driver, in contrast, he now has no need of the rules, for his moves have become by and large implicit, automatic, embedded in his mind. He need no longer think *about* them when in the act of driving.

11. However, elsewhere, Chew remarks that much science as it is known today retains certain remnants of nineteenth-century teleological absolutism, and hence it requires a language based on some unquestionable framework. No given theoretical model derived from such a science can be entirely satisfactory, for, in reality, there can be potentially a "limitless variety of partially successful models" (Chew, 1970, 26).

12. Chew himself states that: "A physicist who is able to view any number of different partially successful models without favoritism is automatically a bootstrapper" (Chew, 1970, 27).

13. Significantly, Eddington (1958a, 244) points out, and he is one of the first to do so, that the mind knows nature through subjective conjectural acts, and hence it can regain from nature no more than it puts into nature. Along these lines, Wigner (1970, 171-84) states that a consistent theory of the quantum level cannot be forthcoming without the inclusion of and reference to consciousness, for ultimately the knower is at one with the known.

14. This Borgesian quote is the epigraph to a collection of essays on the "many worlds interpretation of quantum mechanics" (De Witt and Graham, 1973). As will become evident, it conveys a very concise image of the universe according to this interpretation!.

15. This *simultaneity* is not that against which Derrida, reacted. As will be observed below, such *simultaneity* can only exist in a domain other than that which is present to consciousness *of* or seeing *as*—i.e., in the domain of potentials rather than actuals.

16. *Simultaneously* is used here in a contradictory sense, for it is, logically speaking, and in light of DC and MC, impossible for an "observer" to

separate itself from the "observed" *and* "observe" the "observed" *simultaneously.* Yet somehow, contradictorily, unspeakably, and unthinkably, it must be done. So we must admit that it *is* possible.

17. The "observer," according to modern physics, is not necessarily a human being, but can be any part of the universe interacting with any other part.

18. See, from various perspectives, Gribbin (1979), Toben (1975), White (1977), and Progoff (1973), and for a more technical treatment, Wheeler (1973).

19. In this light, Wheeler (1973, 151-52) tells us that: "Instead of founding quantum mechanics upon classical physics, the "relative state" [i.e., "many worlds"] formulation uses a completely different kind of model for physics. This new model has a character all of its own; is conceptually self-contained; defines its own possibilities for interpretation; and does not require for its formulation any reference to classical concepts (brackets mine)."

20. In other words, what I am implying is that the deconstructionists in general are relatively conservative. Even the most scandalizing notions among the deconstructionists, or for that matter the avant-garde humanists—for example, that "language as differentiation and as knowledge bears no necessary correspondence to reality" (Said, 1975, 38)—seems pale in comparison to the "new physics."

21. It has already been admitted that the "new physicists" discussed here have not received universal acceptance, even in their own fields. Their speculative hypotheses, though an attempt to remedy what they perceived to be the inadequacy of the Copenhagen interpretation, are at this point either not fully verified empirically or they are blatantly unverifiable. Perhaps it is a tribute to the scientific community that the scientists tend to view all new hypotheses with reversed skepticism. This is unfortunately not the case many times in the humanities, where new ideas are usually either categorically rejected, or, if emanating from venerable anointed priests of a given cult, are uncritically embraced. Obviously we are relatively more gullible than the scientists, though, as Feyerabend (1975) reveals, the same cultism persists even in the sciences.

22. Admittedly, structuralists and neo-structuralists such as Barthes (1971, 9-10) claim vehemently that there is nothing that will more surely kill research than a fixed method. However, method, as they refer to it, is generally that of the nineteenth-century science, and even of positivism during the present century. Graff (1979) rightly maintains that Bloom, de Man, Derrida, Miller, and Hartman misconceive positivism, assuming it still to be the vogue among scientists. In reality, the heyday of positivism is now history, as almost all scientists will tell us. In spite of this, perhaps the present infatuation with deconstruction is ultimately for the wrong reasons. Since deconstruction can, though naively, be reduced to a small set of rules for discovering a text's *aporia*—though this comment does not discount my own "reduction" of deconstruction on pages 52 and 53 of this chapter— it seems that, as Donaghue (1980, 41) remarks, there is "a suggestion of scientific method in Deconstruction which appeals to graduate students who have begun to doubt that the Humanities constitute a discipline."

In contrast, Norris (1982, 98), referring to Hartman in particular and the Yale critics in general, states that: "This is deconstruction 'on the wild side', a criticism that thrives on Derrida's example but rarely seeks to emulate his rigour of argument. Hartman can defend his all-embracing rhetoric by invoking Derrida's powerful deconstructions of philosophical texts. From here it is a short step to the general idea that philosophy is simply another variety of literature, a text pervaded by the same rules of figuration."

Actually, it seems, deconstruction "can only be as useful and enlightening as the mind that puts it to work" (Norris, 1982, 91).

23. Compare Popper's refutation to Peirce's quote in footnote 32 of chapter one. See also, for a comparison of Peirce and Popper, Rescher (1978), and Freeman and Skolimowski (1974).

24. Popper contrasts Einstein to Freud, Adler and Jung. The former, "said that if the red shift effect (the slowing down of atomic clocks in strong gravitational fields) was not observed in the case of white dwarfs, his theory of general relativity would be refuted. No description whatsoever of any logically human behavior can be given which would turn out to be incompatible with the psychoanalytic theories of Freud, or of Adler, or of Jung" (Popper, 1972, 38, n. 5).

25. However, see a critique of Popper's critique of metaphysical hypotheses in Grünbaum (1979) and O'Hear (1980). See also Fried and Agassi (1976) and Agassi (1977).

26. Similarly, Hutten (1962, 222), another philosopher of science, points out that: "Every theory must contain some error if it is to be true. If it did not, it would be impossible to correct it by later experience and more advanced theories. Such a theory would, in fact, be closed itself or belong to a closed system: it would be a pseudo-theory."

27. If, in the sense of Derrida, the TC is defined as an absence within us which is ineffable, then we are in a Platonic dilemma of having to attempt to "say what *is not*." However, this becomes no irremediable problem for Popper, for what *is not* a theory must, by refuting that theory and replacing it with an alternative, over time become the articulation of what *is*, which once again contains, implicitly as it were, what *is not*. Ineffability has become, at least partly, effable.

28. Perhaps one reason for Popper and Derrida appearing to be similar yet the inverse of one another is because the latter's critique of Husserl is against a form of science which was almost in its totality rejected by Popper. For example, Husserl assumed that scientific ideas-theories were timeless and univocally true (Derrida, 1978b, 82). For Popper, in contrast, the meanings of words can over time never be clear, and hence theories are constantly changing. Moreover, all theories are no more than interpretations, and to understand a theory, over time, like deconstructing a text, is an "infinite task" (Popper, 1974a, 28).

29. This reaction to language analysis and precise definitions of all terms is part of Popper's criticism of logical positivism. The positivists start with established scientific theories, accepting them as true, and then begin

clearing up minute problems of language use so as to axiomatize the entire system.

30. In fact, says Popper, an eventual move to increase clarity must be *ad hoc*, piecemeal, for absolute communication can never occur. It cannot occur because of a lack of precise meanings, for it is *"impossible to speak in such a way that you cannot be misunderstood"* (Popper, 1974a, 30). This is necessarily so, because, commensurate with Derrida, there is, and there can be, no absolute identity of meaning.

31. *"Never let yourself be goaded into taking seriously problems about words and their meanings. What must be taken seriously are questions of fact, and assertions about facts: theories and hypotheses; the problems they solve; and the problems they raise"* (Popper, 1974a, 19).

32. However, Popperian "hermeneutics" is not that of most phenomenologists. In the first place, Popper is interested only in reconstruction of the text's problem situation, not in its univocal meaning. And in the second place, for Popper, there can be no fixed norms for determining correct from incorrect interpretations. We are not capable of generating *the one and only true meaning of a text.* Instead of norms, *ad hoc* assumptions must be posited, and then subjected to critical inquiry. On the other hand, for a good example of the problems inherent in applying Popperian "hermeneutics," see Hirsch (1967), who obviously uses many of Popper's ideas.

33. It might also appear that another clash between Popper and Derrida lies in the former's "realism." One might claim that Popper's science is referential while Derrida's conception of texts, or of the world for that matter, is that of self-referentiality. Yet in the final analysis, as Popper is prone to believe and as we shall see in chapter three, science, with its emphasis on conjectures more than on observations, and on critical and logical refutation more than on meaning in a positive sense, is also over the long haul self-referential.

34. For a discussion of "quantum logic" accessible to the layperson, see Heelan (1970a, 1971). "Quantum logic" will be treated in further detail in chapter seven.

35. It is interesting to speculate on the reasons for which Popper's disciples have one by one, and on distant grounds, set about intellectually to castrate their master, while this has not occurred among the Derrideans. Could it be that Popper's open method itself encourages criticism, refutation, and even a form of "deconstruction," while Derrida's convoluted style and occult anti-method foments a mystical cult of adulators? It is too soon to know, of course, since the Derridean converts are relatively recent.

36. Actually, science, as well as the humanities, has been traditionally defended by small groups which held their own standards as sacrosanct and all others taboo. Certainly, special professions such as science, philosophy, and literary criticism must set up certain norms, otherwise there could be no professionals. But these norms need not be absolute and immune to change. When viewing the history of mankind, there is not a single norm which can remain valid under all conditions; madness can become reason, given changing circumstances. Hence "reason" and "logic," as well as

"irreason" and "illogic," must eventually join other abstractions which can potentially lead toward dogmatism such as writing and speech, nature and culture, etc.

37. See Derrida's (1974b) essay on metaphor.

38. The problem here is that the deconstructionist's "center," unlike Popper's "bold conjectures," is established *a priori*. That is, the "center"— the point in the text revealing the "metaphysics of presence"—is preconceived, and it is determinately there, though not yet opened to view.

39. Significantly, if a system is inconsistent (i.e., "falsified"), it becomes capable of producing any and all truths; that is, future hypotheses.

40. This being the case, the rules of formal logic do not, and can never, exactly apply. The scientist consequently, and whether he realizes it or not, "usually develops a *practical logic* that permits him to get results amidst chaos and incoherence. Most of the rules and standards of this *practical logic* are conceived *ad hoc*, they serve to remove a particular difficulty and it is not possible to turn them into an organon of research" (Feyerabend, 1978, 199). Feyerabend shortly afterward quotes Einstein's familiar comment that the scientists, working with *ad hoc* rules and methods, must appear to the epistemologist as "unscrupulous opportunists." If successful, then, the scientist, like the deconstructionist, must know all the tricks.

41. Immediately it is observed that most obviously Feyerabend believes it is possible to escape the system of conventional reason, logic and methods, and it might be said in extension, metaphysics. Though Feyerabend's means of accomplishing this task might be considered debatable, the objective in later sections of this inquiry will be to outline as concisely as possible how such a step "outside" may be possible.

42. In general the "paradigm" or "*Weltanschauung*" hypothesis follows this notion of incommensurability, whose chief proponents, besides Feyerabend, are Kuhn (1970a), Polanyi (1958), Toulmin (1953), and Hanson (1958). See also Suppe (1977) for an excellent survey.

43. Deconstructive critics, as pointed out by Gasché (1979), adhere to an "incommensurability" of sorts between literary theories and interpretations. However, Gasché rightly questions whether this "incommensurability" is indeed as acute as they claim.

44. This for Feyerabend was the problem of the Copenhagen interpretation, which fused aspects of classical physics with Einsteinian physics.

45. However, this does not imply that the larger framework is capable of generating a neutral language with which to translate the terms of the smaller frameworks into one another. There can be no synthesis in the full sense, only, so to speak, oscillation from one frame to another, or better said, to the many: a multiple "double-bind."

46. But see Norris (1983) for distinctions between the later Wittgenstein and Derrida.

47. Although generally in agreement with this formulation, elsewhere (Merrell, in press) I argue that there is always some semantic "overlap" between even the most radically contradictory theories (see also other critiques of this "radical meaning variance" theory from diverse perspectives

in Achinstein, 1968; Kordig, 1971; Phillips, 1973, 1977; Scheffer, 1967; Trigg, 1973). However, since the objective here is to survey Feyerabend and relate his view to that of Derrida, let us accept him at face value for the moment.

48. De Man (1971, 144) suggests that: "However negative it may sound, deconstruction implies the possibility of rebuilding." Perhaps we can go no further than stating such a possibility. If deconstructive rather than merely destructive, deconstruction, as a negative theology, as a negative diacritical approach, lays bare the terrain for future erection of a new edifice, but it thus far has hardly created any definite image of that edifice.

49. This, once again, is no legitimate critique of deconstruction. It is surprising however that the same sin against either "reason" or "irreason," whichever the case may be, is nothing new, even in the sciences. It has been common practice in the Western World for centuries.

50. The deconstructionist might cite as the best example of "irrational" discourse Derrida's (1977) reply to Searle in GLYPH 2. This, however, is a very reasoned "irrationalism," a refusal to meet the opponent on his own grounds, and an oblique attack from an incommensurable and unexpected framework. Feyerabend would likely have little patience with such "methods."

C H A P T E R   T H R E E
Deconstruction Meets a Mathematician

1. Miller (1976a) refers to the Yale crowd—himself, de Man, Bloom, and Hartman, and including Derrida—as the "uncanny critics" whose radicalism sets them apart not only from "reasoned criticism," but from the entire stream of Western World metaphysics. However, as we have noted provisionally, and as will be illustrated further, these critics are actually quite conservative when compared to some contemporary physicists and the maverick philosophers of science.

2. This "logic of undecidables" is, as was argued in chapter two, like a circle. Meanings pass into one another, "simultaneously," and *ad infinitum* (see Derrida, 1972a, 207).

3. In this light, interestingly enough, Hans (1981, 101) tells us that instead of creating a "negative theology," as most deconstructionists assert, Derrida: "has mapped out a new direction by thematizing the old one. He has simply become caught up in his own rhetoric, and this has left him flat in the midst of his own kinds of predictability and security—not by design but rather because his view itself precludes anything that would give it fresh nourishment."

4. On the other hand, Said (1978, 702) suggests that the general appeal of deconstruction stems not from any clear-cut method, for there should be none, given deconstructionist premises. Rather, the technique seems pedagogically easily teachable, diffusable, and practicable. One must learn only a relatively small set of terms with no precise meanings which can be used in a variety of ways. Jakobson's (1960) sextet of terms, derived from communication theory, and Burke's (1973) pentad have held a similar attrac-

tion. In either case, the "method" appears at the outset lax enough that one can pick and choose what happens to fit best at the moment; there is apparently no rigid heuristic. However, it must be remembered that, as was pointed out above, the actual merit of the "method" ultimately depends on the skill of the deconstructor. But cannot the same be said of Popper and Feyerabend's ideal scientist?

5. In this respect Pfeffer (1972, 103) remarks that: "The sciences, precisely as Nietzsche had urged and anticipated with profound clarity, repudiated the possibility of rational certainty and predictable causality, and acknowledged the need for a revision of the meaning and function of truth. With the discoveries of Heisenberg concerning the principles of physics and Goedel concerning mathematical ambiguity, the sciences have arrived at the state where they breed paradoxes for reason itself."

6. It must be conceded that, with the notions of DC, MC, and the TC, a critique of *simultaneity* is also implied (see especially Derrida, 1974a, 85; 1978a, 3-30). This is further evidence that Derrida is part of a broad-based transformation in the Western world-view.

7. "Gödel" is rapidly becoming a "buzz word." His theorems, though in a way quite simple, require for their proof an exceedingly complex formulation the complete understanding of which, I must admit, is beyond my grasp, and beyond the full comprehension of all but a few specialists. Recently, however, some excellent expositions of Gödel's theorems have appeared. Among the most accessible are Bronowski (1966, 1978), Bernstein (1978), Quine (1962) and Smullyan (1978). Hofstadter (1979) gives a very extensive review, relating Gödel to art, music, language, and artificial intelligence research. More difficult and relatively technical reviews are found in Nagel and Newman (1958) and DeLong (1971).

8. Significantly, Hutten (1956, 36–37) points out how undecidability involves meaning and hence semantics. Furthermore, with respect to scientific knowledge, he tells us that: "Gödel's theorem, far from being a catastrophe, has emphasized the semantic character of scientific theory, and so provided a better insight into the formal structure of a system. And it shows up what we may call the 'piecemeal method of science': we can never set up a single universal, comprehensive system of knowledge which contains all the knowledge there is."

9. It is appropriate here to mention that Derrida demonstrates some familiarity with Gödel's proof, though he does not directly acknowledge the fact (see especially Derrida, 1978b, 53-54; 1978a, 162; 1972a, 248-49; 1980).

10. Popper (1974a, 131) referring to Gödel, reveals that:

[T]he evolution of physics is likely to be an endless process of correction and better approximation. And even if one day we should reach a stage where our theories were no longer open to correction, since they were simply true, they would still not be complete—and we would know it. For Gödel's famous incompleteness theorem would come into play: in view of the mathematical background of physics, at best an infinite sequence of such true theories would be needed in order to answer the problems which in any given (formalized) theory would be undecidable.

11. Gödel's proof, it must be mentioned, does not apply to all formal systems. It has been demonstrated that certain systems, such as elementary Boolean algebra, are decidable (Spencer-Brown, 1979). More complex systems, however, are not.

12. For example, complementing Gödel's demonstration that there are undecidable formulas, Alonso Church proved that there are no decision procedures for certain systems. A. M. Turing along similar lines showed the incomputability of computer systems, and ultimately, of the human "computer," and Tarski proved that truth is not definable within a system but only from within its respective meta-system, a notion which bears similarity to Gödel's incompleteness theorem. In combination, these "limitative theorems" demonstrate that "every axiomatic system of any mathematical richness is subject to severe limitations, whose incidence cannot be foreseen and yet which cannot be circumvented" (Bronowski, 1966, 4; see also Stent, 1978, 191-205, on the limitations of human knowledge).

13. Interestingly enough, Peirce's admonishings were obviously forgotten, or ignored, at the turn of the century when, under Hilbert's program, there was an attempt to reduce all mathematics to logical formulations.

14. In this respect see also Musès (1972) and Ullmo (1964).

15. In other words, this would be precisely the state of affairs that, according to Kuhn, Feyerabend, and other "paradigm" philosophers of science, has always prevailed between incommensurable theories.

16. Of course there are obvious differences between music and language, on the one hand, and mathematics and language on the other (see Merrell, 1981, for a brief discussion).

17. See also note 14 of this chapter.

18. Popper, it bears mentioning, calls himself a "realist." Unlike Gödel and many contemporary "idealistic" scientists, he maintains belief in a complete and real world. What is incomplete and indeterminate is our effort to understand that world.

19. According to Schlegel (1967, 192), both in our attempt to know the natural world and in the expression of this knowledge in language, there are "limitations on completeness of knowledge when the describing tool, be it elementary particle or logical proposition, becomes the same as that which we are describing." By analogy, the same can be said of the language of metaphysics and art, or the mind's attempting to understand its own working. I believe Derrida would agree here.

20. On the nature of all imaginary worlds or fictions (i.e., artistic, scientific, mathematical, mythical, etc.), see Merrell (1983).

21. With respect to Derrida's notion of *supplement* (simultaneously a completion and an addition to), it has been pointed out that there can always be a *supplement* to a *supplement* no end. This might appear similar to the frame switching referred to here by means of which, presumably, the deconstructor's "double-bind" might be resolved. However, firstly, the Derridean use of "double-bind" excludes any permanent solution, and secondly, human finitude (and fallibility) cancels the possibility of a given individual's or a collection of individuals' reaching the ultimate, self-sufficient frame.

22. See Polanyi (1958, 1966) on focal and subsidiary or peripheral awareness, which I employ in constructing a theory of fiction perception (Merrell, 1979, 1983, in press).

23. For example, Abrams (1977, 435) remarks that: "the deconstructive method works, because it can't help working; it is a can't fail enterprise, there is no complex passage of verse or prose which could possibly serve as a counterinstance to test its validity or limits. And the uncanny critic, whatever the distinctiveness of the text to which he applies his strategies, is bound to find that they all reduce to one thing and one thing only."

24. See Schrödinger's (1961) article, one of the most penetrating, on the inexact nature of science.

25. Of course it is by now clear that the *deconstructive principle* bears similarity with the Gödelian paradox.

26. Goldbach conjectured that every even number is the sum of two primes. For instance, $10 = 7 + 3, 20 = 13 + 7, 26 = 17 + 9$, and so on. Fermat's theorem is that: $X^{n+2} + Y^{n+2} = Z^{n+2}$ where X, Y, Z, and n are variables existing within the range of natural numbers. Much time has been dedicated to these problems, but solutions (i.e., proofs) have not been found.

27. Derrida (1978b, 56) significantly reveals the indeterminacy of the decidability of the *deconstructive principle:* "[W]hat is mathematical determinability in general, if the undecidability of a proposition, for example, is still a mathematical determination? Essentially, such a question cannot expect a determined response, it should only indicate the pure openness and unity of an infinite horizon."

28. Musès (1972, 111) remarks that: "Just as the deepest meaning of number is qualitative, so the deepest mathematics is also qualitative, as topologists were among the first to suspect." Of course the arts and the humanities are qualitative throughout, and at a certain qualitative level we can assume that they share commonality with mathematics and the sciences. This is, precisely, the level of the *pre-rational decision* referred to here.

29. Lakatos, in his very interesting book, *Proofs and Refutations* (1976), debunks the traditional notion of absolute proofs in mathematics. Admittedly, his hypothesis does not appear to have acquired unanimous support among mathematicians. But, then, this is further testimony that some mathematicians, like some scientists and logicians, can be as conservative as most humanists.

30. Along these lines, and according to Leitch (1983, 251), the fact that: "every text lends itself to deconstruction and to further deconstruction, with nowhere any end in sight, generates a structure of aporia. So too does the insight that no escape outside the logocentric enclosure is possible since the interpreter must use the concepts and figures of the Western metaphorical tradition. And the experience of the unavailability to discourse of a literal bottom or undifferentiated ground leads to a version of aporia. There's no way out. Interpretation is endless."

C H A P T E R   F O U R
Immanence Knows No Boundaries

1. Significantly, the paradoxes of Zeno, "in some form, have afforded grounds for almost all the theories of space and time and infinity which have been constructed from his day to our own" (Russell, 1926, 183).

2. For example, Parmenides' description of "being" bears no similarity to ordinary experience. In fact, it denies time as well as particulars: "What is is uncreated and imperishable, for it is entire, immovable and without end. It was not in the past, nor shall it be, since it is not, all at once, continuous. ... Now it is divisible, since it is all alike; nor is there more here and less there, which would prevent it from cleaving together, but it is full of what it is. So it is all continuous" (Kirk and Raven, 1957, 273-75).

3. It seems that Derrida is Heraclitean in the sense of Nietzsche's Dionysian world of "eternal self-creation, of self-destruction" (Nietzsche, 1913, 432). Moreover, with respect to the emphasis on writing, Heraclitus preceded Derrida, for according to Kahn (1979, 3); "In a literary age which we think of as still primarily 'oral', Heraclitus' influence made itself felt exclusively through the power of the written word." Yet Heraclitus, unlike Derrida, is still close to the standard archaic view of language that truth is embodied in names and is available to whoever knows how to read their meaning.

4. It also bears mentioning here that Sartre (1966, 83), before Derrida, refuted the notion of an experienced plenary presence. The experience of communication at the precise instant of communication is impossible, because the subject's "now" is not identical to the object's "now." They are apart in time, separated by an almost-infinitesimal instant by at least the speed of light and by the duration of neuronal firings in the brain. Nor can the simple present be experienced introspectively, in solitude, as Beckett's characters tell us. This denial of presence is actually also a necessary outgrowth of relativism, as reported by Einstein, that "there is no such thing as simultaneity, there is no such thing as 'not,' independent of a system of reference" (Barnett, 1968, 48).

5. Of course, there is a difference between Popper's use of "repetitions" and that of Derrida. Popper never relates the term to the equivalent of signifier-signified; it always and exclusively involves experience of language and of the world. For Derrida, on the other hand, it would appear that there can be no real deductive logic. Rather than inductive repetition—identities—from which a generality can be arrived at, there are only differences. And instead of deduction, there is only presupposition-laden rhetoric with no ultimate and ultimately true axioms—no "center." Derrida, as will be discussed below, is a sort of super-empiricist. For him what *is* experienced at the moment is simply all there *is*. But, as we shall see also, this super-empiricism does not escape some of the problems of induction.

6. Derrida's (1974a, 66-67) temporal and temporalizing aspect of the TC, however, does not exactly fit into Popper's conception with respect to

non-human organisms. The animal organism, according to Popper, has no consciousness *of* repetition, *of* past and therefore *of* future, at least in the human sense. Consciousness *of* past and future, and *of* repetition, is not possible without a human experience of time and a propensity consciously for abstracting, and without some capacity for making judgments. But at some level the animal organism possesses at least the rudiments of such a capacity. Bateson (1972) tells about experiments in which a dog is trained to distinguish between a circle and an oval, and then when the two forms are changed so as to appear more and more alike, the animal loses its ability to distinguish between them and even manifests "neurotic" tendencies. *Order became chaos*, for it lost its ability to abstract. Beckett's anti-hero becomes "lost," similarly, when two things become nearly identical. This process can be reversed. For example, Jakobson and Halle (1956) point out that learning a language entails the increasing ability to differentiate and to perceive differentiation between previously undifferentiable sounds—*chaos becoming order*, for the proper abstraction is now possible. As mentioned above, maximum noise (lack of abstraction and differentiation) completes the cycle to become perceived as sameness, even identity.

7. At one point, Derrida (1973, 135), like Bohm, does imply, though vaguely, how his own scheme might itself be deconstructed and replaced by a more general alternative.

8. Very definitely, Bohm and other contemporary physicists proceed beyond "objectivism and relativism," which, according to R. Bernstein (1983), characterizes the general spirit of our times.

9. This charge of nihilism against deconstruction is common. Actually it is oversimplistic, a blow below the belt. Many deconstructionists have never ceased to reiterate their defense of deconstruction as non-nihilistic (see especially Miller, 1979). In all honesty, and without extending the discussion, here, I tend to agree.

10. These *differences* for Leibniz, called *differentials* in modern calculus, are ideally infinite in number along a curve. With an infinity of *differences* of *differences*, ideally a circle can be "squared," everything can be made into everything else, and no-*thing*, consequently can be really and truly identical to itself, for all is One. Zeno demonstrated that we can impose our mind on the world to produce counterintuitive results which prove that what we see is not what there is. In othe words, the One, Identity, is the true reality. Berkeley, a sort of modern Zeno, accomplished the inverse, arguing that *differentials*, which lead by an act of mind to the One, were counterintuitive and nothing more than fictitious abstractions of the world, and that actually what there is is no more than what we see. So reality is not one but many, the many of concrete, subjective perception. Derrida, it seems, reinverts the argument once again, suggesting that there is an underlying reality (of DC, MC, and the TC) which has been lost due to Western World abstractions and logic; that is, Derrida appears to believe that *differences* are real. The many of concrete subjective perception is in reality nothing more than increasingly minute differentiation. The virtually unlimited movement of DC, then, is virtually the Absolute, for identity is no more than an act of the abstracting mind (see also, in this respect, Heideg-

ger, 1969, 50-51). It appears that what in Western metaphysics is fictitious, in anti-metaphysics can become real, and vice versa.

11. The law of contradiction is also ineffectual; since all points are identical to all other points, their opposite cannot exist. It should be mentioned here that the abolishment of Aristotelian principles of logic has been a popular pastime in this century. To cite a few instances, in 1908 L.E.J. Brouwer abrogated the excluded middle principle in his "intuitionist logic." Count Korzybski (1933) abolished the law of identity in his "non-Aristotelian" foundations of a "new science." During the following decade, Lupasco (1947) constructed a "logic of contradiction" as an alternative to traditional logic. And more recently Melhuish (1973) uses a logic of "contradictory complementarity," inspired by Bohr and Heisenberg, in formulating his "paradoxical nature of reality."

12. See Chang (1971), also Herrigel's (1971) interesting book on the art of archery in Zen.

13. Peirce, it must be mentioned, was during his earlier days a nominalist of sorts (see Fisch, 1978).

14. Nevertheless, it must be emphasized that Peirce, like Bohm and Popper, believed that our grasp of such levels of generality can never be complete, or completely true: "The principle of continuity is the idea of fallibilism objectified. For fallibilism is the doctrine that our knowledge is never absolute but always swims, as it were, in a continuum of uncertainty and of indeterminacy. Now the doctrine of continuity is that *all things* so swim in continua" (Peirce, 1960, 1.171). Compare Peirce's "swimming" with Derridean *play!*

15. Since Derrida (1973) critiques Husserl's concept of "points," of "punctuation," it might be contended that a similar charge could be leveled against Peirce. However, Peirce's notion of mediacy (similar to MC and the TC) qualifies his use of the term, which, if the same, is not exactly used within the "metaphysics of presence."

16. Here it will be countered that Derrida would deconstruct Peirce's "Platonism," especially in light of Derrida's (1978b) critique of Husserlean "Platonism." The nature of this "Platonism," however, will be discussed in chapter five in light of Popperian-Derridean thought.

17. See Burr (1972). Significantly, Bohm (1971) also uses the hologram model for his notion of the "undifferentiated wholeness" of the universe.

18. This property, it will be recalled, is comparable to Leibniz's "monads," which reflect the entire universe.

19. These are speculations some of which enjoy little empirical evidence (but see Wilber, 1982). They are, however, hardly less speculative than many of the recent hypotheses in astrophysics and quantum mechanics that are, likewise, not yet subject to empirical validations or falsifications—"quarks" and "white holes" being cases in point.

20. This assertion will be discussed in section nine of the present chapter, and Peirce's *abduction* will be considered further in chapter seven.

21. In other words, Beckett's character's questions, which continue to "pour out of his mouth" from somewhere, though he knows not where,

emanate continuously, as a process, which becomes *differentiated* to his consciousness only mediately, after the fact. And even though these questions are actualizations *from* and *with respect to* the silence of which they are *not*, his conscious mind, striving to work toward the boundary where silence begins, is engaged in a futile act, for his words become increasingly *differentiated* without there being the possibility, due to his finitude, of reaching oneness, the silence.

22. This four-dimensional "block," as has been pointed out particularly by Le Shan (1969, 1974), Capra (1975), Talbot (1980), Zukav (1979) and others, is similar to the absolute *(Nirvāna)* in Oriental thought. It is also comparable to Permenides' One.

23. See Park (1972, 11-21) who argues convincingly that time does not actually pass: the passage of time is a "myth" created by consciousness. In fact, since every "moment" of past and future exists *simultaneously* in the "block," then we *are*, at *each* "instant" in our lives, always and already contained "within" it! Also, from a not-too-fictional, yet ironic, standpoint, see Borges's (1964b, 171-87) "New Refutation of Time," which presents the universe in one static "block," in which all exists in a single "time." This notion is similar, Rucker (1977, 121) points out, to that of Gödel (1959) who demonstrated that if *simultaneity* is a relative concept, then space-time cannot be a conglomeration of successive "nows." Viewed from above, from a cosmic perspective, past and future exist in one frozen "now."

I am aware that I am gingerly trodding on quicksand, running the risk of immediately being branded a logocentrist, a victim of the "myth of presence." In contemporary thought, at least since Heidegger, we have the notion that, to abbreviate hopefully without oversimplifying, *being is time*, that the subject, contrary to Husserl's claim, is not atemporal. Derrida, in full support of this notion, asserts temporality, and non-transcendence, for temporality and finitude must lie at the very core of our existence. The entire ontological framework of Western World philosophy has been in part overturned. Science's quest for truth with the confidence that it is attainable is also rebutted. But, I must reiterate that, judging from the above sections, it has become evident that much of contemporary physics and the philosophy of science is not suffering from logocentrism to the extent that some critics would have it. They have, sometimes gracefully, at other times with effort, and still at others not without a degree of anguish (i.e., Einstein's case) slipped outside the logocentric circle.

24. Admittedly this Einsteinian notion of the "block" is in the nineteenth-century tradition of the scientist's describing a nature apart from himself. In contrast, for the philosophers of "process" (Peirce, James, Bergson, Whitehead), as well as quantum theory, the emphasis is on interaction between observer and object, on the scientist as part of the system. The paradox of Einstein's system is that the scientist remains bound within an immanent universe, but at the same time he conceives of it *as if* he were somehow able provisionally to step "outside" it—an act of mind.

Significantly, Derrida (1974a, 61) criticizes L. Hjelmslev's taxonomy of language on the grounds that it is an attempt to isolate the entire linguistic system, and give it a transcendental otherworldly origin, with Hjelmslev as the Supreme Objective Observer. It might be contended that Einstein's problem is comparable, and that the posited existence of the "block" is thoroughly a "metaphysics of presence." The distinction, however, rests in that the "block," as I understand it, is not a system in the Hjelmslevian sense. It is a potential to be actualized; it can never be a presence *for* consciousness.

25. Yet James (1977) in defending his notion of a "pluralistic universe," attempted to reconcile the idea of a "block-universe," or oneness, with incessantly changing manyness.

26. In other words, Derrida (1973, 95) tells us that: "When I say I, even in solitary speech, can I give my statement meaning without implying, there as always, the possible absence of the object of speech—in this case, my self?" "I" is a *deferred presence*, for "I" or "I am" cannot be *in* the "block," for it is necessarily also a *deferred actualization*. Moreover, extending "I am" to "I am mortal" is feasible, but: "*I am immortal* is an impossible proposition" (Derrida, 1973, 54). This must be, for particulars cannot exist in the "block," and for an imaginary infinite being to make the statement implies that he, on so doing, has "stepped out" of the "block," and therefore become mortal, hence the proposition is still impossible.

27. Peirce's argument is this—and, incidentally, it effectively reveals the paradox, very central to this inquiry, of our basic human penchant for an intuitive and logical demand for immediacy and at the same time its logical and phenomenological impossibility:

> [W]e must have an immediate consciousness of the past. But if we have an immediate consciousness of a state of consciousness past by one unit of time and if that past state involved an immediate consciousness of a state then past by one unit, we now have an immediate consciousness of a state past by two units; and as this is equally true of all states, we have an immediate consciousness of a state past by four units, by eight units, by sixteen units, etc.; in short we must have an immediate consciousness of every state of mind that is past by a finite number of units of time. But we certainly have not an immediate consciousness of our state of mind a year ago. So a year is more than any finite number of units of time in this system of measurement; or, in other words, there is a measure of time infinitely less than a year. Now, this is only true if the series be continuous. Here, then, it seems to me, we have positive and tremendously strong reason for believing that time really is continuous. (Peirce, 1960, 1.169, also 7.653).

28. However see Hartshorne (1973) for the differences between the Peircean notion of continua and quantum mechanics.

29. Significantly, after Beckett struggles through his almost interminable array of *mutually cancellatory* words, his protagonist finally arrives, at the end of *How It Is* (1964) wallowing in a sea of muck, "where all is identical." His words have become in essence quasi-infinitely differentiated. Symbolically, total *difference* has approached total *indifference*. Absolute Chaos has become virtually The Order.

30. Therefore, according to Feyerabend, and Derrida, there can be no univocal meaning, for the word carries no special message given it by absolute and present Being. There can be nothing more than a fabric of inter-

related sentences, and any meaning that exists can only be derived from relations between them, not from anything in them.

31. For development of this thesis, from various perspectives, see Hofstadter (1979), McCulloch (1965), Pribham (1971), Ornstein (1973), and Ten Houten and Kaplan (1973). And for further discussion, see Merrell (1983).

32. Significantly, Sarfatti (1974) argues that an application of Gödel to physics implies that no theory of physics dealing with physical objects can explain physics. Metaphysical statements will be necessary for such an endeavor. Likewise, no theory of brain-events can explain mind-events, no theory of actual signs can explain DC, and, concomitantly, no rule of a game can be used to change itself.

33. I must emphasize that this "somewhere else" has, as we shall see, nothing in common with onto-theological doctrines. The mind, in the sense of Peirce, is, inexorably, immanent. Mediate (differential) consciousness *of* cannot encompass it, for consciousness is included *within* it.

34. See Weyl (1963), and for a popular treatment in physics, Talbot (1980) and Gerach (1978).

35. This "light cone" is not that of a "consciousness" in the ordinary meaning of the term. Just as the "observer" in quantum mechanics can be any "particle," so each and every "particle" has its "light cone," and a reaction between a given "particle" and all others is made possible only within the "future" and "past" of that "particle," and "elsewhere" being at a given moment in time inaccessible to it.

36. For example, see Toben (1975), Gribbin (1979), and Sarfatti (1974). "Tachyons," the hypothetical "particles" or "entities" mentioned above, can presumably travel faster than light in the "elsewhere" beyond actualized events in space-time, for they are beyond actuals, in the potentia. *Simultaneity* appears to be therefore a possibility after all. Sarfatti (in Toben, 1975) among others further speculates that information may be passed between "particles" by means of "tachyons." If this is so, then there may be parallels between instantaneous "tachyonic" transmission of messages over long distances and Jung's (1973) concept of "synchronicity," an acausal, atemporal connecting principle which he uses to account for telepathy and other paranormal forms of consciousness. Provocative though these ideas may be, however, little evidence has yet been accumulated to support them.

37. See Rucker (1977) for further discussion.

38. In other words, just as the linelander's and the flatlander's universes were conceived to be infinite from within, but from without they were viewed as finite but unbounded, there is no reason to believe that the same is not true of the spherelander's universe. This, finally, touches on our own twentieth-century outlook, which has been foreseen by Cusanus (1954), among others. He argued that the universe is boundless in the sense that it has neither circumference nor center. It is not infinite, yet it cannot be finite, for there are no definite boundaries within which it can be enclosed. For Cusanus, such a universe is unintelligible without the concept of God, who is at a "center" equidistant from all points, and hence he is infinite; he and he alone can comprehend the universe on his own. Significantly, sphereland, or our own universe, can be conceived according to

relativity theory as unbounded (or "infinite") but at the same time finite. Yet this appears acceptable to the twentieth-century mind, for God has now been conveniently displaced from the system—i.e., the system has been de-onto-theologized. As pointed out in footnote 22 of this chapter, Einstein conceived formally and mathematically of this relativity universe *as if* he were outside it. A useful relativist metaphor has been created to endow us with a godless certainty; yet we are always already within our cosmology.

39. On the other hand, everything on earth would lie open to view for the 4-D being. The money in a bank vault, the bottom of the ocean, even our own innards (see Rucker, 1977, 1-10).

40. See Rosen (1973, 1975) for implications of the Möbius strip for explaining non-empirical phenomena.

41. In other words, the Klein bottle is a higher-order topological structure than the Möbius strip. In essence it consists of a right-twisted Möbius strip fused to a left-twisted Möbius strip, hence entailing a 4-D framework.

CHAPTER FIVE
The Unlimited Web of Writing

1. Elsewhere Derrida (1974a, 44) puts forth the thesis that "writing in general covers the entire field of linguistic signs," whereas speech does not.

2. Significantly, some studies have indicated certain parallels between the genetic code—which appears to be identical for all organisms—and human language—which has no readily distinguishable analogue in animal communication (see Beadle and Beadle, 1966; Gerard, Kluckhohn, and Rapoport, 1956; Jakobson, 1973; Masters, 1970). Derrida refers to Jakobson on the notion that from a physically continuous stream of oral speech there can be differentiated a discontinuity of discrete units, or "distinctive features." It is for this reason, that an all-or-nothing opposition between speech and (phonetic) writing must be renounced (see also Merrell, 1982). Writing is by nature, and empirically, discontinuous. And both writing and speech consist of meaningless "bits" (graphemes-phonemes) which combine by a set of rules to form meaningful wholes. This, precisely, is the parallel between (phonetic) writing and speech, as well as the genetic code.

3. The thesis goes something like this: The marks are all there is; they do not contain, inherently, any meaning. There is meaning only in the context of a reading, and hence, given DC and MC, there exists potentially an infinity of meanings. The text's signification, then, is virtually no-*thing* unless it is being observed, actualized—a formulation comparable, we must recall, to that of the "new physics." Barthes (1972, 258) with this infinite meaning variance in mind, suggests that rather than talking about truth, we should speak of the validity and coherence of the text. However, as demonstrated in chapter three, this project implies the notion of undecidability, and syntactic considerations of undecidability or provability cannot ultimately be divorced from semantic considerations of truth.

4. It is, interestingly enough, the "blinding and unbearable" visual "sign" which predominates in Christian mysticism in contrast to the more

direct form, the non-visual pure experience, of Eastern mysticism (Keys, 1972; Fischer, 1975; Nicolás, 1978).

5. For a further, and very adequate, critique of the primacy of the visual, as well as of the notion that mind "mirrors" reality, see Rorty (1979).

6. Significantly, Spencer-Brown claims that in his calculus, "mathematical language has become entirely visual, there is no proper spoken form, so that reverbalizing it we must *encode* it in a form suitable for ordinary speech. Thus, although the mathematical form of an expression is clear, the reverbalized form is obscure" (1979, 92). This seems comparable to Derrida's pristine purity of the algebraic grapheme. The main difference in translating Spencer-Brown's mathematics to verbal form is that in the mathematical writing, there is freedom to mark the two dimensions of the plane—horizontal and vertical—whereas speech (or phonetic writing) is unidimensional, linear, temporal. Spencer-Brown goes on to state that: "Much that is unnecessary and obstructive in mathematics today appears to be vestigal of this limitation of the spoken word" (1979, 92).

7. The notion that radically distinct languages contain within themselves distinct "logics" is closely aligned with the Sapir-Whorf language relativity hypothesis—which has, incidentally, influenced both Feyerabend and Kuhn. Whorf (1956, 238) stated, before Derrida, that: "Modern thinkers have long since pointed out that the so-called mechanistic way of thinking has come to an impasse before the great frontier problems of science. To rid ourselves of this way of thinking is exceedingly difficult when we have no linguistic experience of any other and when even our most advanced logicians and mathematicians do not provide any other—and obviously they cannot without the linguistic experience." In addition, Derrida's (1974a, 85) contention that our concepts of time and linearity are bound up in our phonetic notion of speech and in our writing is paralleled, though for different reasons, throughout Whorf's writing. Non-European languages, Whorf (1956, 134-59) claims, reveal a relatively atemporal and non-linear perspective of the world.

8. Interestingly enough, Derrida (1972a, 205) alludes to the ideal Mallarmean blank text as "white against black," which imposes silence on the absence of the title or the text that could have been but is not. This, like an inversion of Peirce's blackboard example, implies potentially an infinity of possibilities to be actualized over time.

9. In this sense, writing, the ideal Derridean form of writing, is not simply the name of the act of setting down marks, or the name of the marks themselves, but, in interaction with the observer, the physical marks are/become signs, conceived in terms of their non-physical character, which has no signified except another sign. This interconnection of signs breeds, at the more complex level, "intertextuality." Understandably, the phenomenologist may complain that Derrida deprives us of "literature in its relation to truth" (Riddel, 1976, 587). Derrida gives us literature already in quotes, already related (potentially related) to all other literary texts. Each text is meaningful not because it inherently contains truth, but only in its *play* of DC.

10. Over the long haul, then, what was "true" can/must become "false," and vice versa, hence "truth" can never be known, only "falsities"—Popper's game is once again comparable to deconstruction, but in a strangely inverted way.

11. See Merrell (1982) for earlier development of Popper's argumentative function, but for a different purpose: to develop the "epistemological foundations" of written texts.

12. Similarly, knowledge, claims Popper, as well as Feyerabend and other "paradigm" philosophers such as Kuhn, Polanyi, and Hanson, is necessarily hypothesis or theory impregnated (see Popper, 1972, 71f).

13. Significantly, Popper sharply contrasts his method of conjectures and hypothesis formation with the Husserlean method of directly grasping the essence of Truth. Intuition, maintains Popper, as does Peirce, is fallible, hence always to a degree uncertain. Therefore any and all conjectures can give rise to new problem situations, and if they are guided by intuition, they can be no more than tentative (Popper and Eccles, 1977, 172). The deconstructionist must surely agree.

14. Concomitantly, to reiterate, it seems that the strategy of the deconstructionist consists of isolating that which is *always determinate* (the "uncanny moment," "navel," or *aporia*) against that which is indeterminate (by means of DC, MC, and the TC, and other catchwords such as *pharmakon, supplement, hymen, dissemination,* etc.), but at the same time when that *determinate point* in the text is isolated and dis-covered, it becomes simultaneously an *indeterminacy*. The operational imperative behind this deconstructive act appears to be: *It is determinate that there is no determinacy.* Or: *It is decidable that there is no decidability*—paradoxically, and in light of the *deconstructive principle.*

15. This relativism includes, among other forms, the *Weltanschauung* or "paradigm" view of scientific theories.

16. Popper (1972, 159) warns, however, that: "We must beware, . . . of interpreting these objects as the thoughts of a superhuman consciousness as did, for example, Aristotle, Plotinus, and Hegel."

17. According to Popper (1972, 149) the counterpart in nature of World 3 is to be found in the exosomatic developments, by means of inborn capacities, of non-human organisms, such as spider webs, bird nests, beaver dams, etc. In these cases, as in human "objective knowledge," the physical substrates left by these non-human organisms "transcend" their makers since they remain as monuments testifying to inborn capacities, or "knowledge."

18. Interestingly, both Derrida (1978b, 94-97) and Popper (1972, 107-8) would agree that if a set of books is destroyed, the "knowledge" they contained might eventually be reconstituted, though it would always be different; since World 2 would have changed, the created object of this new World 3 would be a variation of the former, and consequently the material substrates in World 1 would be different as well. This testifies, as well, that successive interpretations of the same book do not afford univocal meaning.

19. To repeat, Popper's "transcendence" of World 3 objects is not the mystical "otherworldliness" of transcendental phenomenology. It is, in con-

trast, the natural product of exceedingly complex brain processes possessed to a greater or lesser degree by all higher animal organisms.

20. Here, it bears mentioning, Popper's World 3 is relative to Peirce's notion of the *real*. Peirce believes that the *real* exists, but what is *real* depends upon the opinion of the community at a given time and place. That is, the *real* exists in two ways, $real_1$ which is independent of the subjective mind (and hence unknowable, in its totality), and $real_2$ which is dependent upon collective convention (and hence in constant transition). $Real_1$ is "objective" while $real_2$ is "intersubjective." But knowledge of $real_2$ can approach, though never be equal to, $real_1$, and therefore it is part of the "objective," like Popper's World 3 (see Almeder, 1971, 1975). In this sense, then, Peirce in particular and the pragmatists in general do not necessarily deny the equivalent of Popper's World 3. $Real_2$ is not purely a World 3 phenomenon, but a state of mind, like World 2. And $real_1$ is independent of all minds but contains the myriad possibilities for $real_2$.

21. Significantly, Frye (1957), himself an advocate of a sort of "archetypal intertextuality," mentions that the realm of literature itself, rather than the individual work, is an autonomous order, an "ideal order." This seems comparable to Popper's conception of World 3 objects also.

22. Here we perceive a certain similarity between World 3 objects and Gottlob Frege's "objective contents of thought." For example, we tend to say, "My opinion about today's political situation is . . ." but we don't usually say, "My Pythagorean theory is . . ." The former is a World 2 statement while the latter is a Popperian or Fregean objective public statement.

23. O'Hear's (1980) critique of Popper comes into view here. Popper's mixture of *discovery* and *invention* is, O'Hear claims, contradictory. *Discovery* implies that that which is discovered already existed autonomously. *Invention*, in contrast, is a creation of the mind. At the outset, it seems that Popper wants to mix Platonist mathematics and thought with intuitionist mathematics and thought, an unlikely and contradictory combination. On the other hand, Popper does not exactly give these World 3 undiscovered objects any sort of Platonic ontological reality. Like Heisenberg's (1958, 186) notion of elementary particles, "they form a world of potentialities or possibilities rather than one of things or facts." In this respect, then, Popper's hypothesis is at least partly vitiated.

24. A false conjecture necessarily enjoys status in World 3, since the subsequent "falsification" of that conjecture, and its corresponding counterstatement, also having been integrated into World 3, depends upon it (Popper, 1974a, 180-87). Extrapolating from this notion, in light of the above chapters, it can be inferred that if World 3 ultimately can contain the potential for all "truths" as well as all "falsities," then it is a vast set of *mutually cancellatory entities*. In other words, it must be like the continuum of potentials, a set of unactualized possibilities. Compare this formulation to Peirce's $real_1$ in footnote 20.

25. It might be objected here that the Romantic poet exalts the subjective "I," and therefore his poetry does not adequately correspond to Popper's idea of World 3 objects. However, though Popper does not touch on this problem, he would probably respond that good poetry is the particular-

ized manifestation of general ("objectivized") human emotions and sentiments; therefore, it pertains to World 3 (see also, from another view, Graff, 1979, 37).

26. Peirce's (1960, 2.54) concept of libraries as "stores of knowledge" also bears some resemblance to World 3.

27. Recall, in this light, the nature of texts in Borges's Tlön.

C H A P T E R   S I X
Who's Afraid of Anomalies?

1. However, Bohr (1934, 22) warns that: "there is set a fundamental limit to the analysis of the phenomena of life in terms of physical concepts, since the interference necessitated by an observation which would be as complete as possible from the point of view of the atomic theory would cause the death of the organism. In other words: *the strict application of these concepts which are adopted to our description of inanimate nature might stand in a relationship of exclusion to the consideration of the laws of the phenomena of life.*"

2. This notion, prevalent in Oriental philosophy for centuries, that there is no ultimate division between consciousness (mind) and reality, is gaining a foothold in contemporary physics (see Bohm, 1979; Eddington, 1958b; Floyd, 1974; Musès and Young, 1972; Walker, 1970; Toben, 1975; Wigner, 1970; Wilber, 1982). Interestingly, Peirce developed a similar idea:

> [A]ll mind is directly or indirectly connected with all matter, and acts in a more or less regular way; so that all mind more or less partakes of the nature of matter. Hence, it would be a mistake to conceive of the psychical and physical aspects of matter as two aspects absolutely distinct. Viewing a thing from the outside, considering its relations of action and reaction with other things, it appears as matter. Viewing it from the inside, looking at its immediate character as feeling, it appears as consciousness. (Peirce, 1960, 6.268)

On this topic Derrida is, strangely enough, silent. However, by extrapolation from Derridean thought, it can be speculated that there is ultimately no division between conscious mind and the system of writing (i.e., the infinite potential of "intertextuality"). Furthermore, if this is so, then, like Borges's Tlön, there can be no ultimate division between "intertextuality" and the world. This is a thought against which all but George Berkeley and a handful of others would fearfully recoil, for it annihilates the idea of a physical world "out there" and tends to give credence to a mysterious form of subjective idealism. Science, it seems, is pushing toward precisely this image. But Popper would, however, adamantly disagree with this conception.

3. In other words, most likely without having read Derrida and certainly uninfluenced by him, it appears that Popper has accomplished the impossible: he has debunked the Western World *epistémè*. Popper (1962, 12) points out that "in science there is no *'knowledge,'* in the sense which Plato and Aristotle understood the word, in the sense which implies finality."

Newton's physics was simply true for Kant; it was *epistémè*. But we now know that Newton was superseded by Einstein, and that, someday, Einstein must undoubtedly take a back seat to anyone who can effectively construct a more general theory. This activity, the game of science, is more appropriately for Popper the formulation of tentative hypotheses by bold conjectures as counterarguments *(doxa)* rather than belief in the acquisition, once and for all, of indubitable knowledge *(epistēmē)* (Popper, 1963, 104). This is also comparable to Peirce's notion of human fallibilism and his pragmatic theory of knowledge (see Apel, 1980, 77-92).

4. In this vein perhaps the most interesting study with respect to the union between Western science and Eastern thought is by Le Shan (1969, 1974) who juxtaposes statements by Western philosopher-scientists and Eastern sages, and presents them before knowledgeable subjects, who cannot distinguish the sources with any degree of consistency.

5. Yet it must be emphasized that science, with its hypothetico-deductive approach, is non-onto-theological, though, at the same time, it has closed the circle to, paradoxically, arrive at some of the same conclusions as Eastern mysticism which, in essence, is at variance with the "empiricism" of Newtonian science.

6. The term in quotes is from the later Wittgenstein (1953). A "form of life" entails language use within its particular socio-cultural context, meaning being derived from that use. It is in part this aspect of Wittgenstein's thought that Garver (1973) compares to Derrida.

7. Significantly, there are similarities between Derrida's "radical empiricism" and that of James, the bulk of whose philosophy is edified on this concept. James attempts to make a cut between empiricism—which posits the experience of disjoint atoms—and rationalism—based on a unity but at the expense of appeals to transcendental principles. James believes that conjunctive (i.e., unifying) relations are embodied in experience, not imposed from without. Moreover, like Derrida, identity doesn't apply to experience, for in real situations not only do relations suffer incessant transformations, but the environment, as well as the experiencer, change; and these relations mushroom out in many directions rather than linearly. Hence there is no origin as a disjoint break with something, nor can there be any self-presence at a given moment. All is in process. And, although one may be able to isolate experiences in which logical relations hold by ignoring all those in which they do not, such artificial cuts are only mutilated parts of a vast natural network where no such relations hold, and thus they cannot be said to reflect the nature of the world. For James, then, differential relations are experienced and hence they are *"as real as anything else in the system"* (James, 1967, 195).

8. I will not be so naive as to suppose that by revealing these problem situations I am therefore "deconstructing deconstruction." The motivation underlying the following exercise is derived from an attempt to make evident some problems of "radical empiricism," and the above quote from Derrida merely happens to contain a few key points I wish to discuss. As an added footnote, I believe it is by now apparent that in principle I agree

with much of Derrida, but I also believe that some practitioners of deconstruction should be more aware of the broad implications of the "method."

9. Significantly, Funes sees, and he wonders, but he is incapable of hypothesis formation, of thought, or of empiricism *after the fact of a tentative conjecture*.

10. There is actually another problem closely tied to this one. What we know is always finite, but what we don't know, given the epistemological assumptions in this inquiry, is always infinite. Hence if one is in a true state of "errance," within this infinitely vast unknown, there must prevail a set of *mutually cancellatory* possibilities, and therefore with no *a priori* hypothesis, nothing can be selected.

11. Negation is, as pointed out above, rather than unary, according to its usual conception in traditional metaphysics, binary. It cannot *be* except *with respect to* some-*thing* (see Cowan, 1975; Merrell, 1983).

12. The deconstructionist would undoubtedly deconstruct my use of *indifference*. For Derrida (1974a, 71), nothing less than "infinite being can reduce the difference in presence. In that sense the name of God, at least as it is pronounced within classical rationalism, is the name of indifference itself." However, as will be argued in this and the following chapter, if the notion of DC is taken to its extreme, the product can be none other than *indifference*.

13. For instance, John Cage strives to reject all desire to control sounds and let them simply represent themselves, divorced from human expression, emotion, sentiment. This, like other avant-garde movements in the arts, Meyer (1967) calls "anti-teleological."

14. Funes's total perceptual grasp if taken to its extreme form is analogous to Pierre Simon de Laplace's hypothetical Superobserver, which, if cognizant of the state of the entire universe at an instant, could determine, by laws of cause and effect, all past and future states. Twentieth-century relativity abolished this mechanistic ideal.

15. It might appear that a defense of Lévi-Strauss is forthcoming within the Popperian framework: if "new information" can always invalidate— "falsify"—a theory, then the methodology involved is not necessarily empiricist, but "falsification." But actually, according to Feyerabend, and even, by extrapolation, to Popper, scientific theories are not "completed or invalidated by new information." They are replaced by competing theories that are more adequately (and rhetorically) defended by their creators. Empirical evidence can always be twisted to fit a given hypothetico-deductive construct such that it appears that the evidence is empirical, though, in retrospect, it may become apparent that it was not. Thus "experience" is, ultimately the "proof" of nothing; theory is a free creation of the mind—*play*.

16. Once again, totalization is never possible, even from non-empirical frameworks, as witnessed above in the cases of Bohm, Feyerabend, Popper, and others.

17. For a controversial review of these fallacies in the context of scientific thought, see Suppe (1977).

18. Here we discover what appears to be the distinction between Derrida's "radical empiricism" and that of James. For the latter, the original experience (like Peirce's Firstness), preceding perception and conception (like Peirce's Secondness and Thirdness) is an undifferentiated unity, without distinctions. Perceptions and conceptions are selections, from this orderless chaos, which form the basis for further perceptions and conceptions at conscious as well as non-conscious levels. The question, to which James does not address himself, is: How is the first percept possible? For Derrida all origins are irretrievable, and hence there can be no account of a beginning. But the problem is that we cannot really know how to begin—the induction problem.

19. From various views, on the critique of the Romantic ego-centered world of art, see Sypher (1962), Meyer (1967), and Foucault (1971). For a counter-reaction against this view, see Morris (1979).

20. Along these same lines, Hans (1981, 85) rightly asserts that Derrida puts an end to man, commensurate with the modernist view, but at the same time, with his stress on the omniscience of language which is the product of and the fullest expression of man, he merely diffuses his anthropomorphism.

21. "[I]f only they'd stop committing reason, on them, on me, on the purpose to be achieved, and simply go on, with no illusion about having begun one day or ever being able to conclude, but it's too difficult, too difficult, for one bereft of purpose, not to look forward to his end and bereft of all reason to exist, back to a time he did not" (Beckett, 1955, 384-85).

22. This, equally, is the problem in critiquing deconstructive *play*. If it is prior to and encompasses every-*thing*, then there can be no-*thing against which* to view it and *against which* to critique it. Beckett is certainly aware of this paradox with respect to his universe of words. When words cease pouring forth, silence ensues. And since silence excludes words, there can be no outside vantage point from which words can be perceived.

23. That is: "My propositions serve as elucidations in the following way: anyone who understands me eventually recognizes them as nonsensical, when he has used them—as steps—to climb up beyond them. (He must, so to speak, throw away the ladder after he has climbed up it.)" (Wittgenstein, 1961, 6.54).

CHAPTER SEVEN
Beckett's Dilemma: or, Pecking Away at the Ineffable

1. See also Rescher (1976), and a counterargument to Goodman by Bunch (1980).

2. This example follows the epistemology of the "radical meaning variance" theorists, namely Feyerabend (1975), Hanson (1958), and Kuhn (1970a). Scientific "paradigms," according to this view and as pointed out in previous chapters, are incommensurable and consequently non-

translatable since, with the advent of a radically new theory (i.e., Einsteinian relativity or quantum mechanics) the meanings of all terms used in that theory undergo mutation.

3. This situation is analogous to, as argued in chapter six, the "inductive fallacy" (see in this respect also Popper's, [1959, 1963] criticism of induction).

4. Significantly, Wittgenstein's "rabbit/duck" example is precisely that used by Hanson (1958), one of the "radical meaning variance" theorists.

5. A "standing wave" can be created by connecting a rope to a stationary object and causing it to move up and down, to oscillate. It is not a "traveling wave" such as water or light waves.

6. See Merrell (1982) for elaboration of this "oscillation" model.

7. It might appear that here I depart radically from Peirce. Peirce contends that intuition in the Cartesian sense is a myth. On the contrary, he claims, our knowledge of our internal world is derived wholly from our observation of external events. Signs (or thoughts) refer to other sign-thoughts previously experienced, *ad infinitum*, and there exists no bedrock of clear and distinct, innate ideas. Moreover, consciousness *of* experience is not an immediate affair; it can only occur mediately, and over time, by referring to other signs-thoughts (see also Merrell [1982] for a formulation of this notion from a different angle). The leaps and bounds of cognition I am speaking of do not depend on innate ideas or concepts. They entail a capacity, by means of some cognitive mechanism and by inferential reasoning processes, to jump from one level of thoughts-signs to another. With this I believe Peirce would agree, for it involves what he calls—and which will be discussed briefly below—*abduction*.

8. According to the formulation in chapter six, increasing differentiation (i.e., $love_1$, $love_2$, $love_3$, ... $love_n$) represents part of the background against which what came as a surprise, as it were, could be foregrounded. But for the surprise (i.e., $love_1$ → "rose") to occur, there must have been the expectation that something (i.e., $love_1$) would ordinarily be the case, that is, there must have been an expected stopping "point," or "center." In a system of absolute *indifference*, on the other hand, "rose" could not be foregrounded and *set apart from* and *related to* $love_1$.

9. The inconsistency inherent in this formulation, as well as those of previous sections, is no reason to wallow in existential anguish. The consistency of our conceptual constructs is not, as evinced by many of the prominent intellectuals quoted in this book, a necessity. And the thesis of the consistency of our empirical world is, after all, only one alternative among many. In fact, Rescher and Brandom (1979, 40) propose that a paradox-embracing approach enjoys certain advantages:

> One can treat paradox as a matter of *local* inconsistency or singularity, an occasional difficulty, but not a pervasive disaster. It is possible—nay perhaps even probable—that the tolerance of such a liability might be offset by advantages elsewhere. It becomes worth examining whether the negativity of paradox might perhaps be offset by the positivity of systematic advantages attaching to the procedures that permit them—the avoidance of complications, systematic simplicity and convenience, comprehensiveness of content,

uniformity of approach etc. It thus becomes a matter of comparative cost-benefit analysis to see whether the negativity of paradox-acceptance might not in fact be counterbalanced by certain systematic advantages over its paradox-avoiding rivals.

10. See Goodman (1976) from whom in part these two terms were adopted/adapted.

11. I am speaking here of Western World phenetic writing. This is not necessarily intended to be a refutation of Derrida's concept of "writing."

12. In fact, Kuhn (1970b) admits that he later recognized what he had not originally perceived, for he had left his concept by and large unanalyzed.

13. This "lattice" is a variant of "quantum logic." For a layperson's exposition see Heelan (1970a, 1971) and Zukav (1979). For a more technical account, see Greechie and Gudder (1973). This use of "quantum logic" will undoubtedly be branded by some as *logocentric*. But the point is that "quantum logic" is a far cry from the logos of Gottlob Frege, Husserl, the early Wittgenstien, or logical positivism. It is, definitely, a non-Aristotelian formulation.

14. In terms of this study, a "context logic" contains context-dependent sentences the values of which are derivable from their connections with other possible, but not necessarily actualized, complementary sentences. Examples from everyday life are numerous: the language of work and the language of play, the language of pure science and the language of technology, the language of peace and the language of war, etc. "Context logic" is also non-Boolean, for its ordering can be no more than partial and non-distributive since its elements are complementaries rather than identities or contradictories and since there is not necessarily any implication—"if-then" clauses. That is to say, the "logic" does not follow the canons of traditional logic (see Heelan, 1970a, 1970b, 1971).

15. Actually, Heraclitus (as well as Korzybski) would approve of such a form of communication, for it would to a great extent, portray his universe of incessant change.

16. With respect to analogous problems of using scientific terms, elsewhere (Merrell, in press) and following Capek (1961) and Heisenberg (1958), I have argued that such terms as "mass," "particle," "space," etc. can be used with "syntactic" precision in the context of a text, but "semantically" there may be a "lag" such that the meanings of the terms have failed to undergo proper mutation, for the writer, the reader, or both. The best such cases are found in the distinctions in the meanings of these terms between the Newtonian and Einsteinian frameworks.

17. Significantly, Beckett's allusions to Zeno's paradoxes and to never ending decimals is a portrayal of his creative act, especially his prose. He stated in 1956 (quoted in Fletcher, 1964, 194) that: "The French work brought me to the point where I felt I was saying the same thing over and over again. For some authors writing gets easier the more they write. For me it gets more and more difficult. For me the area of possibilities gets smaller and smaller. ... At the end of my work there's nothing but dust."

18. However, Derrida (1973, 159) later seems to allude to ineffability in the absolute sense.

19. Beckett once said: "I'm not interested in stories of success, only failure" (quoted in Bair, 1978, 349).

20. "Beckett leaves only one thing intact: the capacity of human consciousness to reflect upon itself" (Hassan, 1967, 30). After Beckett's earlier heroes tend to be rather schizophrenic, oscillating from "inner" to "outer" and back again (Barnard, 1970), his later antiheroes are freed from the physical world to withdraw into the less confining circle of the mind. Finally, in *How It Is* (1964) Beckett comes frighteningly close to actually saying/ writing nothing. Even the protagonist's presence in the mud within which he inches forward is a flaw; he mars the nothingness of the continuum— the mud. Yet his is a necessary and ephemeral flaw, for he came forth from the mud, and will return to it.

21. "In recent years there has been some danger of Mr. Beckett being sentimentalized. Self-defensively we are driven to persuade ourselves that his plays are not really filled with terror and horror, but are, at bottom, jolly good fun. Well, they are not jolly good fun. They are amongst the most frightening prophesies of, and longing for, doom ever written" (Harold Hobson, quoted in Bair, 1978, 469).

22. Compare to Derrida's "logic of non-choice," which prevails at the text's grammatological "navel."

23. In order that this intellection be unrestricted, significantly many of Beckett's characters desire insanity, which is tantamount to freedom of commitment to "rationalism," freedom to create, at least mentally, and freedom from social norms—all of which Feyerabend, interestingly enough, prescribes for the "play of science."

24. Hesla (1971) and Morot-Sir (1976) amply demonstrate how Beckett is not only anti-Cartesian, but also distinguishable from the thought of Husserl, Sartre, and other existentialists, especially in his infinite regress of consciousness *of*, and his portraying, through his prose, the futility of searching for origins.

25. Beckett states that: "I think anyone nowdays, who pays the slightest attention to his own experience finds it the experience of a non-knower, a non-conceiver ... The other type of artist—the Apollonian—is absolutely foreign to me" (quoted in Shenker, 1956).

Here Beckett discards the notion of truth through art, identifying himself with the Dionysian creator. Dionysian art focuses on the mystery, the horror, and the suffering of human existence. It also entails the very mystery of creation, which is not accessible to rational inquiry. But to receive such insight, the artist himself must suffer those same human degradations (see Copeland, 1975, 38-43). This aspect of Dionysian art, with which Nietzsche identified himself also, seems strangely foreign to the well-entrenched deconstructionists—ironically.

26. For example, Beckett's Molloy and Malone don't know exactly where they are or how they got there. They simply start talking, with no pretentions of knowing anything:

But what's all this about not being able to die, live, be born, that must have some bearing, all this about staying where you are, dying, living, being born, unable to go forward or back, not knowing where you came from, or where you are, or where you're going, or that it's possible to be elsewhere, to be otherwise, supposing nothing, asking yourself nothing, you can't you're there, you don't know who, you don't know where, the thing stays where it is, nothing changes, within it, outside it, apparently, apparently. (Becket, 1955, 370)

P O S T S C R I P T

1. See Booth's (1979) lucid exposition on the "powers and limits of pluralism." Somewhat commensurate with the type of radical pluralism I am suggesting here, Booth concludes his introductory chapter with a perplexing dilemma:

> Finally, can we imagine a genuine pluralist of pluralisms, one who can accept and use many different umbrellas—a plurimodist of plurimodes, a metalinguist of metalanguages? But how could such a one, praising and relating many ways of praising and relating but encountering other pluralists of pluralisms who insist on different ways—how could he avoid an infinite regress of ever more vacuous pluralisms?
>
> I cannot promise a finally satisfactory encounter with these staggering questions, produced by my simple effort to be a good citizen in the republic of criticism. Beginning what looked like a fairly innocent search for productive ways of dealing with critical conflict, I have landed in very threatening territory indeed. (Booth, 1979, 34)

Booth's "pluralism of pluralisms" must ultimately entail a vast set of *mutually cancellatory affirmations and negations* not unlike Beckett's work. Threatening territory? Perhaps, to the not-too-curious seeker at least—and I don't believe Booth would be included here. But frankly, I see no way out, I doubt that there is any, within human reason and framed in human language that is.

References

Abbott, Edwin A.
1952. *Flatland.* New York: Dover Publications.

Abel, Lionel
1974. "Jacques Derrida: His *'Differance'* with Metaphysics." *Salmagundi*, 25, 3–21.

Abraham, Ralph
1976. "Vibrations and the Realization of Form." In *Evolution and Consciousness: Human Systems in Transition*, eds. P. Jantsch and C. H. Waddington, pp. 134–49. Reading, Massachusetts: Addison-Wesley.

Abrams, M. H.
1977. "The Limits of Pluralism II: The Deconstructive Angel." *Critical Inquiry*, 3, No. 3, 425–38.

Achinstein, Peter
1968. *Concepts of Science, A Philosophical Analysis.* Baltimore: Johns Hopkins University Press.

Agassi, Joseph
1977. *Towards a Rational Philosophical Anthropology.* The Hague: Martinus Nijhoff.

Almeder, Robert
1971. "The Idealism of Charles S. Peirce." *Journal of the History of Philosophy*, 9, No. 4, 477–90.
1975. "The Epistemological Realism of Charles Peirce." *Transactions of the Charles S. Peirce Society*, 11, No. 1, 3–17.

Altieri, Charles
1976. "Wittgenstein on Consciousness and Language: A Challenge to Derridean Literary Theory." *Modern Language Notes*, 91, No. 6, 1397–1423.

Apel, Karl-Otto
1980. *Towards a Transformation of Philosophy.* Translated by G. Adey and D. Frisby. London: Routledge & Kegan Paul.

Bair, Deirdre
1978. *Samuel Beckett.* New York: Harcourt, Brace, Jovanovich.

Barnard, G. C.
1970. *Samuel Beckett: A New Approach.* New York: Dodd, Mead.

Barnett, Lincoln
1968. *The Universe and Doctor Einstein.* New York: Bantam.

Barthes, Roland
1971. "Ecrivains, Intellectuels, Professeurs." *Tel Quel*, 47, 3–18.
1972. *Critical Essays.* Translated by R. Howard. Evanston: Northwestern University Press.

1974. *S/Z*, Translated by R. Miller. New York: Hill & Wang.

Bateson, Gregory
1972. *Steps to an Ecology of Mind.* New York: Ballantine Books.

Beadle, George and Muriel
1966. *The Language of Life.* Garden City, New Jersey: Doubleday & Co.

Beckett, Samuel
1955. *Molloy, Malone Dies, The Unnamable.* New York: Grove Press.
1957. *Proust.* New York: Grove Press.
1964. *How It Is.* New York: Grove Press.

Bernstein, Jeremy
1978. *Experiencing Science.* New York: Basic Books.

Bernstein, Richard J.
1983. *Beyond Objectivism and Relativism; Science, Hermeneutics, and Praxis.* Philadelphia: University of Pennsylvania Press.

Bilaniuk, Olexa-Myron, and E. C. George Sudarshan
1969. "Particles Beyond the Light Barrier." *Physics Today*, 22, No. 5, 43–51.

Black, Max
1962. *Models and Metaphors: Studies in Language and Philosophy.* Ithaca: Cornell University Press.

Bloom, Harold
1975. *A Map of Misreading.* New York: Oxford University Press.

Bohm, David
1951. *Quantum Theory.* Englewood Cliffs: Prentice-Hall.
1957. *Causality and Chance in Modern Physics.* Philadelphia: University of Pennsylvania Press.
1962. "A Proposed Topological Formulation of the Quantum Theory." In *The Scientist Speculates*, ed. I. J. Good, pp. 302–14. New York: Basic Books.
1965. *The Special Theory of Relativity.* New York: W. A. Benjamin.
1971. "Quantum Theory as an Indication of a New Order in Physics. Part A: The Derivation of New Orders as Shown through the History of Physics." *Foundations of Physics*, 1, 359–81.
1979. *A Question of Physics: Conversations in Physics and Biology.* Conducted by P. Buckley and F. D. Peat, pp. 124–50. Toronto: University of Toronto Press.

Bohr, Neils
1934. *Atomic Theory and the Description of Nature.* Cambridge: Cambridge University Press.
1958. *Atomic Physics and Human Knowledge.* New York: John Wiley & Sons.

Boler, John P.
1964. "Habits of Thought." In *Studies in the Philosophy of Charles Sanders Peirce*, eds. E. C. Moore and R. S. Robin, pp. 382–400. Amherst: University of Massachusetts Press.

Booth, Wayne C.
1979. *Critical Understanding: The Powers and Limits of Pluralism.* Chicago: University of Chicago Press.

Borges, Jorge Luis
1964a. *Labyrinths, Selected Stories and Other Writings,* eds. D. A. Yates and J. E. Irby. New York: New Directions.
1964b. *Other Inquisitions, 1937-52.* Translated by R. L. C. Simms. Austin: University of Texas Press.

Braithwaite, R. B.
1962. "Introduction," to Gödel's *On Formally Undecidable Propositions of Principia Mathematica and Related Systems.* Translated by B. Meltzer, pp. 1–32. Edinburgh: Oliver & Boyd.

Broglie, Louis de
1959. "A General Survey of the Scientific World of Albert Einstein." In *Einstein: Philosopher-Scientist,* ed. P. A. Schilpp, Vol. 1, pp. 109–27. New York: Harper & Brothers.

Bronowski, Jacob
1966. "The Logic of the Mind." *American Scientist,* 54, No. 1, 1–14.
1978. *The Origins of Knowledge and Imagination.* New Haven: Yale University Press.

Bruner, Jerome
1957. "Going Beyond the Information Given." In *Contemporary Approaches to Cognition: A Symposium Held at the University of Colorado,* pp. 41–69. Cambridge: Harvard University Press.

Buczynska-Garewicz, Hanna
1982. "Sign Versus the Perfect Beginning." In *Studies in Peirce's Semiotic, Toronto Semiotic Circle Monographs, Working Papers and Prepublications,* ed. D. Savan, pp. 5–23. Toronto: Victoria University.

Bühler, Karl
1934. *Sprachtheorie.* Jena: Fischer.

Bunch, B. L.
1980. "Discussion: Rescher on the Goodman Paradox." *Philosophy of Science,* 47, No. 1, 119–23.

Burger, Dionys
1968. *Sphereland: A Fantasy about Curved Space and an Expanding Universe.* Translated by C. J. Rheinboldt. New York: Thomas Y. Crowell.

Burke, Kenneth
1973. *The Philosophy of Literary Form.* Berkeley: University of California Press.

Burr, Harold Saxton
1972. *The Fields of Life.* New York: Ballantine Books.

Capek, Milic
1961. *The Philosophical Impact of Contemporary Physics.* New York: American Book Co.

Capra, Fritjof
1975. *The Tao of Physics*. Berkeley: Shambhala Publications.

Chang, Garma C. C.
1971. *The Buddhist Teaching of Totality: The Philosophy of Hwa Yen Buddhism*. University Park: Pennsylvania State University Press.

Chew, G. F.
1968. "Bootstrap: A Scientific Idea." *Geoscience*, 23 Aug., 161, 762–65.
1970. "Hadron Bootstrap: Triumph or Frustration?" *Physics Today*, 23, 23–28.

Cohn, Ruby
1962. *Samuel Beckett: The Comic Gamut*. New Brunswick: Rutgers University Press.

Copeland, Hannah Case
1975. *Art and the Artist: In the Works of Samuel Beckett*. The Hague: Mouton.

Costa de Beauregaard, Oliver
1966. "Time in Relativity Theory: Arguments for a Philosophy of Being." In *The Voices of Time*, ed. F. T. Fraser, pp. 417–33. New York: George Braziller.

Cowan, Daniel A.
1975. *Mind Underlies Space Time: An Idealistic Model of Reality*. San Mateo, California: Joseph Publishing Co.

Culler, Jonathan
1976. "Presupposition and Intertextuality." *Modern Language Notes*, 91, No. 6, 1380–96.
1982. *On Deconstruction: Theory and Criticism After Structuralism*. Ithaca: Cornell University Press.

Cusanus, Nicolas
1954. *Of Learned Ignorance*. Translated by G. Haran. New Haven: Yale University Press.

Dantzig, Tobias
1930. *Number: The Language of Science*, 4th ed., revised. New York: Free Press.

Davis, James
1972. *Peirce's Epistemology*. The Hague: Martinus Nihjoff.

DeLong, Howard
1971. *A Profile of Mathematical Logic*. New York: Addison-Wesley.

Derrida, Jacques
1972a. *La dissémination*. Paris: Editions de Minuit.
1972b. *Positions*. Paris: Editions de Minuit.
1972c. *Marges de la philosophie*. Paris: Editions de Minuit.
1973. *Speech and Phenomena, And Other Essays on Husserl's Theory of Signs*. Translated by D. B. Allison. Evanston: Northwestern University Press.

1974a. *Of Grammatology.* Translated by G. C. Spivak. Baltimore: Johns Hopkins University Press.

1974b. "White Mythology: Metaphor in the Text of Philosophy." *New Literary History*, 6, No. 1, 5-74.

1977. "Limited Inc." *Glyph 2: Johns Hopkins Textual Studies*, pp. 162– 254. Baltimore: Johns Hopkins University Press.

1978a. *Writing and Difference.* Translated by A. Bass. Chicago: University of Chicago Press.

1978b. *Edmund Husserl's* Origin of Geometry: *An Introduction.* Translated by J. P. Leavey. Stony Brook, New York: Nicolas Hays.

1980. "The Law of Genre." *Glyph 7: Johns Hopkins Textual Studies*, pp. 206–12. Baltimore: Johns Hopkins University Press.

Desmonde, William H.
1971. "Gödel, Non-Deterministic Systems and Hermetic Automata." *International Philosophical Quarterly*, 11, No. 1, 49-74.

Dewan, E. M.
1976. "Consciousness as an Emergent Causal Agent in the Context of Control System Theory." In *Consciousness and the Brain*, eds. G. G. Globus, G. Maxwell, and I. Savodnik, pp. 181–98. New York: Plenum Press.

De Witt, Bryce, and Neill Graham, eds.
1973. *The Many-Worlds Interpretation of Quantum Mechanics.* Princeton: Princeton University Press.

Dobbs, H. A. C.
1972. "The Dimensions of the Sensible Present." In *The Study of Time*, eds. J. T. Fraser, F. C. Haber, and G. H. Müller, pp. 274–92. New York: Springer-Verlag.

Donaghue, Denis
1980. "Deconstructing Deconstruction." *The New York Review*, 27, No. 10, June 12, 37-41.

Eco, Umberto
1976. *A Theory of Semiotics.* Bloomington: Indiana University Press.
1979. *The Role of the Reader: Explorations in the Semiotics of Texts.* Bloomington: Indiana University Press.

Eddington, Arthur
1958a. *The Philosophy of Physical Science.* Ann Arbor: University of Michigan Press.
1958b. *The Nature of the Physical World.* Ann Arbor: University of Michigan Press.

Einstein, Albert
1950. *Out of My Later Years.* New York: Philosophical Library.
1959. "Autobiographical Notes." In *Albert Einstein: Philosopher-Scientist*, ed. P. A. Schilpp, Vol. 1, pp. 3–95. New York: Harper & Brothers.

Federman, Raymond
1970. "Beckettian Paradox: Who is Telling the Truth?" In *Samuel Beckett Now*, ed. M. J. Friedman, pp. 103–17. Chicago: University of Chicago Press.

Feyerabend, Paul
1967. "On the Improvement of the Sciences and the Arts, and the Possible Identity of the Two." In *Boston Studies in the Philosophy of Science*, Vol. 3, eds. R. S. Cohen and M. W. Wartofsky, pp. 387–415. Dordrecht-Holland: D. Reidel.
1970. "Against Method: Outline of an Anarchistic Theory of Knowledge." In *Minnesota Studies in the Philosophy of Science*, Vol. 4, eds. M. Radner and S. Winokur, pp. 17–130. Minneapolis: University of Minnesota Press.
1975. *Against Method.* London: NLB.
1976. "On the Critique of Scientific Reason" In *Method and Appraisal in the Physical Sciences: The Critical Background to Modern Science, 1800-1905*, ed. C. Howson, pp. 309–39.. Cambridge: Cambridge University Press.
1978. *Science in a Free Society.* London: NLB.

Fisch, Max
1978. "Peirce's General Theory of Signs." In *Sight, Sound, and Sense*, ed. T. A. Sebeok, pp. 31–70. Bloomington: Indiana University Press.

Fischer, Roland
1975. "Cartography of Inner Space." In *Hallucinations: Behavior, Experience and Theory*, eds. P. K. Siegel and L. J. West, pp. 197–239. New York: John Wiley & Sons.

Fletcher, John
1964. *The Novels of Samuel Beckett.* London: Chatto & Windus.

Floyd, Keith
1974. "Of Time and Mind: From Paradox to Paradigm." In *Frontiers of Consciousness*, ed. J. White, pp. 296–320. New York: Avon Books.

Fortune, Dion
1935. *The Mystical Qabalah.* London: Ernest Benn.

Foucault, Michael
1971. *The Order of Things.* New York: Pantheon Books.

Freeman, Eugene, and Henryk Skolimowski
1974. "The Search for Objectivity in Peirce and Popper." In *The Philosophy of Karl Popper*, Book II, ed. P. A. Schilpp, pp. 464–519. La Salle, Illinois: Open Court.

Fried, Yehuda, and Joseph Agassi
1976. *Paranoia: A Study in Diagnosis.* Dordrecht-Holland: D. Reidel.

Frye, Northrop
1957. *Anatomy of Criticism.* Princeton: Princeton University Press.

Garver, Newton
1973. "Preface." In Jacques Derrida's *Speech and Phenomena*, Trans-

lated by D. B. Allison, pp. ix–xxix. Evanston: Northwestern University Press.

Gasché, Rudolphe
1979. "Deconstruction as Criticism." *Glyph 6: Johns Hopkins Textual Studies*, pp. 177–215. Baltimore: Johns Hopkins University Press.

Gerach, Robert
1978. *General Relativity from A to B.* Chicago: University of Chicago Press.

Gerard, R., C. Kluckhohn, and A. Rapoport
1956. "Biological and Cultural Evolution: Some Analogies and Explorations." *Behavioral Sciences*, 1, 234–51.

Gödel, Kurt
1959. "A Remark About the Relationship Between Relativity Theory and Idealistic Philosophy." In *Albert Einstein: Philosopher-Scientist*, Vol. 2, ed. P. A. Schilpp, pp. 535–62. New York: Harper & Brothers.

Gombrich, E. H.
1960. *Art and Illusion.* Princeton: Princeton University Press.

Goodman, Nelson
1965. *Fact, Fiction and Forecast.* New York: Bobbs-Merrill Co.
1972. *Problems and Projects.* Indianapolis: Hackett Publishing Co.
1976. *Languages of Art.* Indianapolis: Hackett Publishing Co.
1978. *The Ways of Worldmaking.* Indianapolis: Hackett Publishing Co.

Goody, Jack
1977. *The Domestication of the Savage Mind.* Cambridge: Cambridge University Press.

Graff, Gerald
1979. *Literature Against Itself: Literary Ideas in Modern Society.* Chicago: University of Chicago Press.

Greechie, R. J., and Stanley P. Gudder
1973. "Quantum Logics." In *Contemporary Research in the Foundations and Philosophy of Quantum Theory*, ed. C. A. Hooker, pp. 143–73. Dordrecht-Holland: D. Reidel.

Greenlee, D.
1973. *Peirce's Concept of Sign.* The Hague: Mouton.

Grene, Marjorie
1974. "Bohm's Metaphysics and Biology." In *The Understanding of Nature: Essays in the Philosophy of Biology*, ed. M. Grene, pp. 180–88. Dordrecht-Holland: D. Reidel.
1976. "Life, Death, and Language: Some Thoughts on Wittgenstein and Derrida." *Partisan Review*, 43, No. 2, 265–79.

Gribbin, John
1979. *Time-Warps.* New York: Dell Publishing Co.

Grünbaum, A.
1979. "Is Freudian Psycho-Analytic Theory Pseudo-Scientific by Karl

Popper's Criterion of Demarcation?" *American Philosophical Quarterly*, 16, 131–41.

Hans, James S.
1981. *The Play of the World*. Amherst: University of Massachusetts Press.

Hanson, Norwood R.
1958. *Patterns of Discovery*. London: Cambridge University Press.
1965. "Notes Toward a Logic of Discovery." In *Perspectives on Peirce*, ed. R. J. Bernstein, pp. 42–65. New Haven: Yale University Press.

Harari, Josué V.
1979. "Critical Factions/Critical Fictions." In *Textual Strategies: Perspectives in Post-Structuralist Criticism*, ed. J. V. Harari, pp. 17–72. Ithaca: Cornell University Press.

Hartman, Geoffrey
1975. *The Fate of Reading and Others Essays*. Chicago: University of Chicago Press.

Hartshorne, Charles
1952. "The Relativity of Non-Relativity: Some Reflections on Firstness." In *Studies in the Philosophy of Charles S. Peirce*, eds. P. P. Wiener and F. H. Young, pp. 215–24. Cambridge: Harvard University Press.
1973. "Charles Peirce and Quantum Mechanics." *Transactions of the Charles S. Peirce Society*, 9, No. 4, 191-201.

Hassan, Ihab
1967. *The Literature of Silence*. New York: Knopf.

Heelan, Patrick
1970a. "Complementarity, Context-Dependence, and Quantum Logic." *Foundations of Physics*, 1, No. 2, 95–100.
1970b. "Quantum and Classical Logic: Their Respective Roles." *Synthese*, 21, 2–33.
1971. "Logic of Framework Transpositions." *International Philosophical Quarterly*, 11, 314–34.

Heidegger, Martin
1969. *Identity and Difference*. Translated by J. Stambaugh. New York: Harper & Row.

Heisenberg, Werner
1958. *Physics and Philosophy*. New York: Harper & Row.

Heisenberg, Werner, et al.
1962. *On Modern Physics*. Translated by M. Goodman and J. W. Binns. New York: Collier Books.

Hempel, Carl G.
1946. "A Note on the Paradoxes of Confirmation." *Mind*, 55, 79–82.

Herrigel, Eugen
1971. *Zen in the Art of Archery*. Translated by R. F. C. Hull. New York: Vintage Books.

Hesla, David H.
  1971. *The Shape of Chaos: An Interpretation of the Art of Samuel Beckett.* Minneapolis: University of Minnesota Press.

Hirsch, E. D. Jr.
  1967. *Validity in Interpretation.* New Haven: Yale University Press.

Hoffman, Banesh
  1972. *Albert Einstein: Creator and Rebel.* New York: New American Library.

Hofstadter, Douglas R.
  1979. *Gödel, Escher, Bach: An Eternal Golden Braid.* New York: Basic Books.

Horton, Robin
  1967. "African Traditional Thought and Western Science." *Africa,* 37, 50–71 and 155–87.

Husserl, Edmund
  1964. *The Phenomenology of Internal Time-Consciousness.* Translated by J. S. Churchill. Bloomington: Indiana University Press.

Hutten, Ernest H.
  1956. *The Language of Modern Physics: An Introduction to the Philosophy of Science.* London: George Allen & Unwin.
  1962. *The Origins of Science: An Inquiry into the Foundations of Western Thought.* London: George Allen & Unwin.

Jakobson, Roman
  1960. "Linguistic and Poetics." In *Style in Language,* ed. T. A. Sebeok, pp. 350–77. Cambridge: MIT Press.
  1973. *Main Trends in the Science of Language.* London: George Allen & Unwin.

Jakobson, Roman, and Morris Halle
  1956. *Fundamentals of Language.* The Hague: Mouton.

James, William
  1967. *The Writings of William James,* a comprehensive edition. New York: Random House.
  1977. *A Pluralist Universe.* Cambridge: Harvard University Press.

Jarvie, I. C., and J. Agassi
  1967. "The Rationality of Magic." *British Journal of Sociology,* 18, 55–74.
  1973. "Magic and Rationality Again." *British Journal of Sociology,* 24, 236-45.

Jeans, James
  1958. *The Mysterious Universe.* New York: E. P. Dutton.

Jung, Carl G.
  1973. *Synchronicity: An Acausal Connecting Principle.* Translated by R. F. C. Hull. Princeton: Princeton University Press.

Kahn, Charles H., ed.
1979. *The Art and Thought of Heraclitus.* Cambridge: Cambridge University Press.

Kemeny, John G.
1959. *A Philosopher Looks at Science.* Princeton: Van Nostrand.

Kenner, Hugh
1961. *Samuel Beckett: A Critical Study.* New York: Grove Press.

Keys, James
1972. *Only Two Can Play This Game.* New York: Julian Press.

Kirk, G. S., and J. E. Raven, eds.
1957. *The Presocratic Philosophers.* London: Cambridge University Press.

Koestler, Arthur
1963. *The Sleepwalkers, A History of Man's Changing Vision of the Universe.* New York: Grosset & Dunlap.

Kordig, Karl R.
1971. *The Justification of Scientific Change.* Dordrecht-Holland: D. Reidel.

Korzybski, Alfred
1933. *Science and Sanity: An Introduction to Non-Aristotelian Systems and General Semantics.* Lancaster, Pennsylvania: International Non-Aristotelian Library Publishing Co.

Kristeva, Julia
1969. *Semiotiké: Recherches pour une sémanalyse.* Paris: Seuil.
1970. *Le Texte du roman: approche sémiologique d'une structure discursive transformationelle.* The Hague: Mouton.

Kuhn, Thomas S.
1970a. *The Structure of Scientific Revolutions.* Chicago: University of Chicago Press.
1970b. "Reflections on My Critics." In *Criticism and the Growth of Knowledge,* eds. I. Lakatos and A. Musgrave, pp. 231–78. London: Cambridge University Press.

Laing, R. D.
1969. *The Politics of the Family.* New York: Random House.

Lakatos, Imre
1976. *Proofs and Refutations: The Logic of Mathematical Discovery,* eds. J. Worrall and E. Zahar. London: Cambridge University Press.

Lakatos, Imre, and Alan Musgrave, eds.
1970. *Criticism and the Growth of Knowledge.* London: Cambridge University Press.

Lamont, Rosette
1970. "Beckett's Metaphysics of Choiceless Awareness." In *Beckett Now,* ed. M. J. Friedman. Chicago: University of Chicago Press.

Lao-Tzu
1963. *Tao Te Ching.* Translated by D. C. Lau. Middlesex: Penguin Books.

Laszlo, Ervin
1972. *Introduction to Systems Philosophy: Toward a New Paradigm of Contemporary Thought.* New York: Harper & Row.

Leitch, Vincent B.
1983. *Deconstructive Criticism: An Advanced Introduction.* New York: Columbia University Press.

Lentricchia, Frank
1980. *After the New Criticism.* Chicago: University of Chicago Press.

Le Shan, Lawrence L.
1969. *Toward a General Theory of the Paranormal: A Report of Work in Progress.* New York: Parapsychology Foundation, Inc.
1974. *The Medium, the Mystic, and the Physicist.* New York: Viking Press.

Lévi-Strauss, Claude
1963. *Structural Anthropology.* Translated by C. Jacobson and B. C. Schoepf. New York: Doubleday & Co.
1966. *The Savage Mind.* Chicago: University of Chicago Press.
1969. *The Raw and the Cooked.* Translated by J. and D. Weightman. New York: Harper & Row.

Lupasco, Stéphane
1947. *Logique et contradiction.* Paris: Presses Universitaires.

Macksey, Richard, and Eugenio Donato, eds.
1970. *The Languages of Criticism and the Sciences of Man: The Structuralist Controversy.* Baltimore: Johns Hopkins University Press.

Magliola, Robert
1984. *Derrida on the Mend.* West Lafayette, Indiana: Purdue University Press.

Malcolm, Norman
1959. *Dreaming.* London: Routledge & Kegan Paul.

Man, Paul de
1971. *Blindness and Insight: Essays in the Rhetoric of Contemporary Criticism.* Oxford: Oxford University Press.

Margenau, H.
1959. "Einstein's Conception of Reality." In *Albert Einstein: Philosopher-Scientist,* ed. P. A. Schilpp. Vol. 1, pp. 245-68. New York: Harper & Brothers.

Masterman, Margaret
1970. "The Nature of a Paradigm." In *Criticism and the Growth of Knowledge,* eds. I. Lakatos and A. Musgrave, pp. 59-89. London: Cambridge University Press.

Masters, Roger D.
   1970. "Genes, Language, and Evolution." *Semiotica*, 2, 295-320.
McCulloch, Warren Sturgis
   1965. "What the Frog's Eye Tells the Frog's Brain." In *Embodiments of Mind*, by W. S. McCulloch, pp. 230-50. Cambridge: MIT Press.
Melhuish, George
   1973. *The Paradoxical Nature of Reality*. Bristol: St. Vincent's Press.
Merrell, Floyd
   1979. "How We Perceive Texts." *Dispositio*, 3, No. 7-8, 167-73.
   1981. "On Understanding the 'Logic' of Understanding: A Reincarnation of Some Peircean Thought." *Ars Semeiotica*, 4, No. 2, 161-86.
   1982. *Semiotic Foundations: Steps Toward an Epistemology of Written Texts*. Bloomington: Indiana University Press.
   1983. *Pararealities: The Nature of Our Fictions and How We Know Them*. Amsterdam: John Benjamins.
   In press. *A Semiotic Theory of Texts*. The Hague: Mouton Publishers.
Meyer, Leonard B.
   1967. *Music, the Arts, and Ideas: Patterns and Predictions in Twentieth-Century Culture*. Chicago: University of Chicago Press.
Miller, J. Hillis
   1976a. "Steven's Rock and Criticism as Cure II." *Georgia Review*, 30, 330-48.
   1976b. "Ariadne's Thread: Repetition and the Narrative Line." *Critical Inquiry*, 3, No. 1, 57-77.
   1977. "The Critic as Host." *Critical Inquiry*, 3, No. 3, 439-47.
   1979. "The Function of Rhetorical Study at the Present Time." In *The State of the Discipline, 1970s-1980s* (a special issue of the ADE Bulletin, No. 62), pp. 10-18.
Morot-Sir, Edouard
   1976. "Samuel Beckett and Cartesian Emblems." In *Samuel Beckett: The Art of Rhetoric*, eds. E. Morot-Sir, H. Harper, and D. McMillan III, pp. 25-104. Chapel Hill: Studies in the Romance Languages and Literatures.
Morris, Wesley
   1979. *Friday's Footprints: Structuralism and the Articulated Text*. Columbus: Ohio State University Press.
Musès, Charles A.
   1972. "Working with the Hypernumber Idea." In *Consciousness and Reality*, eds. C. A. Musès and A. M. Young, pp. 448-69. New York: Outerbridge & Lazard.
Musès, Charles, and Arthur Young, eds.
   1972. *Consciousness and Reality*. New York: Outerbridge & Lazard.
Musil, Robert
   1965. *The Man Without Qualities*. Translated by E. Wilkins and E. Kaiser. New York: Capricorn Books.

Nagel, Ernest, and James R. Newman
1958. *Gödel's Proof.* New York: New York University Press.

Nicolás, Antonio T. de
1978. *Meditations through the Rg Veda: Four-Dimensional Man.* Boulder, Colorado: Shambhala Publications.

Nietzsche, Friedrich
1913. *The Complete Works, The Will to Power II,* ed. O. Levy, Vol. 15. Edinburgh: T. N. Foulis.

Norris, Christopher
1982. *Deconstruction: Theory and Practice.* London: Methuen.
1983. *The Deconstructive Turn: Essays in the Rhetoric of Philosophy.* London: Methuen.

Northrop, F. S. C.
1959. *The Logic of the Sciences and the Humanities.* New York: World Publishing Co.

O'Hara, J. D.
1970. "Introduction." In *Twentieth Century Interpretations of Molloy, Malone Dies, and The Unnamable,* pp. 1-25. Englewood Cliffs: Prentice-Hall.

O'Hear, Anthony
1980. *Karl Popper.* London: Routledge & Kegan Paul.

Ornstein, Robert E., ed.
1973. *The Nature of Human Consciousness.* San Francisco: W. H. Freeman.

Park, D.
1972. "The Myth of the Passage of Time." In *The Study of Time,* eds. J. T. Fraser, F. C. Haber, and G. H. Muller, pp. 110-21. New York: Springer-Verlag.

Pascal, Blaise
1910. *Thoughts.* Translated by W. F. Trotter. New York: P. F. Collier & Son.

Peirce, Charles S.
1958. *Collected Papers of Charles Sanders Peirce,* ed. A. W. Burks, Vols. 7 and 8. Cambridge: Harvard University Press.
1960. *Collected Papers of Charles Sanders Peirce,* eds. C. Hartshorne and P. Weiss, Vols. 1-6. Cambridge: Belknap Press of Harvard University Press.

Pfeffer, Rose
1977. *Nietzsche: Disciple of Dionysius.* Lewisberg, Pennsylvania: Bucknell University Press.

Phillips, Derek L.
1973. *Abandoning Method: Sociological Studies in Methodology.* San Francisco: Jossey-Bass Publishers.
1977. *Wittgenstein and Scientific Knowledge: A Sociological Perspective.* Totowa, New Jersey: Rowman & Littlefield.

Planck, Max
1933. *Where Is Science Going?* London: George Allen & Unwin.

Polanyi, Michael
1958. *Personal Knowledge: Towards a Post-Critical Philosophy.* (Chicago: University of Chicago Press.
1966. *The Tacit Dimension.* Garden City: Doubleday & Co.

Popper, Karl R.
1947. "Logic Without Assumptions." *Proceedings of the Aristotelian Society,* 67, 251–92.
1959. *The Logic of Scientific Discovery.* New York: Harper & Row.
1962. *The Open Society and Its Enemies,* Vol. 2. Princeton: Princeton University Press.
1963. *Conjectures and Refutations: The Growth of Scientific Knowledge.* New York: Harper & Row.
1972. *Objective Knowledge: An Evolutionary Approach.* London: Oxford University Press.
1974a. *Unended Quest: An Intellectual Autobiography.* LaSalle, Illinois: Open Court.
1974b. "Reply to My Critics." In *The Philosophy of Karl Popper,* Vol. 2, ed. P. A. Schilpp, pp. 959–1197. LaSalle, Illinois: Open Court.
1974c. "Scientific Reduction and the Essential Incompleteness of All Science." In *Studies in the Philosophy of Biology,* eds. J. J. Ayala and T. Dobzhansky, pp. 259–84. Berkeley: University of California Press.
1982. *Quantum Theory and the Schism in Physics,* ed. W. W. Bartley, Vol. 3. Totowa, New Jersey: Rowman & Littlefield.

Popper, Karl R., and John C. Eccles
1977. *The Self and Its Brain.* New York: Springer-Verlag.

Pribram, Karl
1971. *Languages of the Brain: Experimental Paradoxes and Principles in Neuropsychology.* Englewood Cliffs: Prentice-Hall.

Prior, A. N.
1957. *Time and Modality.* Oxford: Clarendon Press.

Progoff, Ira
1973. *Jung, Synchronicity, and Human Destiny: Noncausal Dimensions of Human Experience.* New York: Dell Publishing Co.

Puthoff, Harold, and Russell Targ
1977. *Mind-Reach.* New York: Delacorte.

Quine, Willard van Orman
1962. "Paradox." *Scientific American,* 206, 84–95.

Rescher, Nicholas
1976. "Peirce and the Economy of Research." *Philosophy of Science,* 43, 71–98.
1978. *Peirce's Philosophy of Science.* Notre Dame: University of Notre Dame Press.

Rescher, Nicholas, and Robert Brandom
1979. *The Logic of Inconsistency: A Study of Non-Standard Possible World Semantics and Ontology.* Totowa, New Jersey: Rowman & Littlefield.

Riddel, Joseph
1976. "From Heidegger to Derrida to Change: Doubling and (Poetic) Language." *Boundary 2,* 4, No. 2, 571–92.

Roberts, Don
1973. *The Existential Graphs of Charles S. Peirce.* The Hague: Mouton.

Robinson, Michael
1969. *The Long Sonata of the Dean: A Study of Samuel Beckett.* New York: Grove Press.

Rorty, Richard
1979. *Philosophy and the Mirror of Nature.* Princeton: Princeton University Press.

Rosen, Steven J.
1976. *Samuel Becketl and the Pessimistic Tradition.* New Brunswick, New Jersey: Rutgers University Press.

Rosen, S. M.
1973. "A Plea for the Possibility of Visualizing Existence." *Scientia,* 108, 9–12.
1975. "Synsymmetry." *Scientia,* 110, 539–49.

Rucker, Rudolf v. B.
1977. *Geometry, Relativity and the Fourth Dimension.* New York: Dover Publications.

Russell, Bertrand
1926. *Our Knowledge of the External World.* London: George Allen & Unwin.

Said, Edward
1975. *Beginnings: Intention and Method.* New York: Basic Books.
1978. "The Problems of Textuality: Two Exemplary Positions." *Critical Inquiry,* 4, No. 4, 673–714

Santillana, Giorgio de
1961. *The Origin of Scientific Thought: From Anaximander to Proclus, 600 B.C. to 300 A.D.* Chicago: University of Chicago Press.

Sarfatti, Jack
1974. "Implications of Meta-Physics for Psychoenergetics Systems." *Psychoenergetics Systems,* Vol. 1, pp. 3–10. London: Gordon & Breach.

Sartre, Jean Paul
1966. *Being and Nothingness.* Translated by H. Barnes. New York: Citadel Press.

Scheffer, Israel
1967. *Science and Subjectivity.* New York: Bobbs-Merrill.

Schlegel, Richard
1967. *Completeness in Science.* New York: Appleton-Century-Croft.

Schlossberg, Edwin
1973. *Einstein and Beckett: A Record of an Imaginary Discussion with Albert Einstein and Samuel Beckett.* New York: Links Books.

Schrödinger, Erwin
1957. *Science, Theory and Man,* Translated by J. Murphy and W. H. Johnston. New York: Dover Publications.
1961. "The Not-Quite-Exact Sciences." In *The Fate of Man,* ed. C. Brinton, pp. 452–62. New York: George Braziller.

Shenker, Israel
1956. "Moody Man of Letters." *New York Times,* 6 May, Sec. 2, 1 and 3.

Singh, Jagjit
1966. *Great Ideas in Information Theory, Language and Cybernetics.* New York: Dover Publications.

Smullyan, Raymond M.
1978. *What Is the Name of This Book?* Englewood Cliffs: Prentice-Hall.

Spencer-Brown, G.
1979. *Laws of Form.* New York: E. P. Dutton.

Sperry, R. W.
1966. "Brain Bisection and Mechanisms of Consciousness." In *Brain and Conscious Experience,* ed. J. C. Eccles, pp. 298–313. New York: Springer-Verlag.
1969. "A Modified Concept of Consciousness." *Psychological Review,* 76, 532–36.
1970. "An Objective Approach to Subjective Experience: Further Explanation of a Hypothesis." *Psychological Review,* 77, 585–90.

Spivak, Gayatri Chakravorty
1974. "Translator's Preface." In *Of Grammatology,* J. Derrida. Translated by G. C. Spivak, pp. ix–xc. Baltimore: Johns Hopkins University Press.

Stent, Gunther
1975. "Limits to the Scientific Understanding of Man." *Science,* 187, 1052–57.

Suppe, Frederick, ed.
1977. *The Structure of Scientific Theories.* Urbana: University of Illinois Press.

Sypher, Wylie
1962. *Loss of the Self in Modern Literature and Art.* New York: Random House.

Talbot, Michael
1980. *Mysticism and the New Physics.* New York: Bantam Books.

Tarski, Alfred
1956. *Logic, Semantics, Metamathematics.* Translated by J. H. Wordger. Oxford: Clarendon Press.

Ten Houten, Warren, and Charles D. Kaplan
1973. *Science and Its Mirror Image, A Theory of Inquiry.* New York: Harper & Row.

Toben, Bob
1975. *Space-Time and Beyond: Toward an Explanation of the Unexplainable.* New York: E. P. Dutton.

Todorov, Tzvetan
1968. "Introduction." *Le Vraisemblable,* a special issue of *Communications,* 11, 1–4.

Toulmin, Stephen
1953. *The Philosophy of Science.* New York: Hutchinson.

Trigg, Roger
1973. *Reason and Commitment.* London: Cambridge University Press.

Ullmo, Jean
1964. "The Agreement between Mathematics and Physical Phenomena." In *The Critical Approach to Science and Philosophy,* ed. M. Bunge, pp. 350–59. Glencoe: Free Press.

Walker, Evan Harris
1970. "The Nature of Consciousness." *Mathematical Bio-sciences,* 7, 131–78.

Weiss, Paul
1952. "The Logic of the Creative Process." In *Studies in the Philosophy of Charles Sanders Peirce,* eds. P. P. Wiener and F. H. Young, pp. 166–82. Cambridge: Harvard University Press.

Weyl, Hermann
1963. *Philosophy of Mathematics and Natural Science.* rev. ed. Translated by O. Helmer. New York: Atheneum.

Wheeler, John A.
1973. "Assessment of Everett's 'Relative State' Formulation of Quantum Theory." In *The Many-Worlds Interpretation of Quantum Mechanics,* eds. B. S. DeWitt and N. Graham, pp. 151–53. Princeton: Princeton University Press.

White, John, and Stanley Krippner, eds.
1977. *Future Science: Life Energies and the Physics of Paranormal Phenomena.* New York: Doubleday & Co.

Whitehead, Alfred North
1938. *Modes of Thought.* New York: MacMillan Publishing Co.

Whitehead, Alfred North, and Bertrand Russell
1927. *Principia Mathematica,* 2nd ed. Cambridge: Cambridge University Press.

Whitrow, G. J.
  1969. *The Natural Philosophy of Time.* New York: Harper & Row.

Whorf, Benjamin Lee
  1956. *Language, Thought and Reality,* ed. J. B. Carroll. Cambridge: MIT Press.

Wiener, Norbert
  1948. *Cybernetics: Or, Control and Communication in the Animal and the Machine.* Cambridge: MIT Press.

Wigner, E. P.
  1969. "The Unreasonable Effectiveness of Mathematics in the Natural Sciences." In *The Spirit and the Uses of the Mathematical Sciences,* eds. T. L. Saaty and F. J. Weyl, pp. 123–40. New York: McGraw-Hill.
  1970. *Symmetries and Reflections, Scientific Essays.* Cambridge: MIT Press.

Wilber, Ken, ed.
  1982. *The Holographic Paradigm and Other Paradoxes.* Boulder, Colorado: Shambhala.

Wittgenstein, Ludwig
  1953. *Philosophical Investigations.* Translated by G. E. M. Anscombe. New York: MacMillan Co.
  1961. *Tractatus Logico-Philosophicus.* Translated by D. F. Pears and B. F. McGuinness. London: Routledge and Kegan Paul.
  1972. *On Certainty.* Translated by D. Paul and G. E. M. Anscombe. New York: Harper & Row.

Young, Arthur
  1976. *The Geometry of Meaning.* San Francisco: Delacorte Press.

Zeman, J. Jay
  1977. "Peirce's Theory of Signs." In *A Perfusion of Signs,* ed. T. A. Sebeok, pp. 22–39. Bloomington: Indiana University Press.

Zervos, Christian
  1952. "Conversation with Picasso." In *The Creative Process: A Symposium,* ed. G. Brewster, pp. 55–60. New York: New American Library.

Zukav, Gary
  1979. *The Dancing Wu Li Masters: An Overview of the New Physics.* New York: William Morrow & Co.

Index